ST. JOSEPH
POLISH CEMETERY

Inscriptions from the
"Old Section"

Compiled by

Gene (Genevieve) Stachowiak Szymarek

HERITAGE BOOKS
2012

HERITAGE BOOKS

AN IMPRINT OF HERITAGE BOOKS, INC.

Books, CDs, and more—Worldwide

For our listing of thousands of titles see our website
at
www.HeritageBooks.com

Published 2012 by
HERITAGE BOOKS, INC.
Publishing Division
100 Railroad Ave. #104
Westminster, Maryland 21157

International Standard Book Numbers
Paperbound: 978-1-55613-076-2
Clothbound: 978-0-7884-9258-7

DEDICATION

To my loved ones who rest here
especially

Great-Grandfather Jozef Laskowski

one of the first Poles in St. Joseph County, Indiana
arriving in 1859 and living to the age of 105

and

to my beloved husband, John F. Szymarek

INTRODUCTION

St. Joseph Polish Cemetery covers a very large area and is divided in two parts: the Old Section which consists of Sections A through and including Section H, and the Perpetual Care (PC) section which is designated as PC1 - PC2 - etc. This book primarily covers all of the Old Section. You will find a few gravesites designated PC1 - these are included because the author had personally researched these particular families.

Utmost care has been taken to translate into the English language all pertinent information which appeared on any Memorial. I have also taken the liberty of including the maiden names of most wives as I found them recorded in the Marriage Records at the County Court House in South Bend, Indiana. This, I hope, will be helpful to anyone attempting to complete their family research.

Gravesites with no designated Section were obtained from other sources and does not indicate they are interred in the Old Section. One should contact the St. Joseph Undertaker and Cemetery Association at 824 S. Mayflower Road, South Bend, IN 46619 for exact locations.

AFTOWSKI, Joseph J Jr 4 July
1885 - 1961 (A)
Mary 1891 - 1972 (nee: Rybak)
(A)
Edward 1910 - 1910 (A)
(Anthony A Ciesiolka same lot)
AFTOWSKI, Joseph 1858 - 1911
(A)
Eleanora 1860 - 1923 (nee:
Wesolowski) (A)
Valentine 1860 - 23 Feb 1926
Brother (A)
Valentine 1900 - 1926 Son (A)
John 1886 - 1961 (A)
ALBRECHT, Wladyslaw 1866 -
14 Nov 1913 (B)
Maryanna 29 July 1876 - 1954
(nee: Lisiecka) (B)
---- 1877 - no date (B)
Klemence 1907 - 1908 (B)
Wanda -no dates- (B)
Wladyslawa -no dates- (B)
ALEXANDROWICZ, Anna 1864 -
1938 Mother (H)
ALEXANDER, Hipolit 1889 -
1965 (H)
Kelly 1895 - 1964 (H)
Constance 1890 - 1970 (nee:
Zaliska) (H)
ALLEN, Eleanor 1899 - 1951 (F)
(Wladyslaw & Praxeda Andrys-
iak, & Emma Haines same lot)
AMBROZIAK, Lucas 1882 - 1945
Father (E)
Frances 1892 - 1969 Mother (E)
(Felix Klimczuk same lot)
ANDREWS, Fred 1907 - 1977 (F)
Frances 1911 - 1970 (F)
ANDRYSIAK, Michael 1876 -
1949 Father (A)

ANDRYSIAK (continued)
Josephine 1877 - 1967 Mother
(nee: Wentland) (A)
Henry J 1907 - 1940 Son (A)
ANDRYSIAK, Frances 20 Sept
1887 - 20 March 1907 (A)
Jozef Mar 1851 - 28 May 1932
(A)
Antonina 1853 - 1937 (A)
Zofia 1889 - no date (A)
ANDRYSIAK, Piotr 1886 - 9 Dec
1928 (A)
Agnieszka 1885 - 1932 (nee:
Kolacz) (A)
Bronislaw 1907 - 11 Feb 1932
Son (A)
ANDRYSIAK, Eleanora 1892 -
1919 (A)
Walenty Jan 1839 - 20 Dec 1921
Father (A)
Frances Sept 1842 - 1927 Mother
(nee: Nowak) (A)
Alexander 1884 - 20 May 1926
(A)
ANDRYSIAK, Wojciech 1869 -
1952 Father (A)
Agnieszka 1871 - 1931 Mother
(nee: Cyranowski) (A)
Gertrude K 1905 - 1932 Daughter
(A)
(Lot next to Agnes sis: Mary
Jarecki w/o Jacob Rydzinski)
ANDRYSIAK, Kazimierz 1872 - 5
Sept 1936 (B)
Eleanora 1873 - 1933 (nee:
Stypczynski) (B)
ANDRYSIAK, Wladyslaw 1870 -
1918 Father (F)
Praxeda (Sadie) 1878 - 1926
Mother (nee: Lewinski) (F)

ANDRYSIAK (continued)
(Eleanor Allen and Emma Haines same lot)
ANDRYSIAK, Joseph 1921 - 1941 Son (H)
(Magdelena Cholaz same lot)
ANDRZEJEWSKI, Joseph 1858 - 1908 Father (A)
Josephine 1855 - 1938 Mother (A)
John 1883 - 1905 Son (A)
Joseph 1879 - 1944 (A)
ANDRZEJEWSKI, Michael 1864 - 10 Aug 1935 Father (B)
Anna 1865 - 1923 Wife (B)
---- 1833 - 1911 Mother (B)
ANDRZEJEWSKI, Adam 1869 - 1945 Father (D)
Wladyslawa 1879 - 1949 Mother (D)
Stephanie 1906 - 1917 (D)
Wanda 17 Mar 1917 - 1918 (D)
Marion 1902 - 1976 (D)
ANDRZEJEWSKI, Wladyslaw 1877 - 1931 Father (D)
Bronislawa 1879 - 1960 Mother (D)
Florence 1915 - 19-- (D)
Antony J 13 Aug 1901 - 18 Nov 1967 WWII Indiana Pfc Battery B 448 AAA BN CAC (D)
ANDRZEJEWSKI, Stanislawa 12 Apr 1880 - 18 Oct 1929 Mother (D)
Antony 12 Apr 1883 - 16 Feb 1939 Father (D)
Edward 5 Aug 1911 - 13 Aug 1934 (D)
ANDRZEJEWSKI, John C 9 Dec 1880 - 18 Sept 1942 WWII Indiana 2Lt Inf (D)
Albert 1920 - 1929 (D)
Joan C 1888 - 1942 Mother (D)
ANDRZEJEWSKI, Michaelene 1844 - 1924 (Nee: Mallok) (C)
Wawrzyniec 1836 - 1915 (C)
(Martha and Helen Paege same lot)
ANDRZEJEWSKI, Ignacy 13 Jan 1864 - 6 Oct 1933 (C)
ANTOLINI, Helen 1898 - 1959 (E)
William 1898 - 19-- (E)

ANTOLINI (continued)
(Robert E Vermilyer same lot)
ANTONOWICZ, Michael 1881 - 1945 Father (C)
Sophie 1887 - 1964 Mother (C)
ANTONOWICZ, Antoni 16 June 1895 - 5 Jan 1920 "Born in Poland" (Polish War Veteran) (E)
ARENDT, Michael 1866 - 29 Jan 1933 (A)
ARANOWSKI, Henryetta 1917 - 1925 (A)
(Michal and Apolonia Skarupinski same lot)
ARNOLD, Anna 1887 - 1952 (nee: Piotrowski) (B)
(Szymon & Agnieszka Piotrowski same lot)
AST, Henry 1883 - 1961 (B)
Mary 1889 - 1958 (B)
Alice 1911 - 1912 (B)
ASZKLAR, Victoria 1904 - 1967 (C)
Joseph 1889 - 1956 (C)
Jan 23 May 1899 - 4 June 1937 (C)
Lucya 1871 - 1938 Mother (C)
Franciszek 1886 - 5 Dec 1913 (C)
Wojciech 1857 - 30 May 1929 Father (C)
AUDENAERT, Sue Ann 1959 - 1960 Baby (C)
(John Karcewski & Lillian M Wlodarek same lot)
BABACZ, Jozef 1864 - 1943 Father (F)
Elzbieta 1868 - 1926 (nee: Jeziorski) Mother (F)
BABACZ, Wojciech no date - 29 March 1927 (Old Sec)
BADORA, Maryann no date - 21 May 1953 (F)
(Wm Marshal same lot)
BADOWSKI, Nikodem 2 March 1882 - 1947 (C)
Anna 29 June 1889 - 24 Jan 1972 (nee: Jankowski) (C)
Angela 1911 - 1915 (C)
Wanda A 1922 - 1960 (C)
BADOWSKI, Prakseda 1863 -

2

BADOWSKI (continued)
1918 (nee: Gorniak) Grandmother (D)
Joseph 1892 - 1 Feb 1930 (D)
Marianna 1895 - 1930 (nee: Nowak) (D)
(Bronislaw Hojnacki-brother same lot)
BADUR, Edward John 1893 - 24 Oct 1942 Indiana S2C US Navy (F)
Joan R 3 Apr 1930 - 27 Apr 1980 (F)
BAJER, Frank J 1882 - 1948 (A)
Frances 1882 - 1961 (nee: Pulaski) (A)
BAJDEK, Josephine 1893 - 1975 (E)
Konstanty 2 Aug 1890 - 1976 (E)
Helen 26 Mar 1891 - 1921 (nee: Botka) (E)
(Ludwik & Antonina Niezgodski & Franciszka Przeradzka same lot)
BAJDEK, Mary 1891 - 1953 (nee: Klosinski) (F)
Stanislaw 1887 - 1976 (F)
John 1928 - 1928 (F)
BALCZERZAK, Jan 1892 - 5 Feb 1934 Father (D)
Wladyslawa 1892 - 1945 Mother (D)
BALDWIN, Randy C 1945 - 1952 (A)
(Stanley Fisher same lot)
BALKA, Catharine 1891 - 1969 (nee: Witucki) (B)
Casimir F 1882 - 1952 (B)
(Helen Niedbalski and Sophie Witucki same lot)
BALKA, George no date - 12 July 1919 (-)
BALON, Anna 1884 - 1967 Mother (D)
Joseph Sr 1885 - 1956 Father (D)
(George Piwowarczyk same lot)
BALUKIEWICZ, Katarzyna 1884 - 1941 (nee: Dziewa) (A)
Wladyslaw 1885 - 19-- (A)
BANACKI, Petronella 1884 - 1913 (nee: Rozniakowski) Wife (C)
Helena 1875 - 1945 with picture

BANACKI (continued)
Mother (C)
Robert 1880 - 1961 with picture Father (C)
BANACKI, Joseph 1887 - 1961 Father (D)
Weronika 1915 - 1932 Daughter (D)
Catharine 1889 - 1967 Mother (D)
BANASIEWICZ, Ralph 1919 - 18 June 1934 Son (G)
Maryann B 1886 - 1956 Mother (G)
BANASZAK, Antoni 1859 - 1914 (A)
Magdalina 1869 - 1950 (nee: Szarletta) (A)
BANASZAK, Martha 1883 - 31 Dec 1959 (F)
Franciszek 1867 - 18 April 1950 (F)
(Pearl Nowastowski same lot)
BANASZAK, Peter 1867 - 1942 (G)
Maryann 1866 - 1944 (nee: Smiegielski) (G)
BANEK, George 1850 - 1 March 1925 (B)
BANICKI, Salomea 1883 - 1973 (nee: Burzynski) 1st husband - John Dobrzykowski (B)
Leon 1889 - 18 Feb 1937 WWI (B)
BANICKI, Magdaline 1860 - 1922 (nee: Hennet) (B)
Harry 1905 - 1915 (B)
Martin 1858 - 4 Oct 1910 (B)
Elgin 1903 - 9 May 1931 (B)
BANICKI, Ignacy 1854 - 1938 Father (C)
Maryanna 1856 - 1943 (nee: Olejniczak) Mother (C)
(Waclaw Olejniczak same lot)
BANICKI, Veronica 9 Dec 1897 - no date Mother (D)
Edward E no date - 17 Oct 1931 Father (D)
BANICKI, Frank L 12 Aug 1896 - 6 Feb 1959 WWI Indiana Pvt 6 Regt FA Repl Draft (F)
Bronislawa 1903 - 1933 Wife & Mother (F)

3

BANICKI (continued)
(Wojciech & Helena Maciejewski same lot)
BANICKI, Wanda 1891 - 1978 (H)
Alfreda 1925 - 19-- (H)
Peter 23 Apr 1894 - 1974 (H)
Ben no dates (H)
BANICKI, Wojciech no dates - 4 May 1925 "Polish Veteran" (F)
BANICKI, Jim 8 Dec 1934 - 8 Oct 1975 Son (F)
(Nancy Lukaszewski same lot)
BANIEWSKI, Steve 1892 - 1931 (B)
BARBER, Victor 1881 - 1962 (D)
(Vera Walkowiak, A Gaik, A & B Wrotnowski, & Louis Hany-zewski same lot)
BARCZYKOWSKI, Frank Jr 1881 - 1960 (A)
Hattie 1887 - 1957 (nee: Rzycka) (A)
Alice 1926 - no date (A)
Richard 1924 - no date (A)
BARCZYKOWSKI, Adalbert 27 Nov 1881 - 21 Nov 1918 (B)
Sophia 4 March 1888 - 1965 (nee: Delinski) (B)
BARCZYKOWSKI, Helen 1912 - 1934 Mother (B)
(Adalbert - Sally - Joseph Krakowski same lot)
BARDICK, Stephen 1911 - 1970 Father (D)
BARGIELSKI, Anthony 1879 - 1953 Father (D)
(Stanislaw Zbrzezny same lot)
BARGIELSKI, Stanley A 1913 - 1966 (D)
Maryann 1914 - 1961 (D)
(Sylvester Domski same lot)
BARGIELSKI, Franciszka 1875 - 1921 (E)
(Szczepan Traszkowski same lot)
BARKER, William no date - 23 Feb 1982 (H)
(Theodore & Phyllis Kaz-mierczak same lot)
BARKOWSKI, T 1868 - 1956 (A)
A 1864 - 1945 (A)
(K Zieromski same lot)
BARKOWSKI, William A 1888 -

BARKOWSKI (continued)
1965 (A)
Franciszek Nov 1860 - 1940 (A)
Maryanna June 1866 - 1914 (nee: Liszewski) (A)
Antoni 1894 - 1930 Son (A)
(Helena Sarnowski same lot)
BARRON, Leo no date - no date (C)
Stanislaw no date - no date (C)
Tekla no date - no date (C)
BARRY, Martha 3 March 1904 - 16 Feb 1979 (C)
(Praxida and Antony Mrockiewicz same lot)
BARTKIEWICZ, Adam J 23 Jan 1883 - 1961 (C)
Hattie 22 Sept 1893 - 28 Jan 1982 (nee: Wierzbinski) (C)
Maria 1892 - 1920 (nee: Smiecinski) Wife (C)
BARTKOWIAK, Stanislaw 1900 - 1927 (B)
BARTKOWIAK, Michael Oct 1858 - 10 March 1924 (-)
BARTOSIAK, Benjamin 1914 - 1939 (PC)
BARTOSIK, Anthony no dates - 23 June 1918 (-)
BARTOSIEWICZ, Michael 1842 - 20 March 1920 (E)
Barbara 1849 - 1925 (nee: Golubski) (E)
BARTOSIEWICZ, Victoria 1890 - 1938 (nee: Zawacka) (A)
Joseph 21 Dec 1882 - 1960 (A)
Casimir 1928 - 1953 Son (A)
Bernice 7 June 1918 - 1918 (A)
Helen 10 Sept 1915 - 1916 (A)
Frank 1912 - 1913 (A)
Rose 1911 - 1911 (A)
BARTZ, Sabina 1915 - 1948 (D)
(Gladys Rajewski same lot)
BARTZ, Susan Marie no date - 21 June 1963 (F)
(Walter Klosinski same lot)
BARZAN, Jozef no date - 13 Jan 1916 (-)
BARZYNSKI, Walenty 1 Feb 1855 - 3 Jan 1930 (B)
BAUER, Maryanna 1930 - 1931 (A)

4

BAUER (continued)
(John & Josephine Gierse same lot)
BECK, Bronislaw 1897 - 11 Jan 1935 Father (E)
Wilhelm 1866 - 4 Apr 1935 (E)
Wiktoria 1865 - 1938 (E)
Marta 1899 - 1964 (nee: Laskowski) Mother (E)
---- Veteran WWII (E)
BECK, Mary H 1883 - 1978 (D)
Harry M 1880 - 1923 (D)
BECZKIEWICZ, Stella R 1887 - 1940 (Wife John A; nee: Kurakiewicz)
BECZKIEWICZ, Veronica 1855 - 1937 (B)
Peter 1856 - 1934 (B)
Mary 1943 Sister (B)
BECZKIEWICZ, Sadie E 1901 - 1967 (B)
Stanley A 1894 - 1951 (B)
Emilia 1864 - 5 Oct 1932 (nee: Kaiser) (B)
Antoni 1850 - 1910 (B)
Paul V 1932 - 1935 (B)
(Ignatius & Joseph A Werwinski same lot)
BEDNAREK, Jozefa 1878 - 1931 (nee: Rybak) Mother (C)
Ignacy 1871 - 1937 Father (C)
Bert I 1904 - 1954 Son (C)
BEDNAREK, Anna 12 March 1900 - 4 Apr 1924 (nee: Wegner) (F)
Walter J 12 Jan 1900 - 16 March 1935 WWI Veteran (F)
(Bert J and Katharyn Wiatrolek same lot)
BEDNAREK, Albin 1952 Infant (H)
(Andrew Wasielkowski and Janina Sobiech same lot)
BEITLER, Julius A 1877 - 1966 Father (F)
Elizabeth 1880 - 1950 Mother (F)
(Arthur T Smanda same lot)
BELAKOVICH, John 1907 - 1952 (H)
Helen 1911 - 19-- (nee: Wolak) (H)
James T 1942 - 1946 (H)
BELL, Charles T 22 Sept 1956 -

BELL (continued)
28 Oct 1962 "Son of Paul and Joanna Bell" (F)
(Forest & Bernice Ciesiolka, & Matthew F Steinbrunner same lot)
BENNETT, Antonette R 1880 - 1972 Mother (D)
(Ignatius F & Cecylia Mankowski same lot)
BENTKOWSKI, Anna 1830 - 1922 (B)
(Walenty and Jozefa Meller same lot)
BENTKOWSKI, Joseph 3 Jan 1870 - 18 July 1954 (E)
Maryann 1880 - 1955 (nee: Miller) (E)
Walter 25 Feb 1909 - 16 Aug 1979 Pvt US Army WWII (E)
BENTKOWSKI, Stanislaw 2 Apr 1866 - 1962 Father (F)
Stanislawa 1871 - 1936 Mother (F)
Helena 10 June 1906 - 3 Jan 1929 Daughter (F)
BERDZINSKI, Anna 1869 - 1951 Mother (B)
Franciszek 1863 - 29 Nov 1931 Father (B)
BERTMAN, Stanley no date - 20 Oct 1936 (-)
BERUS, Joseph 1884 - 1943 (G)
Carrie 1890 - 1961 (nee: Holewinski) (G)
BIDDLE, Kathleen Ann 20 Sept-30 Sept 1951 (B)
(Jacob Dudek same lot)
BIELECKI, Peter no date - 1937 (A)
BIELEJEWSKI, Marya 1876 - 1967 (H)
Jozef 1872 - 1940 (H)
Stanley 1906 - 1948 (H)
(Stanley J Somogyi same lot)
BIERWAGON, Tekla 1877 - 1961 (nee: Rozplochowski) (B)
Mieczjslaw 1875 - 11 Dec 1928 (B)
Bernice 1857 - 1900 (nee: Andrzejewski) Mother (B)
Cecylia 1886 - 1905 (B)

5

BIERWAGON (continued)
Angela Eugenia 1913 - 1920 (B)
John Ferdinand 1846 - 27 Sept
1925 Father (B)
Sophia 1879 - 1935 (B)
Chester E 1888 - 1954 Father (B)
Chester Stanley Jr 1923 - 1924
(B)
Blanche G 1886 - 1969 (nee:
Pelegia Klota) Mother (B)
(Hedwige Jagodzinski same lot)
BIERWAGON, Joseph 1897 -
1978 (PC)
BIKOWSKI, Leokadya 1896 -
1958 (nee: Janowczyk) (C)
Pawel 1885 - 1945 (C)
Wanda no date - no date (C)
Jozef no date - no date (C)
Mary no date - no date "Our
Baby" (C)
BILINSKI, Walter S no date - 21
Aug 1981 (E)
BILINSKI, Theodore 1886 - 15
Oct 1925 (F)
John no date - 26 May 1923 (F)
(Helen Niespodziany) nee: Krec-
mer w/o Theodore
BILINSKI, Julian 1888 - 1934
Father (G)
Emilia 1893 - 1963 (nee:
Kalinski) Mother (G)
BILINSKI, Kenneth 17 Oct 1946 -
17 Aug 1967 Son (G)
BLACHARSKI, Walter C 19 Dec
1887 - 1964 (A)
Mary C 1894 - 1960 (nee:
Wojciechowski) (A)
Benjamin 1917 - 1951 Son (A)
BLACK, Dewey no date - 18 Sept
1981 (H)
(Caroline & Wojciech Dlugosz
same lot)
BLADECKI, Jacob 1873 - 1955
(C)
Angela (1) 1883 - 1918 (nee:
Grzegorek) (2) Laura Brod-
zinski (C)
BLASCZAK, Jozef 1862 - 1941
(B)
Julianna 1864 - 1948 (nee:
Gratziella) (B)
Walenty 1896 - 28 June 1909 (B)

BLASCZAK (continued)
William 1907 - 19-- Pvt US
Army WWII (B)
BLASZCZYK, Teofil 1880 - 1 Jan
1929 Father (B)
Salomea no date - 5 Aug 1944
(nee: Jurgonski) Mother (B)
(Jan & Maryanna Jurgonski same
lot)
BLUMBERG, Thaddeus 21 Oct
1896 - no date Indiana (F)
(Other information not legible)
(Jozef Mikolajewski same lot)
BLUMBERG, Konstanty 1910 -
17 Oct 1933 (PC)
Edmund 1907 - 21 March 1934
(PC)
Thomas 12 Oct 1845 - 21 May
1936 Uncle (PC)
Stephen 1881 - 21 Apr 1932 (PC)
BOBINSKI, Adolph 19 Dec 1880 -
1961 (C)
Hattie 11 Oct 1885 - 1971 (nee:
Bonek) (C)
John 1891 - 1915 Brother (C)
BOBINSKI, Joseph no date - 3
July 1934 (-)
BOBOWSKI, Antoni 1862 - 17 Oct
1915 (C)
Emilia 1872 - 1948 (C)
(Julian Kozlowski & Jozefa Hoj-
nacki same lot)
BOBROWSKI, Petronella 1860 -
1940 (H)
Michael 1870 - 1939 (H)
(Stanislaw Pacaytes same lot)
BOCHERS, Lisa Marie 7 March
1970 - 7 Dec 1976 (F)
(Michael Szczepaniak & Stella
Vanderhagen same lot)
BOCK, Charles K 9 Sept 1909 - 9
Apr 1970 (B)
(Jan, Mary, & Cecylia Witucki &
Frank Wendland same lot)
BODGE, Helen V 1905 - 1950 (F)
(Katarzyna, Bronislaw & Jan
Rybacki same lot)
BOGACKI, Anna 18-- - 1931
Mother (nee: Marecki) (-)
BOGACKI, Apolonia 1881 - 1950
Mother (PC)
Pawel 1875 - 1948 Father (PC)

6

BOGACKI (continued)
Wladyslaw S 1904 - 1931 (PC)
BOG--RSKI (Not Legible), Ferdinand no date - 1919 (-)
BOGUNIA, Jean 1916 - 1957 (E)
Valentine 1879 - 1961 (E)
Victoria 1889 - 1959 (nee: Szemek) (E)
BOJEWICZ, Anna 1845 - 1908 (A)
Frank 1843 - 1909 (A)
Helen 1874 - 1939 (nee: Kendziorski) (A)
Henry Sr 1865 - 1942 (A)
BOJEWICZ, Larry J 20 June 1892 - 1963 (E)
Clara M 1895 - 19-- (Nee: Fleugal) (E)
BOKSA, Carl 4 Oct 1895 - 4 July 1959 Indiana Pvt 2 Regt FA Repl Depot WWI (B)
BOLKA, Jozef T (1) 9 Mar 1873 - 2 Sept 1913 (A)
Marya 4 Aug 1878 - 1 May 1973 (nee: Stasinski) (A)
(2) Huber
(Jan Stasinski same lot)
BOLKA, Gregory 1900 - 1919 (D)
Stanislaw 1 May 1867 - 13 May 1930 (D)
(Steve Kostruv same lot)
BOLKA, Alfred no date - no date (F)
Jozef (1) 1894 - 13 July 1925 (F)
(Helen Fenwick (2) same lot) nee: Bednarek (F)
BOLKA, Aloysius M 1893 - 11 Aug 1923 (G)
---- 1918 - 1925 Daughter (G)
Franciszka 1900 - 1922 (G)
BONCZYNSKI, Marion 1898 - 20 Oct 1911 (A)
Cecylia 15 Sept 1859 - 13 March 1927 (A)
Franciszek 30 Nov 1860 - 12 Nov 1937 (A)
Walenty 11 Feb 1882 - 5 July 1934 (A)
(Helena Jaskiewicz same lot)
BONEK, Wojciech 1850 - 1925 (B)
Maryanna 1854 - 1937 (nee: Stro-

BONEK (continued)
zewski) Wife (B)
(Jozef Strozewski, Raymond Luczkowski, & Susan Wiltrout same lot)
BONIEWSKI, Steve no date - 14 Jan 1937 Indiana Pvt 669 Aero Sq (H
(Boleslaw & Maryanna Rutkowski same lot)
BONK, Agatha 1884 - 1914 (nee: Postula) (C)
Maryanna 1887 - 1942 (C)
John J 5 March 1883 - 1964 (C)
Valentine - 1915 - 1919 (C)
Adam no dates Infant (C)
BONK, Tomara Sue 9 Oct 1962 - 11 Oct 1962 (H)
Tracy R 2 Feb 1976 - 2 Feb 1976 Baby (H)
Frank D 21 Apr 1910 - 16 Sept 1968 (Indiana MM2 US Navy WWII) (H)
Frances 1908 - 1941 "Married 21 Aug 1933" (H)
BORDEN, Alexander A no dates Father (G)
Eleanora T no dates Mother (G)
Joseph no dates Son (G)
BOREK, Steve 17 June 1889 - 6 July 1956 Father Pvt Co D 60 Pioneer Inf WWI (E)
Magdelena 1890 - 1976 Mother (E)
BORKOWSKI, Wojciech 1864 - 1934 Husband & Father (B)
Stanislawa 1875 - 1944 Wife & Mother (B)
Virginia 1911 - 19-- Daughter (B)
Bridget 1900 - 19-- Daughter (nee: Florkowski) (B)
BORKOWSKI, Andrew 1876 - 1963 (B)
Agnes 1877 - 1932 (B)
(Frances Nowicki same lot)
BORKOWSKI, Antony 1894 - 1930 (A)
BORKOWSKI, Teofilia 1879 - 1975 (B)
Frank 1879 - 26 Dec 1928 Father (B)

7

BORKOWSKI (continued)
Edmund 1909 - 1964 (B)
Arthur J 19 Feb 1916 - 1 Sept
1979 "OM3 US Navy WWII"
(B)
BORKOWSKI, Catharine 1877 -
1949 (nee: Pomtaska) (H)
Kleofas 1865 - 1942 (H)
Michael M 1902 - 1967 (H)
Casimir F 22 Feb 1908 - 3 May
1950 "Indiana Pfc 38 Inf WWII
BSM PN" (H)
BORLIK, Klara 1886 - 1913 (nee:
Grzesk) (A)
(Wladyslaw and Martha Grzesk
same lot)
BORLIK, Steve 16 Apr 1884 -
1965 (C)
Anna 1885 - 1971 (nee:
Makielski) (C)
Mamie 1920 - 1921 (C)
BORLIK, Prakseda 1858 - 1930
(nee: Rozek) Mother (C)
Marcin 1849 - 1940 Father (C)
Frank X 1897 - 1969 (C)
BORLIK, John J 1886 - 1973 (E)
Tillie C 1897 - 1967 (E)
BORLIK, Bartholomew 1850 -
1920 (E)
Caroline 1850 - 1946 (E)
BOROWICZ, Frank no date - 3
May 1920 (-)
BOROWSKI, Maryanna 1875 -
1949 Mother (A)
Ignacy 1873 - 1930 Father (A)
Andrzej J 1900 - 1914 (A)
BOROWSKI, Alexander F 4 Jan
1900 - 13 Oct 1947 "WWI In-
diana SF2C US Navy" (A)
---- 1865 - 1946 Father (A)
---- 1871 - 1939 Mother (A)
BOROWSKI, Walter M 25 Sept
1909 - 13 March 1980 (B)
Clara 1912 - 19-- (nee: Deka)
(B)
(Tekla Staszewski same lot)
BOROWSKI, Antoni 1888 - 1950
(C)
(Antoni and Eleanora Wlodarski
same lot)
BOROWSKI, Stanislaus no date -
1919 (-)

BOROWSKI, Teofil 1905 - 1924
Father (E)
Jozef 1908 - 1943 Son (E)
Jozef 1878 - 1955 Son (E)
Severina 1878 - 1963 Mother (E)
BOROWSKI, Jacob 1880 - 10 Dec
1925 "Born Poland - reached
age 45" (G)
---- no dates Father (G)
---- no dates Mother (G)
BORYC, Jan 1869 - 1 Feb 1950
"Age 81" (A)
Petronella no dates (nee: Kuspa)
(A)
BORYC, Steve no date - 14 May
1933 (D)
BORYC, Mary no dates (F)
(Ray S Sobecki same lot)
BORZESZKOWSKI, Weronika
1870 - 1926 (nee: Klos) Mother
(B)
Tomasz 1857 - 26 Feb 1927
Father (B)
Tekla 1907 - 1912 (B)
Marya 1892 - 1917 (B)
Anna 1890 - 1916 (B)
BOTKA, Sylvester J 20 Dec 1889
- 29 Nov 1933 (E)
BOTKA, John no date - 23 March
1937 (E)
BOTKA, Frances 1870 - 1935
(nee: Sas) (E)
John 1863 - 1930 (E)
BOZA, Agnieszka 1880 - 1944
Daughter (D)
Jakob 1861 - 1942 Son (D)
Marcin 1874 - 1941 Son (D)
Wojciech 1835 - 1930 Father (D)
Katarzyna 1842 - 1918 Mother
(D)
Michael 1874 - 1949 Son (D)
Jan 1872 - 1963 Son (D)
BRAMBERT, Ignace J 1883 -
1952 (D)
Alice M 1884 - 1942 (D)
Thomas 6 Dec 1946 - 7 Dec 1946
(D)
(Mary Jasicki same lot)
BRAMBERT, Pauline 1885 -
1970 Mother (nee: Janicki) (F)
(Frederick Renes & Jacob Celi-
chowski same lot)

BRAMBERT, Wojciech 1857 – 4 May 1920 (C)
BRANSKI, Teofil no date – 30 Nov 1924 (-)
BRANSON, Cecylia and Clara 1938 – 1942 (twins) (F) (Szymon & Agnes Brylewski, Helen & Cecylia Loomis same lot)
BREKUS (See BRACKUS-BRECKUS), Eleanora 1887 – 1913 (nee: Kaniewski) (W/o Vincent Brackus) (A) (Vincent K Kaniewski, Nicesor & Bronislawa Janiszewski same lot)
BRECKUS – Also (BRACKUS) Vincent no date – 1937 (D)
BRODOWSKI, Theresa 1888 – 1954 (D) (Jan Nowak same lot)
BRODZINSKI, Rose 1881 – 1918 (nee: Gasiorowski) Mother (A) (Joe & Hilary Gasiorowski [also Gonsiorowski] same lot)
BRODZINSKI, Stanislawa G 1879 – 1900 (C)
Adam 1877 – 1940 Father (C)
BRODZINSKI, Antoni 1837 – 1936 Father (D)
Maryanna 1847 – 1933 Mother (D)
BRODZINSKI, Frank 1837 – 19 March 1936 (B)
BRODZINSKI, Frank 1863 – 29 Nov 1931 (B)
BRODZINSKI, Boleslaw no dates (C)
BROWNELL, Nancy Kubiak 21 July 1943 – 13 Aug 1972 (with picture) (D) (John J Pinkowski same lot)
BRUSICK, Frances 19 March 1887 – 1950 (nee: Marecki) (C)
Joseph 1890 – 23 Feb 1923 (C) (Vincent Grodzicki & Stanley & Alice Lupa same lot)
BRYLEWSKI, Szymon 1855 – 12 Jan 1936 (A)
Agnieszka 1863 – 1936 (nee: Urbanski) (A)
Sophie Roselyn 1897 – 1926 (A) (Cecylia & Clara Branson, Helen

BRYLEWSKI (continued) & Cecylia Loomis same lot)
BRYLINSKI, Anna M 1884 – 1951 (D)
BRYSKI, F 1884 – 1920 "Died at Grebowice, Mala Polska" (D)
BYSTRE, Walter 1903 – 1973 Uncle (H)
Jan 1906 – 1958 Son (H)
Katarzyna 1868 – 1937 Mother (H)
BRZENIAK, Rozalia 1868 – 1930 (nee: Dembinski) (F) (Ladislaus & Blanche Szymanski same lot)
BRZEZINSKI, Leonard 12 Sept 1887 – 16 July 1952 Father (A)
Antonina 1888 – 1967 (nee: Mejer) Mother (A)
Irene 1912 – 1913 Daughter (A)
BRZEZINSKI, Bernice M 1899 – 1967 (nee: Jeziorski) (C)
Frank B 6 Aug 1894 – 20 June 1982 (C) (Clementine Golubic same lot)
BRZEZINSKI, Ignatius 1863 – 1935 (D)
Rose 1867 – 1936 (nee: Grycka) (D)
Michael P 1901 – 29 March 1979 (D) (Martha Kasuirska same lot)
BRZEZINSKI, Alojzy 1917 – 1923 (E)
Tomasz no date – 11 Jan 1921 (E)
Helen 14 May 1908 – 16 June 1980 (E)
Jozef 12 Sept 1906 – 24 Aug 1920 (E)
Petronella 23 June 1881 – 16 Dec 1938 (nee: Kowalski) Mother (E)
John F 1874 – 1954 Father (E)
BRZUSZKIEWICZ, Wiktorya 1858 – 1927 (F)
Stanislaus 1860 – 10 Nov 1934 (F) (Stanislaw & Hattie Chodzinski same lot)
BUCHOLTZ, Valentine 1865 – 1937 Father (A)

BUCHOLTZ (continued)
Frances 1873 - 20 Feb 1923 (nee: Bejer) Mother (A) (Edward & Henrietta Chavis same lot)
BUCHOLTZ, Antony S 6 Dec 1874 - 1937 (B)
Casiemiera 1876 - 1966 (nee: Kowalski) (B)
Antony no date - 1901 (B)
Clemen no date - 1915 (B)
BUCHOLTZ, Kazimier 1826 - 31 March 1920 (B)
Marya 1833 - 1910 (nee: Bartkowiak) (B)
BUCHOLTZ, Mary Jane 1925 - 1933 (F)
Edwin 1902 - 1957 Father (F)
BUCHOLTZ, Casimir 1898 - 1949 (F)
Eleanor 15 Mar 1903 - 16 Sept 1978 (nee: Pejza) (F)
BUCHOLTZ, Boleslaw 1898 - 20 Feb 1927 Father (F)
Anna 1903 - 1950 Mother (F)
John W 1925 - 1960 Father WWII (F)
BUCZKOWSKI, John no date - 4 Aug 1916 (-)
BUCZKOWSKI, Thomas 1857 - 26 Feb 1927 (E)
BUCZYNSKI, Michael 1842 - 1910 Father (B)
Zofia 1888 - 1911 Daughter (B)
Ewa 1854 - 1931 Mother (B)
(#2 marriage Wawrzyniec Jasinski)
---- 1876 - 1951 Daughter (B)
BUCZYNSKI, Antonette 1884 - 1920 (nee: Stypczynski) (B)
Valentine 1886 - 1954 (B)
Blanche 1898 - 1978 (B)
BUCZYNSKI, Stella 1881 - 1918 (nee: Spychalski) (D)
John 1882 - 1967 (D)
Frances 1888 - 1961 (D)
BUDA, Albin 1888 - 1972 (E)
Anna 1893 - 1966 (E)
Anna no date - 12 Sept 1921 (E)
Ludwik no date - 10 Feb 1943 "Placowka" #125" (Polish Veteran) (E)

BUDA (continued)
(Ludwik Zalas same lot)
BUDNIK, Peter P 1867 - 1938 (E)
(Rev John F Kubacki same lot)
BUDNY, Karol 1874 - 1 Oct 1924 (East Fence)
BUDZINSKI, Andrzej 1876 - 1919 Father (A)
Rozalia 1887 - 1918 (nee: Urbanski) Mother (A)
Julianna no dates Daughter (A)
Stefan no dates Son (A)
Peter 29 June 1905 - 29 May 1946 (A)
BUDZINSKI, Henry no date - 1 Oct 1919 (-)
BUDZINSKI, James J 12 Nov 1960 - 15 Nov 1960 (H)
(Michael & Mary Galus same lot)
BUDZINSKI, Hattie 1903 - 19-- (F)
Casimir J 18 Jan 1901 - 1 Aug 1975 "Indiana Pvt US Army WWII" (F)
(Frank J Witucki same lot)
BURCZAK, Mateusz 21 Sept 1895 - 8 Dec 1928 WWI (F)
BURDICK, Victoria T 1899 - 28 Dec 1979 (nee: Holewinski) (H)
Vincent S 1894 - 24 Sept 1980 (H)
Pauline T 1894 - 1942 Mother (H)
BURLINGTON, Rozalia Elizabeth 1904 - 1973 (H)
(Joseph and Elizabeth Herma same lot)
BURZYNSKI, Julianna 30 Dec 1863 - 29 Aug 1920 (nee: Wozniak) Mother (B)
Walenty 1 Feb 1855 - 8 Jan 1930 Father (B)
BURZYNSKI, Bartholomew no date - 6 Oct 1936 (D)
BURZYNSKI, Michael J 1896 - 28 June 1909 (B)
BURZYNSKI, John C 1884 - 1962 (D)
Mary 1889 - 1966 (nee: Urbanski) (D)
Henrietta 1917 - 1918 (D)

BURZYNSKI, Joseph L 16 Mar
1895 - Sept 1977 (F)
Laura B 10 Feb 1895 - Oct 1973
(nee: Brambert) (F)
Loretta M no date - 17 July 1924
daughter (F)
BUSZKIEWICZ, Franciszek 20
Oct 1890 - 25 July 1938 (C)
Wladyslawa 15 June 1893 - 2
July 1926 (nee: Leda) (C)
BUSZKIEWICZ, Wojciech 20 Oct
1885 - 25 July 1940 "Polish
Veteran" (D)
(Paul W Polinski & Hattie De-
jaegher same lot)
BUSZKIEWICZ, T 1923 - 1923
(D)
Szczepan 1883 - 1943 (D)
Maryanna 1884 - 1968 (D)
Felix P 17 Sept 1919 - 5 Apr
1967 "Indiana Trp 6-8 Cav
BSM PH WWII" (D)
BUTTS, Elfreda Lechtanski 1917
- 1968 (G)
(George & Pearl Niespodziany
same lot)
BUYSSE, Margaret L 1913 - 19--
(nee: Deka) (D)
Leonard C 1908 - 1971 (D)
(Bernard Deka and Esther Deka
same lot)
BUZALSKI, Frank W 1888 - 1953
(E)
Verna 1887 - 1966 (nee: Wegner)
(E)
Raymond no dates Infant (E)
(Napomocyna Pilarski same lot)
BUZIAK, Blanche 1895 - 1965
(nee: Klosowski) (F)
Bernard 1926 - 1927 (F)
Alex 1895 - 19-- (F)
Clemens 1922 - 1940 (F)
BYKOWSKI, Jacob 1851 - 13 Mar
1929 (F)
Martha 1888 - 19-- (nee:
Makielski) (F)
John J 1886 - 19-- (F)
BYRSKI, Frank 1884 - 11 Jan
1920 (E)
BYSTRY, Pearl 1904 - 1972
Mother (H)
Frank 1900 - 1938 Father (H)

BYTNER, Adam 1905 - 1944 Son
(A)
Jozefa 1877 - 19-- Mother (A)
Antoni 1876 - 1943 Father (A)
CADUFF, Rita Muszynski 1933 -
1973 Daughter, Wife, Mother
with picture (H)
(Jakub Kaczmarek & Sophie
Muszynski Merrick same lot)
CAMPBELL, Carrie 1886 - 1922
(A)
(Stanislaus Witkowski same lot)
CANDY, Charles R 1924 - 1925
(D)
(Joseph, Cora, Frank, & William
Kolecki same lot)
CAPCHEK, Demetro no date - 20
Oct 1932 (Old Sec)
CARROLL, David Lee 1944 -
1945 (C)
(John & Mary Piechocki, Mary
Wroblewski, Edward J Wruble,
& Maryanna Saunders same
lot) (C)
CARON, Anna 1908 - 1927 (nee:
Moskwinski) (C)
(Mateusz & Rozalia Moskwinski
same lot)
CASNER, John William no date -
9 July 1945 (F)
(Jan & Helena Nowicki same lot)
CASSLER, Wladzia 1903 - 1953
Daughter (C)
(Michael & Victoria Paluszewski
same lot)
CEBULSKI, John no date - 13
August 1918 Father (B)
CEBULSKI, Franciszka 1854 -
1925 Mother (F)
Antoni 1891 - 1941 Son (F)
CELICHOWSKI, Peter 1885 -
1961 Father (F)
Jozefa 20 June 1862 - 1920
Mother (F)
CELICHOWSKI, Jacob 24 July
1886 - 13 Nov 1942 "Indiana
Pvt 18 Inf" Husband (F)
(Frederick Renes & Pauline
Brambert same lot)
CELICHOWSKI, Frank 11 Sept
1897 - 29 May 1969 "Kentucky
Sgt US Army WWI" (G)

11

CELICHOWSKI (continued)
Martha 1902 - 19-- (G)
Hildegarde 1922 - 1959 (G)
CELICHOWSKI, Leo 1893 - 1971
(H)
Constance 1902 - 1950 (H)
Audry Ann no dates (H)
Ervin 1924 - 1944 S/Sgt (H)
CELMER, Frank no dates - 8
May 1967 (PC)
Mary no date - 10 Jan 1950 (nee:
Kuczwara) (PC)
(Stanley & Eylene Tobolski same
lot)
CENCELEWSKI, Konstanty 1870
- 1954 (A)
Helena 1876 - 1957 (nee: Drews)
(A)
Casimir 1913 - 1941 (A)
Antony 25 Nov 1885 - 2 Jan 1908
(A)
CENCELEWSKI, Joseph 1885 -
1972 (G)
Constance 1895 - 1972 (G)
Chester 1915 - 1923 (G)
Nancy 1957 - 1958 Granddaughter
(G)
CHAVIS, Henrietta L 1909 - 1971
(A)
Edward L 1904 - 19-- (A)
(Valentine & Frances Bucholtz
same lot)
CHELMINIAK, Leo J 1 Apr 1895
- 27 Apr 1980 (A)
Theresa D 1896 - 22 Feb 1973
(nee: Urbanski) (A)
CHELMINIAK, Stanley J 1908 -
1974 (D)
Stella V 1908 - 19-- (D)
Wladyslawa 1886 - 1916 (nee:
Manuszak) Mother (D)
Stanley J 1898 - May 1954
Father (D)
CHLEBEK, Irene 20 July - 24
August 1921
(A)
(Peter, Valentine & Mary Wiec-
zorek & Esther Puzinski same
lot)
CHLEBEK, Wladyslawa 22 May
1902 - 3 May 1927 (B)
(Marcin & Paulina Stankiewicz

CHLEBEK (continued)
same lot)
CHLEBOWSKI, Henry 1911 - 14
Apr 1931 (PC)
CHLEBOWSKI, Maciej I 1885 -
16 Nov 1936 Father (E)
Aniela 1893 - 1964 (nee:
Hanyzewski) Mother (E)
CHMIEL, Vincent 1861 - 1941
(A)
Stella 1866 - 1945 (A)
(Walter & Wanda Klota same
lot)
CHMIEL, Amelia 1848 - 1923
(C)
(Jozef Grontkowski same lot)
CHMIEL, Walter 1897 - 1959
Father (D)
Edna 1900 - 1955 Mother (D)
Arthur V 1924 - 1931 Son (D)
CHMIELEWSKI, Theodore 1885
- 13 Feb 1918 (A)
CHMIELEWSKI, Stanislawa 1883
- 1957 (nee: Kitkowski) Mother
(C)
Jozef 1882 - 1951 Father (C)
Stanislaw 10 Nov 1916 - 19 Nov
1916 (C)
Wladyslaw no dates (C)
CHMIELEWSKI, Michael 1850 -
1929 (C)
Maryanna 1855 - 1929 (C)
John Jr no date - 20 Nov 1930
(C)
(Joseph Turczynski same lot)
CHMIELEWSKI, Adalbert no
date - 24 May 1907 (-)
CHODZINSKI, Anton 20 Mar 1854
- 21 Nov 1932 (with picture)
(C)
Agnes A 1870 - 1938 (nee:
Boryc) Mother (C)
Leo J 22 Mar 1897 - 14 March
1966 "Indiana Buglar Co B 3
Ammo Train WWI (C)
CHOODZNSKI, Stanislaw 1895 -
1955 "Mexican Border Vet
1914-1917" (C)
Hattie 1895 - 1957 (nee:
Brzuszkiewicz) (C)
(Stanislaw & Victoria Brzuszkie-
wicz same lot)

CHODZINSKI, Theodore 13 Jan
1948 - 12 May 1949 (G)
C H O L A C Z, Magdelena 1865 -
1935 (H)
(Joseph Andrysiak same lot)
CHOLAJ, Benny 1930 - 1931 (G)
Alexander J 1896 - 1970 (G)
Helen M 1898 - 19-- (G)
(Stephen Molenda & Edward
Uminski same lot)
CHOLASINSKI, Valentine 1869 -
1941 Father (A)
Mary 1878 - 1950 Mother (A)
Ann V 1907 - 1962 (A)
Martin 10 Nov 1899 - 11 March
1964 "Indiana F2C USNR" (A)
CHOLEWCZYNSKI (or HOLEW-
CZYNSKI), Mary 1901 - 1978
(B)
(Maciej and Jozef Holewczynski
same lot)
CHOLEWCZYNSKI, F no date -
1924 "Sokol ZB No I" (C)
CHOLEWCZYNSKI, Marion 1859
- 1912 (B)
CHRAPEK, Aloysius 1877 - 2
June 1934 Father (D)
Harriet 1880 - 1933 Mother (D)
Henry 18 Jan 1916 - 25 May 1979
"Pfc US Army" (D)
(F Muszynski-Grandmother same
lot)
C H R A P L I W Y, Peter 24 June
1876 - 14 Jan 1936 (H)
Joseph 19 Mar 1906 - 19 Jan
1947 Indiana Pvt 361 Inf WWII
"Purple Heart" (H)
CHROBOT, Franciszek 1873 - 20
Dec 1915 (B)
Marie R no date - 1908 (Chrobot-
Couch) "Grapevine Creek
Camp #7" (B)
Henry A 1905 - 1939 (Son of
Frank & Leokadya Chrobot) (B)
Jacob 1823 - 1905 Father (B)
Julianna 1829 - 26 Jan 1917
Mother (B)
Leokadya 1875 - 1962 (nee:
Grzesk) Mother (B)
(1) Coddier
Helen 1902 - 1952 (d/o Frank &
Leokadya Chrobot) (B)

CHROBOT (continued)
Clement 1900 - 1977 Son (B)
CHROBOT, Raymond L 1919 -
1974 (C)
Stanislawa 1881 - 1948 (nee:
Borlik) Mother (C)
Jan 1880 - 1973 Father (C)
Esther 1913 - 1923 (C)
(Ethel Pinkowski same lot)
CHROBOT, Michael 1874 - 2 Jan
1939 Father (C)
Christine 1873 - 1944 (nee:
Jaroszewski) Mother (C)
Waclaw E 12 Apr 1895 - 22 Dec
1956 "Indiana Pfc WWI" (C)
Marie Mae 11 Nov 1890 - 17 Oct
1954 (C)
CHRUSCINSKI, Antoni no date -
14 Jan 1930 (F)
CHRUSTOWSKI, Jan 1873 - 2
March 1937 Father (B)
Maryanna (#2 wife) 1887 - 1956
Mother (nee: Sobecki) (B)
Jozefa (#1 wife) 1886 - 1909 (B)
(Eva Sobecki - mother same lot)
CHRZAN, Stella 1882 - 1911 (A)
(Myron O Moore same lot)
CHRZAN, Walenty 1866 - 1948
(D)
Pelagia 1871 - 1943 (nee:
Gadacz) (D)
CHRZAN, Maryann 1938 - 1940
(D)
Thomas no date - 30 July 1940
(D)
Lenny & Larry no date - 5 July
1946 (D)
Sophie 1915 - 1967 Mother (nee:
Balczerzak) (D)
Ambrose 1910 - 1969 Father (D)
Jozef 1872 - 1941 Father (D)
Bronislawa 1877 - 1936 Mother
(D)
CHRZAN, Edward 1901 - 1930
Husband (D
(Zigmond Nemeth same lot)
CHRZANOWSKI, Albin 24 July
1909 - 8 Nov 1909 (B)
Stanislaw 1854 - 3 Nov 1924
Father (B)
Rozalia 1869 - 1935 Mother (B)
John J 18 May 1896 - 25 June

CHRZANOWSKI (continued)
1936 "Indiana Cpl 56 Regt
CAC" (B)
CHUDZICKI, Jan 1887 - 1918 (C)
Leokadya no dates (C)
Genewefa no dates (C)
Mary 25 Mar 1888 - 8 Dec 1973
(C)
CHUDZICKI, Nickola 28 Apr 1859
- 28 Apr 1939 (F)
CHUDZICKI, Kenneth 30 Apr
1951 - 7 May 1951 (H)
(Jozef & Rose Lodyga same lot)
CHWALEK, Stanislaw 1867 - 5
Feb 1938 Father (F)
Agnieszka 1855 - 1936
Grandmother (F)
Ferdinand 1910 - 1949 Son (F)
Zofia 1879 - 1949 Mother (F)
CICHOS, Martha 25 May 1881 -
16 Dec 1949 Mother (E)
Thomas 28 Dec 1878 - 3 Jan
1942 Father (E)
(Maryanna Jozwiak same lot)
CICHOS, Thaddeus 1911 - 19--
(H)
Mary 1914 - 19-- (H)
Richard Francis 30 June-1 July
1935 (H)
CICHOWICZ, Stanislaus no date
- 9 Jan 1910 (-)
CICHOWICZ, Bronislawa 1882 -
1936 Mother (H)
Joseph 1877 - 1947 Father (H)
CIECORA, Joseph 1881 - 1948
(F)
Marya 1893 - 1941 (F)
Janina 1891 - 1929 (F)
CIERNIAK, Zofia 1900 - 19--
Mother (D)
Konstanty 1882 - 1932 Father (D)
(Stanislaw and Katarzyna
Monczko same lot)
CIERZNIAK, Joseph 1872 - 30
Jan 1934 (D)
Agnes 1874 - 1953 (D)
CIESIELSKI, Frank 29 Aug 1860 -
26 July 1917 (A)
CIESIELSKI, Leon 1892 - 1956
(C)
Marya 1894 - 1975 (nee:
Adamowski) (C)

CIESIELSKI (continued)
Walter S no date - 25 Mar 1943
with picture "Indiana S/Sgt 355
Bomb Sqd" (C)
Gregory Allen no date - 16 Aug
1942 (C)
CIESIELSKI, Family no names no
dates (G)
(Stefen Klodzinski same lot)
CIESIOLKA, Walenty no dates
"Husband of Katarzyna Nowak"
(A)
John 1867 - 1950 (A)
Catharine 1883 - 1918 Mother (A)
Leo H 1904 - 1927 Son (A)
CIESIOLKA, Ignace no date - 6
Dec 1921 (A)
CIESIOLKA, Antony A 1910 -
1973 (A)
Irene J 1914 - 1968 (nee:
Aftowski) (A)
(Joseph & Mary Aftowski same
lot)
CIESIOLKA, Forest P 1902 -
19-- Husband (F)
Bernice 1905 - 19-- Wife (nee:
Banacki) (F)
CIESIOLKA, Harry A 20 Apr 1911
- 20 Mar 1961 "Indiana S/2
USNR WWII" (G)
Clara Aug 1914 - Sept 1976 (G)
CIESIOLKA, Bill A 1907 - 19--
(H)
Hattie 13 Oct 1911 - 1980 (nee:
Strzelecki) (H)
William Jr 25 Apr 1939 - 1 May
1939 (H)
CIESLIK, Steve 1896 - 1966 Son
(D)
Walter 1904 - 1964 (D)
Constance 1864 - 1931 Mother
(D)
Valentine 1859 - 31 Dec 1938
Father (D)
CINDINSKI, Wojciech no date - 7
Apr 1910 (Old Sec)
CISZEWSKI, Joseph 8 Feb 1880 -
9 June 1919 Father (E)
Walter no dates Son (E)
Anna no dates Mother (E)
Gladys no dates Daughter (E)

CIULA, Joseph M 1890 - 1964 Father (F)
Pearl 1901 - 1944 Mother (F)
Sadie 1921 - 1929 With Picture Daughter (F)
Sharon Lee 13 Aug 1947 - 26 Feb 1948 (F)
CIUPINSKI, Wojciech 1852 - 9 Apr 1910 Father (A)
Mary 1869 - 1926 (nee: Urbanski) Mother (A)
Sylvester 1907 - 1910 (A)
Joanna 1899 - 1915 (A)
(Jadwiga Slampurt and Joseph Fritz same lot)
CLINE, Max A 2 Mar 1914 - 11 Nov 1971 "Indiana Pfc 925 Sig Co WWII" (E)
Stephanie M 1922 - 19-- (E)
Sharon Ann 12 Oct 1957 (E)
(Joseph, Mary, & Antony Dudzinski same lot)
COOK, Frederick B 1894 - 1928 WWI (F)
(Sophie Liszewski same lot)
COOPER, Rose 1901 - 1922 "w/o George H Cooper" (A)
(Martin & Josephine Rybak same lot)
COOPER, Bernice 1891 - 1973 (F)
(Tomasz & Michalena Jankowski same lot)
CRISWELL, Debra 19 Feb 1953 - 19 Nov 1953 (B)
(Joseph & Helen Szocinski same lot)
CUKROWICZ, Franciszek 1878 - 17 Sept 1930 (B)
Anna 1878 - 1936 (nee: Mackowski) (B)
Sigmund 4 Nov 1907 - 2 Aug 1972 "Indiana Cpl 107 Inf Trg Bn BSM WWII" (B)
Thadeusz 1 Apr 1914 - 18 Sept 1914 (B)
Felix 1910 - 1923 Son (B)
(Wladyslaw Galwas same lot)
CUKROWICZ, Antonina 1855 - 1938 (B)
Walter 1888 - 1941 Son (B)
Wojciech 18 Apr 1852 - 10 Apr

CUKROWICZ (continued)
1918 Father (B)
CURZYTEK, Harriet 1912 - 1936 (H)
Andrew 1880 - 1952 (H)
Anna 1888 - 1955 (H)
CUZINSKI, Stanley 1877 - 1945 Father (C)
Mary 1887 - 1960 Mother (C)
CWIDAK, Joseph 1869 - 31 May 1909 (A)
(Mary (Herman) Hanyzewski same lot)
CWIDAK, Jan 1877 - 1960 (A)
Jozefa 1880 - 1957 (nee: Wolter) (A)
Aloysius 10 June 1910 - 19 Dec 1944 Indiana Cpl 94 Mecz Cau Ren Sq WWII (A)
(Jozef Wolter same lot)
CWIDAK, Ksaweryna 1876 - 1943 (nee: Piotrowski) Mother (B)
Stanislaw 1875 - 1951 Father (B)
CWIKLINSKI, Magdaline 1869 - 1920 Mother (A)
Konstanty 1869 - 17 Oct 1916 Father (A)
Stefan 27 Apr 1893 - 16 Feb 1918 WWI (A)
Lucia 1903 - 1920 (A)
(Katarzana Drajus same lot)
CWIKLINSKI, Antoni 1842 - 5 May 1913 (B)
Walenty 1849 - 6 March 1917 (B)
Jozefa 1859 - 1931 (nee: Stasinski) (B)
CWIKLINSKI, Clara M 1905 - 19-- (E)
Walter A 1885 - 1981 (E)
(Roman W Podlas same lot)
CYBULSKI, John A 1893 - 1963 (F)
Clementine C 1909 - no date (F)
Walaria 1894 - 1930 Mother (F)
CYGART, Adam P 1892 - 1965 Father (H)
Franciszka 1881 - 1935 (H)
Piotr 1876 - 19-- (H)
Stella 1890 - 1958 Mother (H)
(Paszkiet-no name-child & Brian C Fritz same lot)
CYMAN, Antony 10 Jan 1883 - 23

15

CYMAN (continued)
Apr 1912 (H)
Jadwiga 1874 - 1942 (H)
Frank 1891 - 19-- (H)
Frank 26 Oct 1880 - 4 June 1965
Indiana BMI USNRF (H)
(Stella Jagla same lot)
CYNDROWSKI, Rose 1889 - 1976
(nee: Guzicki) (D)
John 16 Oct 1890 - 1954 (D)
(Antony & Hedwige Guzicki same lot)
CYTACKI, Teofilia 1904 - 1910 (C)
Bernady 1915 - 1916 (C)
Stefan 1914 - 1923 (C)
Antoni 1872 - 1940 (C)
Stefania 1878 - 1964 (C)
CZAJKOWSKI, Mary 1883 - 1950
(nee: Gniot) (A)
John S 1876 - 1950 (A)
Carrie 1909 - 1922 (A)
CZAJKOWSKI, Frank 1881 - 19 Feb 1919 Father (E)
---- 1883 - 1946 Mother (E)
CZARNECKI, Wanda 1903 - 1918 (D)
Czeslaw J 1869 - 1942 (D)
Elzbieta 1870 - 1947 (D)
Czeslaw T 1899 - 1937 (D)
CZARNECKI, Edmund no date - 2 Jan 1935 (C)
Adam 1863 - 13 Oct 1913 (C)
CZARNECKI, Matthew no date - 2 Sept 1937 (F)
CZARNECKI, Leo J 1892 - 1973 (D)
Theresa 1892 - 1965 (D)
Joan 1 Mar 1935 - 27 June 1939 (D)
Edward 19 Jan 1922 - 17 Feb 1922 (D)
Walter F 1902 - 1966 (D)
Leo A 13 July 1925 - 22 Dec 1968 "Indiana MM3 US Navy WWII" (D)
CZARNECKI, Antony J 22 Dec 1894 - 8 Oct 1981 (E)
Valaria 1902 - 19-- (nee: Zmudzinski) (E)
Frances E no date - 1943 (E)
CZARNECKI, Jozefa S "w/o

CZARNECKI (continued)
Peter" 1872 - 1947 (nee: Szepanek) Mother (D)
John 19 Nov 1903 - July 1927 (D)
Pelagia 23 Feb 1893 - 24 July 1921 (D)
CZARNECKI, Frances 1855 - 1928 Mother (F)
Matthew 1855 - 1937 Father (F)
CZARNECKI, Walter E 22 Nov 1900 - 15 Apr 1935 "Indiana Pfc 2 Air Svc Mech Regt" (H)
Hattie G 1905 - 1967 (nee: Wieczorek) (H)
CZECK, Agatha 1864 - 1926 (nee: Ubik) Mother (F)
John 1861 - 1933 Father (F)
Charles 1906 - 1927 Son (F)
Genevieve 1911 - 1930 Daughter (F)
CZEKALSKI, Jan 1891 - 1916 (D)
CZERGOSZ, Rita L 1925 - 1927 (F)
CZERNIAK, Antonina 1846 - 1936 (nee: Zielinski) Mother (B)
(Jan, Katarzyna, & Franceszek Kromkowski same lot)
CZERNIAK, Kazimiera 1892 - 1979 Mother (F)
Telesfore 1891 - 1947 Father (F)
CZERNIAK, Konstanty 1882 - 24 March 1932 (D)
CZERNUSIEWICZ, Antoni 1891 - 1971 (D)
Marya 16 Oct 1893 - 1946 (nee: Demkiewicz) (D)
Henry 1919 - 1922 (D)
CZERWINSKI, Walenty no date - 27 Nov 1917 Father (B)
Rozalia no dates Mother (B)
Wawrzynic no dates Son (B)
CZUK, Joseph 1893 - 19-- (E)
Josephine 1892 - 1968 Mother (E)
Roman 1922 - 1923 Son (E)
Angela 1924 - 1929 Daughter (E)
CZYZEWSKI, Wladyslaw no date - 7 July 1919 (-)
Stanislaw no date - 8 Jan 1917 -
CZYZEWSKI, Maryanna 29 Aug 1882 - 4 Mar 1950 (nee: Smucinski) (C)

CZYZEWSKI (continued)
Franciszek 4 June 1883 - 12 Aug
1950 (C)
(Jan & Agnieszka Smucinski
same lot)
DABROS, Valentine 1878 - 1933
(D)
DABROS, Adam 1881 - 1949
Father (E)
Helen 1891 - 19-- (E)
Clem 1918 - 1978 WWII Pfc US
Army (E)
DABROWIAK, Jan 1861 - 1928
(F)
Marya 1864 - 1941 (F)
DABROWSKI, Franciszka 1909 -
1915 (B)
Agnieszka 1872 - 1922 (B)
Jozefa 1895 - 1952 (B)
Marcin 1901 - 1941 (B)
Teofil 1876 - 1942 (B)
DABROWSKI, John 7 Oct 1846 -
20 Aug 1909 (B)
DALKA, Jan 1877 - 1951 (A)
Emelia 1876 - 1958 (nee:
Dalkowski) (A)
DALKA, Frank 1864 - 1919 (A)
Jacob Apr 1837 - 11 Mar 1916
(Woodman of the World
Memorial) (A)
DALKA, Dominick no date - 26
Jan 1916 (A)
DALKOWSKI, Anna Sept 1849 -
1937 (nee: Nowak) (E)
Jan Nov 1848 - 1929 (E)
DANIELOWICZ, Casimir A 1873
- 1948 (D)
Frances 1874 - 1931 (nee:
Milewski) (D)
Harry A 1907 - 1946 (D)
DANIELOWICZ, Joseph no date -
15 Feb 1919 (-)
DANIELOWICZ, Adrian J 22 Mar
1935 - 2 May 1954 (F)
Cecylia 1895 - 18 Feb 1967 (nee:
Mikula) (F)
Stephen 2 Sept 1897 - 12 May
1980 (F)
DANIELOWICZ Zuzanna 1871 -
1938 (H)
Michael 1878 - 1968 (H)
DANKOWSKI, Konstancya 1871 -

DANKOWSKI (continued)
22 Nov 1930 (nee: Paszkiewicz)
(D)
Peter 1869 - 17 Jan 1941 (D)
(Konstancya Paskiewicz &
Regina Piechowiak same lot)
DAPIERALSKI, Stanley 1886 - 17
May 1917 (C)
DASZYNSKI, William 1913 -
1915 (A)
Albert 1890 - 1952 (A)
(Andy Geabler same lot)
DASZYNSKI, Agnieszka 1847 -
1911 (nee: Laboda (2) Geabler)
(A)
Maryann 1893 - 1977 (nee:
Bojarski) (A)
Maximillian 1887 - 19-- (A)
DAVIS, Cloe 1901 - 19-- (D)
Milton 1904 - 1968 (D)
(Leo Kubisiak & Henry X Hahn
same lot)
DEGUS, Stephania 1888 - 17 July
1980 (nee: Jablocki) (E)
Vincent 1878 - 1945 Father (E)
(Helen Unewski same lot)
DEGUCZ, Evelyn 10 Jan 1925 -
12 Sept 1925 (F)
Irvin 29 Dec 1927 - 27 Apr 1928
(F)
Felix J 1889 - 1967 (F)
Mary 1897 - 19-- (F)
Patricia 2 Apr 1933 - 3 May 1936
(F)
DEJAEGHER, Hattie 1898 - 1940
Mother (D)
(Paul W Polinski same lot)
DEKA, Stella "w/o Bernard" 1884
- 1969 (nee: Piasecki) (A)
(Wladyslaw K Gadacz same lot)
DEKA, Antony 1878 - 1961 Father
(B)
Bronislawa 1882 - 1932 (nee:
Kreczmer) Mother (B)
DEKA, Richard W 1923 - 1978
"WWII Cpl US Army" (C)
(Jan & Bronislawa Krantz same
lot)
DEKA, Bernard 1878 - 1924 (D)
Esther no dates Mother (D)
(Leonard Buysse same lot)
DELINSKI, Andrzej 1846 - 1929

17

DELINSKI (continued) (B)
Maryann 1852 - 1917 (nee:
Jedrzejczak) (B)
DEMBECKI, Frank 10 Oct 1888 -
12 Sept 1954 WWI Ind Pvt Co
B 158 Depot Brig" (A)
(Michael & Helen Pawlowski, &
Antonette Kay same lot)
DEMBINSKI, Leo no date - 12
Sept 1933 (-)
DEMBINSKI, David 1929 - 1979
Son (F)
Stanley 1899 - 1960 Father (F)
Sophie 1903 - 1960 Mother (F)
Theresa 1927 - 1961 Daughter
(F)
DEMBINSKI, Andrew 1865 - 1962
(F)
Maryann 1882 - 1951 (F)
Joseph 12 Mar 1895 - 27 June
1921 WWI (F)
(Casimir Gorski same lot)
DEMBRUSKI, Jan no date - 11
Oct 1912 (-)
DEMSKI, Julia 1892 - 1914 (nee:
Smiegielski) "Wife of Frank
Smielgielski" (B)
(F Smiegielski same lot)
DEMSKI, Frank 4 Aug 1887 - 14
Jan 1932 (D)
DEMSKI, Sylvestor 1912 - 1930
Son (D)
(Stanley Bargielski same lot)
DERANEK, Katarzyna 1882 -
1919 (nee: Hosinski) "Wife of
Felix Deranek" (B)
(Jan & Victoria Hosinski same
lot)
DERANEK, Anna K 1881 - 1965
(A)
John K 1878 - 1955 (A)
Jan 1854 - 1941 (A)
Wilhelmina 1859 - 1936 (nee:
Emilia Wolf) (A)
Wladyslaus 1883 - 1909 (A)
Julianna 1824 - 1916 (A)
Dennis Mark 28-31 Jan 1949
"Son of HG & HE Deranek" (A)
DERANEK, Ludwik 1865 - 1955
(F)
Franciszka 1866 - 1945 (nee:

DERANEK (continued)
Wegner) (F)
Regina 1904 - 1928 (F)
DERDA, Adam 1874 - 18 Oct
1936 Father (A)
Maryanna 1873 - 1958 (nee:
Kaminski) Mother (A)
Stanislaus 1913 - 9 May 1913 (A)
Alfonse no dates (A)
Mary Jane no dates (A)
DERDA, Mary 1913 - 1927 (F)
Marianna 1886 - 1970 (F)
(Jan Kluga same lot)
DERDA, Adam P 29 June 1899 -
31 Aug 1979 "Pfc US Army
WWI" (G)
Maryanna 1901 - 1944 (nee:
Kromkowski) Mother (G)
Richard 1921 - 1925 (G)
DERDZINSKI, Michael 1874 -
19-- (Old Sec)
DERESZYNSKI, Agnieszka no
dates (B)
(Jozef Kajzer & Wawrzyniec
Tafelski & Zygmund Kolczyn-
ski same lot)
DERUCKI, John S 1890 - 1958 (F)
Cecelia 1895 - 19-- (F)
DERUYCK, Arthur J 1892 - 1971
(F)
Blanche V 1891 - 1970 (F)
DESHONG, Virginia 1917 - 1966
(F)
(Michael & Joanna Niespodziany
same lot)
DEWITT, Julias 1885 - 1957 (B)
Julia 14 Mar 1885 - 1943 (nee:
Drajus) (B)
DEALS, Ronald V 15 Feb 1937 -
16 July 1960 Ind Pfc 502 Inf
101 ABA Div WWII (F)
(Antony Kujawski same lot)
DIETZ, William 1876 - 1917 (C)
Mary 1852 - 1932 (C)
Mary Dietz Szmanda 1881 - 1938
(C)
(Stanislaw Szmanda same lot)
DIETZ, John J 1885 - 1949 (A)
Eva 1886 - 1918 (nee;
Witkowski) (A)
(Thelma & Alex Tokarski same
lot)

18

DIETZ, Waclaw no date - 13 July 1917 (-)
Jozef 10 Mar 1883 - 30 July 1920 (-)
DLUGOSZ, Wojciech no date - 5 Sept 1934 (H)
DLUGOSZ, John no date - 2 Mar 1929 (-)
DLUGOSZ, Zane 1908 - 19-- (F)
Phillip 1906 - 1974 (F)
Edward 1909 - 1965 (F)
Victoria 1887 - 1929 (F)
DLUGOSZ, Caroline 1885 - 1970 (H)
Wojciech 1875 - 1937 (H)
(Dewry Black same lot)
DOBECKI, Maryann 1880 - 1930 (nee: Sniadecki) Mother (D)
Walter 1876 - 1951 Father (D)
DOBECKI, Mary Helen 1883 - 1978 (nee: Walkowiak) (D)
Harry M 1880 - 21 Feb 1923 (D)
DOBROWSKI, Walenty 1878 - 24 Nov 1933 (D)
DOBRZYKOWSKI, Jozefa 1880 - 9 Sept 1918 (nee: Janiszak) (B)
Valaria 1875 - 1941 (nee: Szybowicz) (B)
Jozef 2 Mar 1874 - 8 Sept 1930 (B)
Jan 1882 - 11 Aug 1911 (B)
DOBRZYKOWSKI, Walter 1903 - 19-- Father (PC)
Alvina 1 June 1910 - 18 Aug 1979 (nee: Nowicki) Mother (PC)
DOBRZYKOWSKI, Walter A 1902 - 1956 (G)
Irene K 1900 - 1967 (G)
DOLATOWSKI, Margaret no dates (F)
Michael no dates (F)
DOLNIAK, Jozef M 1861 - 20 Mar 1935 (C)
Katarzyna 1866 - 1939 (nee: Staszewski) (C)
DOLNIAK, Michael 1886 - 1928 (C)
Helen 1889 - 1959 (nee: Mindykowski) (C)
Alex 28 Feb 1917 - 4 Dec 1968 (C)

DOLNIAK, Franciszek 1 June 1888 - 11 June 1914 (C)
DOLNIAK, Wiktorya 1883 - 1930 Mother (D)
Kazimierz 1879 - 1944 Father (D)
DOLNIAK, Joseph 1906 - 19-- (F)
Louise 1904 - 19-- (F)
Richard J no dates (F)
Daniel J 1935 - 1964 Son (F)
(Betty Jane Maciulski same lot)
DOMBECK, Antony 1884 - 1955 Son (G)
Josephine 1848 - 1933 (nee: Ogorkiewicz) Mother "Wife of Michael Dombeck" (G)
John 1874 - 1963 Son (G)
DOMBROS, Frank no date - 18 Apr 1937 (East Gate)
DOMBROWSKI, Mateusz 1882 - 1916 (C)
Mateusz no dates Son (C)
(Stanley Gorajewski same lot)
DOMBROWSKI, Bernice 9 Sept 1898 - 26 Jan 1968 (nee: Gleniewicz) (F)
Alexander 22 Jan 1895 - 26 July 1967 "Baker & Cook School QMC WWI Ill Pvt" (F)
DOMBROWSKI, Casimir Jr 1924 - 1926 (F)
Casimir 21 July 1895 - 1 Nov 1944 "Ind Sgt 61 Inf 5 Div" (F)
(Eugene J Vargo same lot)
DOMINIAK, Andrzej 1885 - 1929 (E)
Stanislawa 1911 - 1922 (E)
Stanislaw 1923 - 1923 (E)
Stella 1891 - 1958 (E)
DOPIERALSKI, William 4 Jan 1911 - 24 Dec 1958 "Ind 9203 Tech Svc Unit WWII" (C)
Stanislaw 1886 - 1916 (C)
(Karolina & Franciszek Kosiak same lot)
DRABIECKI, John 1885 - 5 Apr 1938 (F)
Lucy 1888 - 1967 (F)
Bronislawa 1912 - 1929 (F)
DRAJUS, Katarzyna 1823 - 30 Aug 1908 (nee: Kolesiak) (A)

19

DRAJUS (continued)
(Konstanty Cwiklinski same lot)
DRAJUS, Stanislaw 1915 - 1934 (B)
Marta 1886 - 1960 (nee: Kruszewski) (B)
Stanislaw 1884 - 1920 (B)
Maryanna 1867 - 1907 (nee: Herman) (B)
Jozef 1859 - 1931 (B)
DRAVES, Felix 1872 - 8 Dec 1936 (A)
(Julianna Geryk & Frank Drejer same lot)
DREWS, Felix 1848 - 1936 Father (F)
Maryanna 1859 - 1940 (nee: Napieralski) Mother (F)
(Casimer Hanyzewski & Stanley Waslicki same lot)
DRONGOWSKI, Stanley 1877 - 6 May 1933 (D)
DRUKALA, Thomas 1893 - 1968 Father (D)
Josephine 1894 - 1933 Mother (D)
DRZEMBINSKI, Andrzej no date - 24 Apr 1934 (H)
DRZEWIECKI, Harriet 1911 - 19-- (C)
Irene 1913 - 1914 (C)
Frank B 1880 - 1950 (C)
Mary B 1881 - 1940 (nee: Cwidak) (C)
DRZEWICKI, Szczepan 25 Dec 1877 - 29 Nov 1927 Father (F)
DRZEWICKI, Aloysius 1897 - 1971 (F)
Hattie 1894 - 1979 (F)
Sylvia Hattie 14 March 1927 - 17 Oct 1927 (F)
DUBICKI, Stella 1893 - 1940 Mother (F)
Alex 1888 - 2 Jan 1981 Father (F)
Dorothy 1924 - 1930 (F)
Edward no date - 14 May 1929 (F)
(Sharon J Tucker & William Pawlowski same lot)
DUDEK, Jacob 1866 - 12 Nov 1909 Father (B)

DUDEK (continued)
Jozef 1896 - 1909 Son (B)
Katharine 1873 - 17 Dec 1940 (nee: Nowicki) Mother (B)
Jan 29 May 1903 - 30 Apr 1928 (B)
(Kathaleen Ann Biddle same lot)
DUDEK, Bronislaw 1918 - 17 Nov 1937 (H)
Daniel Richard 28 Aug 1935 - 2 July 1970 "Ind SH3 US Navy Korea" (H)
DUDKA, John Baby no date - 3 Dec 1950 (E)
(Antonina Szajko & Joseph Gurczak same lot)
DUDZINSKI, Mary 1891 - 1965 (E)
Joseph 1895 - 1961 (E)
Antony no date - 23 Sept 1929 (E)
(Max A Cline same lot)
DUDZISZ, Weronika Feb 1876 - 1942 (B)
Benedytka 1908 - 1932 (B)
Karol Jan 1873 - 1 Apr 1917 (B)
Leo 1900 - 1948 (B)
DULCET, Raymond 1922 - 19-- Son (H)
Frances 1891 - 1967 Mother (H)
Thomas 1887 - 1965 Father (H)
Helen 1916 - 1939 Daughter (H)
DUSZYNSKI, Jan 1852 - 6 June 1908 Father (A)
Stanislaw 27 Oct 1889 - 16 May 1916 Reg Army (A)
Anna 1855 - 25 Dec 1927 Mother (A)
DUSZYNSKI, Michael 1848 - 13 Dec 1914 (C)
(John & Elizabeth Herman same lot)
DUSZYNSKI, Frank J no date - 20 April 1931 "Indiana Cpl Coast Artillery" (F)
DUSZYNSKI, Frank 10 Oct 1884 - 27 Apr 1928 (B)
Catharine 22 Oct 1887 - 28 Oct 1963 (nee: Szmanda) (B)
DWORECKI, Stanley T 14 Sept 1890 - 21 Oct 1956 "Indiana Chief Mech 14 Fld Arty WWI"

DWORECKI (continued)
(PC)
Sophie 1889 - 1960 (PC)
DWORECKI, M no date - Feb
1909 (A)
George no date - 4 Jan 1930 (A)
DYCKO, Julianna 1877 - 1957 (C)
Wasil 1864 - 10 April 1939 (C)
D Y L E W S K I, Stanislaw 1880 -
1951 Father (C)
Franciszka 1880 - 1940 Mother
(C)
DYSINSKI, Konstanty no dates (D)
Jozefa no dates (D)
(Edward & Helena Wyruslak
same lot)
DYSKA, Michal 1856 - 1928 (F)
Jozefa 1859 - 1942 Wife (F)
DYSKIEWICZ, Peter 1881 - 1962
(C)
Josephine 1879 - 1963 (C)
(Bert & Stella Kwasnecki same
lot)
DZIEDZIC, Joseph 1889 - 1963
(H)
(John & Frances Stuglik same
lot)
D Z I E K A N S K I, Joseph 28 Feb
1877 - 23 Aug 1932 (D)
Marian 27 Nov 1879 - 14 Sept
1956 (D)
Bernice 1913 - 1945 Daughter (D)
DZIEWA, Antoni no date - 8 Sept
1916 (-)
DZIKOWSKI, Elzbieta no date -
1928 (B)
Waclaw 12 June 1884 - 14 Apr
1980 (B)
Helena 1885 - 2 Sept 1958 (nee:
Lewandowski) (B)
Frank B 1836 - 24 June 1914
Father (B)
DZIUBINSKI, Jozef 1891 - 1924
(G)
(Joseph Kurowski same lot)
DZIUBINSKI, Boleslaw no date -
1928 (G)
E B E L, Roman C 9 Aug 1923 - 5
Feb 1945 "Ind Pfc 143 Inf 36
Inf Div WWII" (F)
EBEL, Edward 1849 - 7 Aug 1924
(G)

EBEL (continued)
Elizabeth 1848 - 1924 (G)
John 7 June 1892 - 16 June 1960
"Ind Wagoner US Army WWI"
(G)
EICHSTADT, Stanley 1882 - 22
Feb 1936 (G)
EITLER, Paul Jr 25 May 1927 -
18 Mar 1980 "SA US Navy
WWII Korea" (G)
Bernice 7 Aug 1925 - 19-- (G)
(Boleslaw Osowski same lot)
ELANTKOWSKI, Julia 1864 -
1925 (A)
Jan 29 May 1864 - 13 Nov 1924
(A)
(Frank R Wesolowski & Albin
Nowinski same lot)
EWALD, Teodor 1870 - 1946 (A)
Katarzyna 1877 - 1954 (nee:
Urbanski) (A)
(Mikolaj Urbanski & Carrie P
Mejer same lot)
EWALD, Frances V 1902 - 1980
(C)
Antony J 23 Dec 1898 - 27 June
1961 "Ind Pvt Btry D 60 Coast
Arty WWI" (C)
Stanley 1900 - 1959 (C)
EWALD, Arthur 1939 - 1941 Son
(D)
Agnes 1921 - 1922 (D)
Herbert no dates (D)
Jozef 1912 - 1930 Son (D)
(Mary Kujawa same lot)
EWALD, Peter P 1894 - 1976 (E)
Lillian D 1901 - 1969 (E)
E W A L D, Michal 1874 - 1923
Father (F)
Maryanna 1881 - 1971 (nee:
Palka) Mother (F)
(Agnieszka Jurczyk same lot)
EWALD, August no dates - 30
April 1907 (-)
EWALD, Fryderyk 1868 - 1932
Father (PC)
Maryanna 1872 - 1951 Mother
"Most Rev Klemens 21 Dec
1906- 5 March 1954 Son or-
dained 30 May 1931" (PC)
E W A N I E C, Wladyslaw 1892 -
1945 Husband (F)

21

EWANIEC (continued)
Felix no dates Father (F)
FABISZAK, Nepomucyna 1875 -
1956 Mother (D)
Tomasz 1867 - 20 Oct 1930
Father (D)
FABISZAK, Martin 1892 - 1957
(E)
Pauline 1889 - 1970 (E)
FALDA, Leonard F 12 Feb 1919 -
22 Nov 1932 (F)
(Jozef Wroblewski same lot)
FALTYNSKI, Jakub no date - 18
Jan 1927 (E)
Maryanna   no   dates   (nee:
Grabarek) (E)
S 1908 - 1950 (E)
John 1894 - 1975 "Pvt US Army
WWI" (E)
FELDMIER, Dallas 4 Oct 1904 -
31 Dec 1977 Mother (D)
(Rudolph Paege same lot)
FENWICK, Helen Bolka 1899 -
1956 (nee: Bednarek) (F)
(Alfred & Jozef Bolka same lot)
FERGER, Andrew no date - 30
Oct 1924 (B)
Tekla Baby no dates (B)
FILIPEK, Mary Baby no date - 20
Sept 1951 (D)
(Esther Rodriguez, Ramiro Lopez
& Angie Paloma same lot)
FILIPECKI, Antony L 1900 -
1967 (F)
Helen V 1902 - 1971 (F)
FISCHER, Roman 1890 - 31 Jan
1932 (F)
FISHER, Boleslaw B 1896 - 1960
Husband (E)
Margaret 1900 - 1930 Wife (E)
(Wiktorya Houser same lot)
FISHER, Stanley 17 Apr 1873 -
1955 Father (A)
Joan   1884   -   1962   (nee:
Nowakowski) Mother (A)
Benjamin 1912 - 1913 (A)
Angela 1912 - 1917 (A)
(Randy C Baldwin same lot)
FISHER, Zygmond Jozef 1893 -
1935 WWI (F)
Catharine 27 Sept 1890 - 15 Oct
1972 (nee: Blasczak) (F)

FISHER, Stanley 1868 - 1925 (C)
FISHER, ---- "Father" no dates
(C)
---- "Mother" no dates (C)
(Mary & John Schymanski same
lot)
FISHER, S no dates (PC)
FISZER, Gertrude no date - 1906
(A)
Walter 1885 - 1962 (A)
FITZKANETS, Andrew no date -
24 Oct 1917 (-)
FIWEK,   Anna   1882   -   1921
(Mausoleum) (E)
Michalena 1854 - 1938 Mother
(E)
FIWEK, Maria Tekla 14 Sept
1925 - 17 Sept 1925 (G)
Stanley J 26 July 1895 - 10 Oct
1961 "Indiana WWI Pvt Co G
39 Inf PH" (G)
FLATOFF, Frances 1900 - 19--
(F)
John 1896 - 1966 (F)
Robert 7 Oct 1929 - 13 Oct 1929
(F)
FLIS, Anna 1879 - 1964 (F)
FLORKOWSKI,   Bridget   1900 -
19-- (B)
(Wojciech Borkowski same lot)
FLORKOWSKI, John K 14 June
1888 - 25 Oct 1911 "Indiana
Pfc Com 67 Inf WWI" (B)
Leon E 1880 - 1952 Son (B)
Julianna 1854 - 1927 Mother (B)
Jozef 1848 - 1926 Father (B)
FLORKOWSKI,   Antony   J   1892 -
1979 (E)
Carrie 1892 - 1967 (nee: Obarski)
(E)
FLOWERS, Peter 10 Jan 1898 -
15 Dec 1933 "Indiana Pvt 10
Inf 14 Div" (D)
(Mary, John, & Vincent Kwiat-
kowski same lot)
FOLEY, Domecela 1906 - 1937
(B)
(Joseph J Kasprzak same lot)
FORYCKI, Ursula no dates (E)
Antony no dates (E)
Josephine no dates (E)
FOX, Christopher 29 Dec 1965 - 1

FOX (continued)
Jan 1966 (F)
(Ray Lisiecki same lot)
FRANKOWIAK, John no date - 4
July 1937 (E)
Maryanna 2 Feb 1851 - 18 Apr
1920 (E)
FRANKIEWICZ, Martha 1892 -
1927 (F)
Steve 26 Oct 1893 - 11 Apr 1959
"Indiana Cook Fld Arty WWI"
(F)
Maryanna 1923 - 1925 (F)
Marcyanna 1869 - 1941 (F)
Ludwik 1869 - 28 Mar 1935 (F)
FRIDRICK, Peter no date - 24
Mar 1924 (-)
FRITZ, Jospeh Baby no dates (A)
(W Ciupinski & Jadwiga Slam-
purt same lot)
FRITZ, Brian C no date - 17 July
1961 (H)
(Adam Frances Piotr & Stella
Cygert Paszkiet (baby) same
lot)
FRONTCZAK, Andrew no date -
25 Mar 1919 (-)
FRYDRYCH, Jan 24 Dec 1852 -
30 June 1913 Father (A)
Pelegia 1857 - 1937 Mother (A)
Anna no date - 12 Nov 1980 (A)
FUJAWA, Rudolph 1885 - 7 Nov
1938 Father (A)
Anna Feb 1885 - 1935 (nee:
Rybak) Mother (A)
(Henry Leda same lot)
FUJAWA, Stanley B 1907 - 1945
Husband (A)
(Edmund Hosinski same lot)
FUJAWA, Bronislawa 1885 -
1961 (nee: Sordel) Mother (C)
Ferdyand 1879 - 1 Nov 1933
Father (C)
Maria 1915 - 1917 Daughter (C)
FUJAWA, Benedict 1925 - 19--
(E)
Louise 1908 - 19-- (E)
Clement 1918 - 1977 "Pfc US
Army WWII" (E)
FUJAWA, Stanislaw 1875 - 6
July 1931 Father (G)
Wiktorya 1879 - 1953 (nee:

FUJAWA (continued)
Gadacz) Mother (G)
Chester L 14 Aug 1905 - 22 Aug
1973 "Ohio Pfc US Army
WWII" (G)
(Marya Switalski same lot)
FUTA, Walenty 14 Feb 1865 - 15
Oct 1910 (B)
Mary K 1875 - 1961 (B)
(John J & Harriet R Nowakowski
same lot)
FUTA, Frank 1892 - 1943 (G)
Mary 1892 - 1957 (nee:
Holewinski) (G)
Bert no dates Brother (G)
Joseph no dates Brother (G)
FYSZER, Jan 16 Dec 1895 - 9
July 1916 (C)
GABRYS, Joseph 10 Jan 1864 - 8
Jan 1927 (A
(Jan Spychalski same lot)
GABRYSIAK, Walter J 1921 -
1973 (E)
(Walter Bilinski same lot)
GABRYSIAK, Joseph V 10 Sept
1916 - 21 Oct 1959 "Ind S/Sgt
743 Ry Opr BN TC WWII" (E)
Frank 1881 - 21 Oct 1959 (E)
Constance 1889 - 1972 (nee:
Lykoska) (E)
GADACZ, Maryanna 24 Jan 1849
- 27 Sept 1919 Mother (A)
(Wife of George Gadacz interred
at Cedar Grove)
Wladyslaw 1875 - 1955 Uncle
(E)
(Frank E Geabler & Paul R Glon
same lot)
GADACZ, Alice 1882 - 1911 (A)
Frank 1881 - 9 Sept 1913 (A)
Joanne 1904 - 1917 (A)
George 1910 - 28 Sept 1930 (A)
GADACZ, Wladyslaw K 28 May
1888 - 30 Oct 1911 (A)
Maryanna 7 Nov 1856 - 13 Aug
1920 Mother (nee: Rybacki) (A)
Michal 17 Aug 1854 - 20 Nov
1929 Father (A)
Janina 1927 - 1928 (A)
(Stella Deka same lot)
GADACZ, Jan C 1863 - 31 May
1939 Father (C)

23

GADACZ (continued)
Franciszka 1862 - 1939 (nee:
Janowiak) Mother (C)
GADACZ, Bert M 19 Dec 1892 -
28 Feb 1980 (D)
(2) Harriet 29 Sept 1897 - 11 Jan
1980 (nee: Paszkiet) Wife (D)
(1) Helena 1893 - 1933 (nee:
Kajzer) Wife (D)
GADACZ (2) John 1906 - 19--
Husband (D)
Mary 14 Mar 1898 - 19-- (nee:
Ciesiolka) (D)
(1) Ted Kazmierczak same lot)
(Husband) (D)
GADACZ, John J 27 Apr 1912 -
19 Apr 1972 "Indiana Pfc US
Army WWII" (H)
Anna 1888 - 1963 Mother (H)
Stanislaw 1885 - 1935 Father (H)
GADACZ, Agnieszka 1891 - 1930
(F)
(Napieralski same lot)
GADOWSKI, George J 1892 -
1974 (F)
Martha D 1893 - 19-- (F)
(Frank Vargyas same lot)
GAIK, A 1890 - 1945 (D)
(Vera Walkowiak, Victor Barber,
A Wrotnowski, & Louis M
Hanyzewski same lot)
GAIK, John 18 Mar 1924 - 12 May
1956 "Indiana T/5 302 Sig Co
WWII" (G)
Jane 1922 - 1969 (G)
Salomea 1893 - 1970 (G)
GAJEWSKI, Joseph 1893 - 1960
Father (C)
Theresa 1895 - 1974 Mother (C)
GALLEGOS, Mary E no date - 30
Aug 1953 (C)
(Michal Rafalski Patricia &
Ralph Myszak same lot)
GALUS, Joseph 14 Jan 1894 - 20
Apr 1912 (D)
GALUS, Michael 1889 - 1969
Father (H)
Mary 1890 - 1976 Mother (H)
Bernice 1917 - 1935 Daughter (H)
(James J Budzinski same lot)
GALWAS, John 1876 - 28 Jan
1944 Father (B)

GALWAS (continued)
Angela 20 Nov 1914 - no date (B)
(1)Agnes no date - 17 Mar 1914
(nee: Dyskiewicz) Mother (B)
(2) Anna Ryska Goralczyk same
lot (B)
Leo 1906 - 1972 (B)
Joseph Baby - no dates (B)
GALWAS, Wladyslawa 5 Aug
1807 - 16 Dec 1900 Mother (B)
---- no dates Father (B)
(Tadeusz Cukrowicz, & Francis-
zek, Anna, & Zygmond Cuk-
rowicz same lot)
GALWAS, Joseph no date - 3 Apr
1914 (-)
GAPCZYNSKI, Lottie 1894 - 1975
(B)
Very Rev Msg Ignatius J 1882 -
1964 "Ordained 21 June 1912"
(B)
Jozefa 1859 - 1940 Mother (B)
Szczepan 1855 - 11 Mar 1929
Father (B)
GAPCZYNSKI, Stanley 12 Nov
1896 - 20 Mar 1973 "Ohio Pfc
US Army WWI" (H)
Theresa 15 Oct 1896 - 20 Dec
1939 (nee: Milewski) (H)
GAPINSKI, Antoni 1870 - 6 Mar
1939 (C)
Marcyanna 1875 - 1956 (C)
Jozefa no dates (C)
Elegius no date - 30 Nov 1917
(C)
Leokadya no dates (C)
GAPSKI, Stephen no date - 9 July
1916 (-)
GARSTECKI, Franciszek 11 Sept
1903 - 17 Jan 1922 (G)
Jozef 1907 - 1927 (G)
Stanley M 8 Sept 1911 - 26 Nov
1947 "Indiana Pvt 52 AA Trg
BN CAC" (G)
Stanley J 1937 - 1954 (G)
Joseph no date - 16 Feb 1930 (G)
GASIOROWSKI- (see GON-
SIOROWSKI - name changed)
Antony 1852 - 29 Jan 1914 (A)
Antonette 1851 - 1911 (A)
(Leo & Mary Palka same lot)
GASIOROWSKI, Joe 1879 - 4 May

GASIOROWSKI (continued)
1908 Father (A)
Hilary 1906 - 1939 (A)
(Rose Brodzinski same lot)
GAWRONSKI, Jozef 1873 - 1948
Father (A)
Stanislawa 1874 - 1947 Mother
(A)
Walter L 5 July 1902 - 29 July
1969 (A)
(Blanche J Kuspa & Jean H
Tobolski same lot)
GAWRONSKI, Theresa 1927 -
1928 twin of Adeline (D)
Adeline 1927 - 1929 twin of
Theresa (D)
(Jozef Gutek same lot)
GAWRYSIAK, Frank W 1911 -
1932 (D)
Walter J 1879 - 1948 (D)
Alexandria M 1880 - 1974 (nee:
Prawat) (D)
Louis D 19 Aug 1917 - 26 Mar
1959 "Indiana T/Sgt Co C 81
Tank Bn" (D)
GEABLER, Andy no dates (A)
(Albert & William Daszynski
same lot)
GEABLER, Frank E 1905 - 1980
(A)
Mary E 1908 - 19-- (A)
(Maryanna Gadacz & Paul Glon
same lot)
GEIST, Martin 4 Sept 1888 - 15
Aug 1957 "Indiana 1/Sgt Btry
F 137 FA WWI" (B)
(---- Wlodarski same lot)
GENCHOFF, Nicholas 1 Jan 1894
- 10 May 1965 (H)
Mary 1892 - 1972 (H)
Gertrude 2 Oct 1920 - 13 Mar
1935 (H)
GERYK (GIERYK), Julianna 1847
- 1932 Mother (A)
Simon 18 Feb 1850 - 21 Feb
1910 (A)
GIERANOWSKI, Rev William
1923 - 19-- (Priest) (G)
Hedwige 1891 - 1978 Mother (G)
Sylvester 1884 - 1952 Father (G)
Edward 1918 - 19-- (G)
GIERSZ, Martin 1830 - 17 Dec

GIERSZ (continued)
1912 (A)
Franciszka 1880 - 1910 (A)
GIERSZ, John 1877 - 1929 (A)
Pauline 1878 - 1948 (A)
Josephine 1917 - 1918 (A)
(Maryanna Bauer same lot)
GIERSZEWSKI, Balbina 1862 -
1943 Grandmother (C)
(Frank & Frances Wilczewski
same lot)
GIERZYNSKI, Franciszek 30
July 1886 - 12 Oct 1915 (C)
Jan 1853 - 12 July 1922 Father
(C)
Mary 1859 - 1921 Mother (C)
GIERZYNSKI, Mary W 1858 -
1946 (B
GIERZYNSKI, Franciszek 1854 -
1927 (E)
Walerya 1889 - 1925 (E)
GILAS, Stanislaw 1880 - 1970
Father (C)
(Jozef & Jozefa Nowak same lot)
GINTER, Konstanty 9 Apr 1820 -
20 Dec 1912 Father (A)
Antonina 10 May 1833 - 20 Aug
1908 Mother "Nee: Ernsdorf,
Born Greater Poland" (A)
Max A 25 Jan 1885 - 19 Sept
1913 (A)
GINTER, Frances 17 Sept 1887 -
19 Nov 1980 (A)
(Jan & Jozefa Paturalski same
lot)
GINTER, John Feb 1862 - 19 Aug
1917 (-)
Andrew no date - 20 Dec 1912 (-)
GINTER, Frances 1881 - 1952
(nee: Lapczynski) (C)
Frank 1876 - 1958 (C)
Leo 1914 - 1916 (C)
Walter 1907 - 19-- (C)
GIZEWSKI, Helena 1919 - 1944
Daughter (D)
(Matthew Hornung same lot)
GLANSK, Walter no date - 14
June 1921 (-)
GLENIEWICZ, Jacob 1877 - 1924
Father (C)
Frances 1877 - 1946 Mother (C)
(Antonette Slesinski same lot)

GLON, Paul R no date - 1926 (A)
Jane P no date - 1926 (A)
(Maryanna Gadacz & Frank E
Geabler same lot)
GLON, Frances 1854 - 1944
Mother (A)
Jozef 1853 - 31 Jan 1914 Father
(A)
Harry 1924 - 1975 (A)
Mary 1897 - 1977 (A)
Leon 1897 - 1971 (A)
GLON, Henry A 1881 - 1947 (A)
Lottie G 1883 - 1971 (A)
Joseph G no dates (A)
Theodore no dates (A)
GLOWACKI, Napomecyna no date
- 7 Nov 1912 (-)
GLOWSKI, Walter no date - 18
Jan 1916 (-)
GLOYESKI, Anthony R 1892 -
1961 Father (C)
Martha T 1893 - 1965 (C)
GLUCHOWSKI, Victoria 1886 -
1969 (D)
Ludwik 1888 - 1 Oct 1937 (D)
GLUMBBUSKI, Adam no date -
28 Nov 1939 "Indiana Pfc 39
Inf 4 Div WWI" (D)
GNIOT, Henryk K 5 May 1887 -
15 Feb 1930 (F)
GNIOT, Hieronim 11 Nov 1891 - 4
Mar 1927 "Indiana Pvt Air Svc
WWI" (G)
Michael 1893 - 22 Aug 1935 (G)
GNOTH, (1) Harold J 1911 - 11
July 1936 Husband (PC)
(Doris Victoria Rose Stachowiak
and (2)John (Mooney) Sekendi
same lot)
GOLICHOWSKI, Maryann 1866 -
1919 Mother (B)
Walenty 1867 - 19 July 1936
Father (B)
GOLICHOWSKI, Eleanor 1911 -
1924 (E)
Michael 1887 - 1919 (E)
Josephine 1886 - 1974 (E)
GOLICHOWSKI, Michael no date
- 16 Jan 1917 (-)
GOLICHOWSKI, Rose 1905 - no
date (F)
Catharine 1862 - 1921 (F)

GOLICHOWSKI (continued)
Michal 1859 - 1939 (F)
Alex 1903 - 1962 (F)
Alex Jr no date - 14 Aug 1931
Son (F)
GOLCZ, Martha 1895 - 1966 (G)
Edward 1893 - 1954 (G)
Victoria no date - 1930 Daughter
(G)
Arthur L 1919 - 1974 Son (G)
GOLCZ, Stanley no date - 23 May
1910 (G)
CT no date - 16 Feb 1930 (G)
GOLUBIC, Clementine 20 Apr
1920 - 28 Mar 1945 (C)
(Bernice & Frank Brzezinski
same lot)
GOLUBSKI, Norbert no date -
1931 (B)
Leonard 1932 - 1940 (B)
(Frank & Pelegia Pietraszewski
same lot)
GOLUBSKI, Irene no dates (C)
(Michael & Marcyanna Krol same
lot)
GOLUBSKI, Steve no date - 20
Jan 1934 "Indiana Pvt 93rd
Eng" "My love goes with you
and my soul waits to join you"
(D)
GOLUBSKI, Michael 1884 - 1969
Father (D)
Mary 1883 - 1963 Mother (D)
GOLUBSKI, Frank X 1892 - 1976
(F)
Anna 1897 - 1968 (nee:
Piotrowski) (F)
Michael 1851 - 19 Mar 1929
Father (F)
Helena 1854 - 1941 (nee:
Lewandowski) Mother (F)
GOLUBSKI, Antony F 1913 - 1975
S2 US Navy WWII (H)
Jadwiga 1892 - 1952 (nee:
Odynski) (H)
Antoni 1888 - 3 Mar 1936 (H)
GOLUPSKI, Eleanora A 29 Oct
1904 - 18 Feb 1974 (A)
Frank J 12 Sept 1904 - 16 June
1974 (A)
(John Samp same lot)

GONSIOROWSKI, (see GASIO-ROWSKI) Martin (h/o Frances Laskowski) 1838 - 25 May 1917 (-)
GORACZEWSKI, Adam 9 Dec 1874 - 8 Apr 1933 Father (B)
Jozefa 12 Feb 1882 - 1970 Mother (B)
(Janina Klosinski, Ignacy & Anna Szafranski same lot)
GORACZEWSKI, Dr Thaddeus C 4 April 1907 - 1951 with picture Father (B)
Marian R 1905 - 1969 Mother (B)
GORACZEWSKI, Klemens B 23 Nov 1852 - 1918 (C)
Maryanna 1865 - 1935 Wife (nee: Rozplochowski) (C)
GORAJEWSKI, Stanley M 1880 - 1966 (C)
(Mateusz Dombrowski same lot)
GORAJEWSKI, Frank 2 Feb 1893 - 23 Sept 1965 Kentucky Pvt 17 Co Transp Corp (E)
Andrew 1864 - 1944 Father (E)
Katharine 1867 - 1945 Mother (E)
Cecylia 2 Sept 1895 - 9 Oct 1919 Daughter (E)
GORAJEWSKI, Margaret 1895 - 1928 (nee: Wroblewski) "Sister of Charles Wroblewski, Wife of Stanley M Gorajewski" (F)
GORALCZYK, Anna 1875 - 28 July 1953 (nee: Ryska) Mother (C)
(2) John Galwas, Husband (C)
(1) Marcen 1876 - 1917 Father (C)
(Magdaline Ryska same lot)
GORALCZYK, Stephen 1887 - 1960 Father (G)
Stella 1893 - 1968 (nee: Gramza) Mother (G)
GORALSKI, Stanislaw 1868 - 20 Nov 1923 Father (C)
Franciszka 1870 - 1920 Mother (C)
Jozef 1897 - 21 Nov 1914 Son (C)
GORKA, Sylvester 1883 - 23 Nov 1926 Father WWI (F)
Martha 1907 - 1944 "Mom" (F)
Helen 1884 - 1971 Mother (F)

GORNIEWICZ, Marcyanna 28 June 1872 - 23 June 1948 Mother (F)
Ignacy 6 Jan 1862 - 28 Sept 1937 Father (F)
(Pelegia Klos same lot)
GORNIEWICZ, Lillian Fisher 27 Nov 1894 - 9 Jan 1971 (F)
(Roman & Stanley Fischer same lot)
GORNY, John 23 June 1858 - 22 Feb 1938 (A)
Rose no dates (nee: Kaniewski) (A)
Frank no date - 28 Oct 1963 (A)
Valentine 1826 - 11 Sept 1907 Father (A)
GORNY-GORNEY, Jakub 1865 - 24 Mar 1937 (A)
Marya 1872 - 1942 Mother (A)
GORNY-GORNEY, Stanley G 14 Aug 1879 - 7 Jan 1933 (A)
Sophie 17 Apr 1902 - 1 Nov 1944 (A)
Rose 14 Aug 1877 - 6 May 1955 (nee: Wlodarek) (A)
(Eleanor Stedman, daughter, same lot)
GORNY, Jakob B 1892 - 1976 (A)
Veronica 1897 - 1977 "Married 16 Nov 1915" (A)
GORNY, Michael 1845 - 22 Feb 1932 Father (B)
Marya 1894 - 1909 Daughter (B)
Antonina 1855 - 1935 Mother (B)
GORNY, Mary Rose no date - 13 Nov 1964 (D)
(Elizabeth Maeyons, Issac Silva, Alvin Putrzewski & Edward Knape same lot)
GORNY, Helena 2 Apr 1890 - 27 Dec 1911 (A)
(Wojciech Pawlak same lot)
GORSKI, Frank no date - 17 Jan 1924 (-)
GORSKI, Jan 1873 - 1 Sept 1927 Father (E)
Michalena 1867 - 1956 Mother (E)
John F 5 June 1901 - 15 June 1970 (E)
Clement J 10 Nov 1898 - 24 May

GORSKI (continued)
1966 "Kentucky Sgt US Army"
(E)
GORSKI, Casimir 15 Feb 1935 - 9
Mar 1935 Son (F)
(Andrew Dembinski same lot)
GORSKI, Bernice 1890 - 1959 (G)
Anton 1893 - 1981 (G)
GOTOWKA, Stanley J 19 Apr
1894 - 22 Dec 1974 "WWI
S/Sgt US Army" (B)
GRABAREK, Vincent 1888 - 1962
(A)
Elizabeth 1895 - 1964 (nee:
Michalski) (A)
(Wojciech & Konstancia
Michalski same lot)
GRABAREK, Stanley J 25 Aug
1913 - 29 Aug 1913 (C)
Stanley C 1885 - 1956 (C)
Josephine 1889 - 1974 (C)
Frank J 14 Oct 1920 - 2 Feb
1944 "Indiana WWII Sgt 7 Inf
3 Inf Div" (C)
GRABOWSKI, John 28 Feb 1887 -
13 Nov 1958 (H)
Celia 5 July 1894 - 27 Apr 1966
(nee: Kujawski) (H)
GRACZYK, Stanislaw 1907 - 14
Jan 1925 Son (A)
(Frank & Jozefa Jaroszewski &
Patricia Ann Kazmierczak
same lot)
GRACZYK, Michael 1880 - 9 Feb
1918 (A)
Casimir 1883 - 1920 (A)
Agnes 1858 - 1923 (nee:
Trafka) Wife (A)
Frank 1846 - 9 Aug 1919 Hus-
band (A)
Stanley 1885 - 1906 (A)
Joseph 1888 - 20 July 1908 (A)
(Josephine Zalas and Rose
Trafka same lot)
GRACZYK, John 20 June 1881 -
27 Aug 1923 (C)
Stanislaw no dates (C)
Kazimierz no dates (C)
Janina Ewa no dates (C)
GRACZYK, Jan 1849 - 1 May
1936 Grandfather (E)
(Jan Stachowski same lot)

GRACZYK, Stella 1913 - 1922 (G)
Mary 1907 - 1924 (G)
Joseph 1871 - 1948 (G)
Antonette 1877 - 1955 (G)
Dorothy 1938 - 1939 Grandchild
(G)
Delores 1938 - 1939 Grandchild
(G)
Eugene 1942 - 1943 Grandchild
(G)
GRADZIELA, Jozef 24 Feb 1924
- 20 July 1924 (B)
Jozef 1859 - 14 Feb 1916 (B)
Maryanna 1836 - 1909
Grandmother (B)
Jozefa 1862 - 1927 Mother (B)
GRAHAM, John no date - 21 Feb
1934 (-)
GRAJCZYK, Stanislaw no date -
14 Jan 1925 (A)
GRAJCZYK, Frank 1846 - 9 Feb
1919 (A)
Michael no date - 9 Feb 1918 (A)
Kazimierz no date - 17 June
1920 (A)
GRAMZA, Theresa 1902 - 1953
"Everyone's Friend" (D)
(Guadalupe L Vallejo same lot)
GRAMZA, Thomas J 12 Mar 1898
- 6 Nov 1950 "Indiana Pvt 150
FA 42 Rainbow Div WWI" (D)
GRAMZA, Michalena 1868 - 1948
Mother (D)
Wincenty 1866 - 1945 Father (D)
Frank 3 Oct 1900 - 9 Aug 1961
"Indiana Pfc Btry F 137 Fld
Arty WWI" (D)
GREEN (correct name: ZIE-
LINSKI) (name changed),
Frank J 21 July 1894 - 9 Aug
1966 "Colorado Cpl Btry B 9
Fld Arty" (A)
(Jan Zielinski, Ludwig Springer
same lot)
GREENWALD, Mary 1868 - 1952
(C)
(William J & Veronica Jaros-
zewski same lot)
GREGOROWICZ, Stanley 1881 -
1949 (G)
Mary 1891 - 1966 (nee:
Szewczyk) (G)

GREMBOWICZ, Maryanna 1883 -
1969 Wife (D)
Wawrzyniec 1885 - 16 May 1932
Husband (D)
GROCHOWSKI, Maryanna 1883 -
1969 Wife (D)
Wawrzyniec 1885 - 16 May 1932
Husband (D)
(Theodosia Osmanski same lot)
GROCHOWSKI, Marya 1918 -
19-- (A)
Boleslaw 1874 - 1922 Father (A)
Jozefa 1879 - 1930 Mother (A)
Sylvester no dates (A)
Alojzy no dates (A)
Julian no dates (A)
(Agnieszka Szczepanek same lot)
GROCHOWSKI, Victor 1899 -
1944 WWI (D)
(Anna Robaska same lot)
GROCHULSKI, Jozefa no dates
(H)
(Alexander & Marya Mejer same
lot)
GROCKI, Julianna I 27 Aug 1902
- 12 July 1967 Mother (F)
(Anna Lipinski same lot)
GROCKI, Henrietta 1 Apr 1924 -
15 July 1926 (E)
(Joseph Trzcina same lot)
GROCKI, Mieczyslaw dates not
legible (G)
GRODZICKI, (1) Vincent 1898 -
22 Oct 1918 Husband (C)
(Frances (nee: Morecki) (3)
Joseph Brusick (2) Stanley
Lupa & Alice Lupa same lot)
GRONTKOWSKI, Charles J 20
May 1896 - 18 Dec 1983
Father (A)
Harriet 1895 - 1969 Mother (A)
(Joseph & Elizabeth Leda same
lot)
GRONTKOWSKI, Jozef 1865 -
1915 (C)
Apolonia 10 June 1876 - 28 Nov
1938 (nee: Chmiel) (C)
Sophie 1892 - 1958 (C)
(Amelia Chmiel same lot)
GRONTKOWSKI, Stephen 1894 -
1951 (F)
(Bert Sokolowski, John Zyto

GRONTKOWSKI (continued)
same lot)
GROTKOWSKI, (2) Peter 1891 -
1978 "Husband Pfc US Army
WWI" (H)
Lottie 20 May 1904 - 15 March
1971 Mother (H)
(Bernard Rutkowski (1) same lot)
GRUDNIEWSKI, Piotr 1883 -
1940 (H)
Victoria 1882 - 1957 (H)
GRUSZKA, Lukasz 1858 - 2 June
1925 Father (F)
Jozefa no date - 17 June 1926
Mother (F)
GRUZA, John J 15 Aug 1892 - 26
Dec 1958 "Indiana Pvt Motor
Tran Corps WWI" (A)
Michael 1855 - 1927 Father (A)
Konstancya 1855 - 1927 Mother
(A)
GRUZA, Valentine no dates (E)
Mary no dates (E)
GRZECHOWIAK, Mary 1880 -
1946 (A)
(Wladyslaw Hyekiel same lot)
GRZEGOREK, Katarzyna 1861 -
1929 Mother (B)
GRZEGOREK, Wiktorya 1867 -
1930 Mother (C)
Walenty 1861 - 1914 Father (C)
H no dates (C)
(Valentine & Mary Kaniewski
same lot)
GRZEGOREK, Tomasz 1852 -
1916 (D)
GRZEGORZEWSKI, Mary 12 Dec
1887 - 27 Dec 1971 (D)
(Catharine Jagla same lot)
GRZELEWSKI, Jozef 1883 - 19
Jan 1943 "Born at Krzyniow
Kalisz Poland" (C)
Boleslaw 1918 - 25 Oct 1940 (C)
Wladyslawa 1885 - 1972 (nee:
Kurek) "Born Kawnica Kalisz
Poland" (C)
(Jan Jerzykowski same lot) #1
Husband
GRZESIAK, John 1887 - 1950 (C)
Frances 1894 - 1976 (C)
GRZESK, Wladyslaw A 4 June
1880 - 23 Oct 1928 Father (A)

29

GRZESK (continued)
Martha 1883 - 1958 (nee: Gieryk)
Mother (A)
Wladyslaw Jr 1913 - 7 July 1935
(A)
(Klara Grzesk Borlik same lot)
GRZESK, Helen T 1 Jan 1888 -
1973 (nee: Borlik) (C)
Julius B 1882 - 1964 (C)
Gertrude A 1917 - 1923 (C)
GRZESK, Szyman 22 Feb 19-- -
no date (-)
GRZESK, Lottie 1899 - 1959 (H)
Felix 1897 - 19 Oct 1936 (H)
GRZESKIEWICZ "Mausoleum
1921" (E)
Stanislaw 1882 - 1924 (E)
Alicia 1912 - 1920 (E)
GRZESKOWIAK, George 1853 -
1907 (A)
Katharine 1849 - 1921 (A)
Frank 1885 - 1957 (A)
Hattie 1887 - 1975 (A)
GRZESKOWIAK, Stella 1886 -
1967 (nee: Urbanski) (A)
Michael A 1886 - 1955 (A)
GRZESKOWIAK, Maryanna 1862
- 1950 Mother (B)
Andrzej 1859 - 1926 Father (B)
Stella 1904 - 1973 Aunt (B)
(Julianna (Mother) Nowicki same
lot)
GRZESKOWIAK, Marcin 1872 -
1943 (F)
Agnieszka 1868 - 1938 (nee:
Bucholtz) (F)
(Charles B. Maternowski same
lot)
GRZESKOWIAK, Stephen 6 July
1895 - 25 June 1961 Indiana
Cpl Co H 47 Infantry (F)
Jan 1855 - 1934 Father (F)
Konstancya 1855 - 1927 Mother
(F)
GRZESCZYK, Stanley 1865 -
1944 Father (D)
Antonette 1870 - 1945 Mother (D)
Bert J 3 March 1924 - 6 March
1924 (D)
GRZESCZYK, Alice 1897 - 1967
(nee: Guzowski) Wife (E)
Harry 17 May 1901 - 6 July 1973

GRZESCZYK (continued)
Missouri Pvt US Army WWI
(E)
Marcin 1858 - 1 Apr 1937 Father
(E)
Anna 1865 - 1925 Mother (E)
GRZYMCZYNSKI, Wojciech 1851
- 27 Aug 1920 (A)
Apolonia 1852 - 1932 (A)
GUENTHER, Clara 1903 - 1944
(E)
(Walter A. Jaronik same lot)
GUMKOWSKI, Alex 1889 - 5 Oct
1953 (D)
Frances 1888 - 12 May 1964 (D)
GUNDECK, Esther 1904 - 1930
(F)
(Frank Jozwiak same lot)
GUNDECK, Antonette 1876 - 29
July 1943 (Nee: Wegnorowicz)
(D)
GURCZAK, Joseph 3 Feb 1895 -
20 June 1963 Missouri Pfc Hq
Co 127 Inf WWI (E)
(Antonina & Franciszek Szajko &
John Dudka same lot)
GUTEK, Jozef no date - 13 Dec
1939 "Placowka #125-(Polish
Veteran)" (D)
(Theresa & Adeline Gawronski
same lot)
GUZICKI, Antonina 1873 - 1954
(C)
Adalbert A 1863 - 29 Nov 1930
(C)
Mary Magdalyn 1914 - 19 Apr
1918 (C)
(Leonard Lukasik & Karen M
Kovach same lot)
GUZICKI, Anthony 1851 - 1933
(D)
Hedwig 1849 - 1945 (D)
(Rose & John Cyndrowski same
lot)
GUZICKI, Michael 24 Oct 1866 -
5 Dec 1956 Father (F)
(Veronica Janczak Korn & Stanis-
law Janczak same lot)
GUZICKI, Rozalia 1868 -1945 "#2
Wife of Michael Guzicki) (F)
(Frank Tomaszewski same lot)
GUZICKI, Joseph G 1893 - 1971

GUZICKI (continued)
(D)
Bernice 1894 - 19-- (nee:
Janicki) (D)
Edwin 1929 - 1973 (D)
(Frances Kalka same lot)
GUZICKI, Stephan 1886 - 1970
Father (G)
(Wife: Helen Luzny interred at
Cedar Grove)
GUZOWSKI, John Feb 1868 - 28
Jan 1936 (A)
Mary July 1872 - no date (nee:
Dalka) (A)
HAHAJ, Walter 25 Apr 1894 - 28
May 1966 Indiana MUS 2/C
327 Fld Arty WWI (G)
Hedwige 1889 - 1962 Mother (G)
HAHN, Henrv X 1901 - 1942 (D)
(Leo Kubisiak same lot)
HAHN, James D 1940 - 1940 (H)
HAINES, Emma 1897 - 1959 (F)
(Wladyslaw Andrysiak and
Eleanor Allen same lot)
HAJDUCKI, Clarence F 20 Sept
1926 - 13 Dec 1969 Indiana
Pfc 677 Mil Pol Bn WWII (B)
Frank John 22 Aug 1895 - 22 Dec
1951 CM3 USNRF Indiana
WWI (B)
Lottie M 7 July 1896 - 4 May
1974 (B)
HALE, Hugh 1903 - 1958 (C)
(John, Mary, Frank, Andrzej, and
Rozalia Hoffman same lot)
HALUDA, John 1886 - 4 Sept
1920 (E)
(Samuel Zukowski and Stanley
Walczak same lot)
HANYZEWSKI, Mary A 1875 - 16
Feb 1958 (nee: Herman) (A)
(1st husband - Joseph Cwidak
and 2nd husband - John
Hanyzewski same lot)
HANYZEWSKI, Michael 19 Aug
1893 - 27 Nov 1936 (C)
(Blazy and Zofia Klodzinski
same lot)
HANYZEWSKI, Louis M 1888 -
1946 (D)
HANYZEWSKI, John no date - 3
Sept 1924 (-)

HANYZEWSKI (continued)
Frank no date - 5 June 1923 (-)
HANYZEWSKI, Albin A 1888 -
1959 (E)
Zana Ray L 1893 - 1924 (E)
Sylwera S 1919 - 1922 (E)
Anna 1865 - 1943 Mother (nee:
Szocinski) (E)
Jozef 1860 - 2 Jan 1934 Father
(E)
(Joseph, Helen, Melvyn, and
Evelyn Kielton same lot)
HANYZEWSKI, Casimir 1885 -
1954 (E)
Magdolina 1885 - 1976 (E)
(Family of Drews and Stanley
Waslicki same lot)
HANYZEWSKI, Carrie
(Leokadya) 1886 - 1941 (G)
Ignatius 1884 - 1951 (G)
(Barbara Ann Piechowicz same
lot)
HANYZEWSKI, Michael no date
- 27 Nov 1934 (H)
HARLOZINSKI, Gertrude T 1918
- 19-- (G)
Matt H 1910 - 1974 (G)
Gerald 1941 - 1942 (G)
Arthur no date - 10 Nov 1948 (G)
HARMACINSKI, Joan J 1883 -
1975 (nee: Kowalski) (H)
Vincent W 1876 - 1963 (H)
HARMACINSKI, Stanley no date
- 6 March 1926 (-)
HARTWICK, Leo J 4 Sept 1896 -
21 Feb 1958 Indiana Pfc 66
Arty Bn Co CAC (E)
Irene 1900 - 1956 Mother (E)
Aloysius 1923 - 1927 with pic-
ture (E)
HARTWICK, George no date - 21
Feb 1938 (D)
Harry H -no dates- (D)
(Tomasz Grzegorek same lot)
HASKO, Mary 1894 - 1912 (A)
(Vincent and Rozalia
Szmankowski same lot)
HASKO, Barney no date - 10
March 1931 (-)
HAYES, William no date - 6 May
1928 (-)
HAZINSKI, M D -no dates- (D)

HAZINSKI, Joseph 1849 - 11 July 1938 (PC)
HAZINSKI, Mieczyslaw 1895 - 11 Feb 1934 (PC)
HAZINSKI, Michael 15 Sept 1858 - 22 Mar 1933 Father (E)
Weronika 1867 - 1953 Mother (nee: Summers (Latosinski) (E)
Michael Robert 6 June 1895 - 29 Oct 1936 S 2/C USNRF WWI (E)
Wanda w/o Lott 1896 - 1961 (nee: Wojciechowski) (E)
Lott L 4 Mar 1893 - 8 May 1974 Pvt U S Army WWI (E)
Richard P 25 Apr 1923 - 24 Sept 1980 Sgt U S Army WWII (E)
HAZINSKI, Valentine 1856 - 1928 (F)
HECHLINSKI, Jan 1877 - 1946 Father (B)
Antonina 1878 - 1965 Mother (nee: Piechoski) (B)
Leokadya 1903 - 1910 Daughter (B)
Sylvester 1909 - 1911 Son (B)
(Marcin Piechocki, Grandfather, same lot)
HECKLINSKI, Casimir J 1904 - 1974 "Beloved Husband and Father" (F)
HEGEDUS, Helen L 8 Apr 1912 - 30 Nov 1962 Wife (C)
(J Roman Klein same lot)
HELAK, Piotr 10 May 1847 - 31 Jan 1907 (B)
Steve P no date - 13 July 1937 Indiana Pvt CL2 Infantry 19 Div (B)
HELAK, William 22 Dec 1896 - 24 Dec 1959 Indiana U S Army (-)
Sophie 1899 - 1933 Mother (-)
HENCELEWSKI, Frank 1880 - 20 July 1916 (D)
HENCELEWSKI, Bernice 1885 - 1961 (D)
Francis 1880 - 1916 (D)
(Felix Kasprzak same lot)
HERMA, Virginia 1933 - 1935 (H)

HERMA (continued)
Joseph 1875 - 1945 Father (H)
Elzbieta 1883 - 1956 Mother (H)
Wladyslaw 1911 - 1919 Son (H)
Wladyslawa 1913 - 1971 Daughter (H)
(Rosalie Elizabeth Burlington same lot)
HERMAN, Andrzej 1836 - 1912 (B)
Maryanna 1835 - 1915 (B)
(Jozef S Zytowski same lot)
HERMAN, Frank 1883 - 1975 (C)
Victoria 1886 - 1974 (nee: Zulkowski) (C)
HERMAN, John 1 Apr 1878 - 8 Dec 1945 Father (C)
Elizabeth 1879 - 8 Jan 1946 Mother (C)
(Michael Duszynski same lot)
HERMAN, Eugene 1927 - 1928 Baby (F)
(Clement and Anna Nijak same lot)
HERMAN, Theresa 1911 - 1945 Wife, with picture (G)
HERMAN, Vincent no date - 23 July 1937 (PC)
HERMAN, Thomas 1875 - 24 Aug 1913 (C)
HES, Lorraine Rose d/o Bert & Rose Karbowski 24 Dec 1925 - 23 Sept 1952 (nee: Karbowski (B)
Mike -no dates- Husband (B)
Michalene Mary no date - May 1952 Daughter (B)
(Bert and Rose Karbowski same lot)
HES, Antoni 11 Mar 1911 - 31 Dec 1911 (B)
Leo J 1914 - 1976 (B)
Alice 1916 - 1974 (B)
HES, Marianna 1855 - 1919 Mother (nee: Tomajczyk) (B)
Stanislaw 1851 - 1925 Father (B)
Michael J 1884 - 1977 (B)
Lucy K 1888 - 1965 (nee: Niemier) (B)
HES, Cecylia w/o Stanislaw Hes -no dates- (nee: Walkowiak) (C)

HES (continued)
(Jozefa, Catharine, and Joseph Walkowiak same lot)
HES, Mike 1899 - 1918 (D)
John 1895 - 1918 (D)
Maciej 1851 - 1943 (D)
Petronella 1863 - 1940 (D)
HES
Alex P 1901 - 1940 (F)
(Jozef Nowak same lot)
HES, Wladyslaw 7 Sept 1892 - 7 March 1923 Father & Husband (G)
(Joseph F Otolski same lot)
HOCH, Charles no date - 12 July 1927 (-)
HOCK, Stanley F 1897 - 1963 Father (F)
-no name- 1923 - 1926 Son (F)
HOCK, Cecylia 27 Nov 1906 - 4 Apr 1961 (F)
Minnie 1871 - 1960 (F)
Charles H 1869 - 1926 (F)
HOFFMAN, Joseph no date - 29 Oct 1933 (-)
HOFFMAN, Agnes 1876 - 1961 (F)
Michael 1881 - 17 Mar 1927 (F)
HOFFMAN, Adam 1900 - 19-- (F)
Stella 1899 - 1974 (F)
(John Krasinski same lot)
HOFFMAN, Hugh Hale 1903 - 1958 (C)
John 1863 - 1947 Father (C)
Mary 1875 - 1951 Mother (nee: Helminiak) (C)
David no date - 1932 age 3 months (C)
Franciszek S 6 Oct 1894 - 6 Nov 1918 "Killed in action on the 6th day of Nov 1918" Cpl U S Army (C)
Andrzej 1865 - 1935 Father (C)
Rozalia 1868 - 1948 Mother (C)
HOJARA, Franklin J Jr 25 June 1917 - 3 May 1967 Indiana Pfc Eng WWII BSM (H)
Stella 1890 - 1935 (nee: Andrzejewski) (H)
Frank J 1889 - 1954 (H)
Franciszek 1914 - 1950 (H)

HOJNACKI, Boleslaw 22 Dec 1883 - 6 May 1939 Father, with picture (F)
Clara Paris 1891 - 1945 (nee: Lukowski) with picture (F)
HOJNACKI, Tekla 1879 - 1922 (A)
(Lukasz Michalski and Weronika Kruszka same lot)
HOJNACKI, Jozefa 1853 - 1923 (C)
(Antoni & Emilia Bobowski, & Julian Kozlowski same lot)
HOJNACKI, Bronislaw 1913 - 25 Nov 1927 Brother (D)
(Prakseda, Jozef, and Marianna Badinski same lot)
HOJNACKI, Sylvester 1915 - 1923 (G)
Roman 1882 - 1950 (G)
Helena 1893 - 1959 (G)
HOJNY, Walter 30 May 1914 - 23 Apr 1965 Indiana Pvt U S Army WWII (C)
HOLEWCZYNSKI (CHOLEW-CZYNSKI), Jozefa 1861 - 1941 Mother (B)
Maciej 1846 - 1912 Father (B)
Katarzyna 1884 - 1908 (B)
(Mary Cholewczynski same lot)
HOLEWINSKI, Stanislaw 1886 - 1933 Brother (G)
Kazimier 1889 - 1922 Brother (G)
Weronika 1867 - 1923 Mother (G)
Antoni 1870 - 1921 (G)
HOLOWSKI, Frank no date - 17 July 1927 (-)
HOLTZ, Peter J 1887 - 1930 Husband AEF WWI (F)
(John and Regina Urban same lot)
HOLUBIAK, Harry 28 Aug 1887 - 8 Jan 1966 (E)
Helen 16 Apr 1883 - 9 June 1970 Wife (E)
HON, Stanley 1876 - 27 Mar 1932 (PC)
HORKA, Wiktorya -no dates- (nee: Wegner) (C)
Ignacy 20 July 1877 - 31 Aug 1956 Spanish American War "1 Regt Wisconsin Inf, Cuba,

HORKA (continued)
Phillipine Islands, Puerto
Rico" (C)
HORKA, Klementyna -no dates-
(C)
(Michael and Katarzyna Wegner
same lot)
HORKA, Frank no date - 21 Aug
1936 (PC)
HORNUNG, Matthew 1865 - 1944
Father (D)
(Helena Giszewski same lot)
HORVATH, Mary Szabo 9 Sept
1884 - 30 April 1953 Mother
(D)
HORVATH, Stephen A 1909 -
19-- (G)
Anne R 1908 - 1979 (G)
(Edward E Melvin same lot)
HOSINSKI, Edmund Joseph 31
Mar 1913 - 25 May 1978 S/Sgt
U S Army WWII (A)
(Stanley B Fujawa same lot)
HOSINSKI, William 1881 - 1946
(B)
Katharine 1883 - 1948 (nee:
Wisniewski) (B)
-no name- -no dates- "Infant
Son" (B)
(Frances Wisniewski and
Florence Wroblewski same
lot)
HOSINSKI, Jan 23 Apr 1856 - 6
Sept 1925 (B)
Wiktorya 20 Dec 1852 - 16 Dec
1917 (nee: Hajduk) (B)
(Katarzyna Deranek same lot)
HOUSER, Wiktorya 23 Dec 1864
- 24 Mar 1931 (E)
(Boleslaw Fisher same lot)
HUBER, Mary A Bolka Huber 4
Aug 1878 - 1 May 1973 (nee:
Stasinski) (A)
(Jozef T Bolka and Jan Stasinski
same lot)
HUDAK, Franciszek 1854 - 11
Apr 1934 (A)
(2 other unmarked memorials
same lot)
HUDAK, Thaddeus E 1907 - 1977
(C)
Sophie B 1910 - 19-- "Married

HUDAK (continued)
24 June 1929" (C)
Justin Frank 1913 - 1940
"Killed" (C)
Edward Stanley 1915 - 1916 (C)
HUDAK, Michael K 8 Aug 1887 -
14 May 1971 Indiana 309
Trench Mortar Bn (C)
Anna 1891 - 1952 (nee:
Borzeskowski)
(Stanislawa Malkowski, Cecylia
Rybicki, and Theresa Miller
same lot)
HUDAK, Marya 1918 - 1921 (D)
Michael 1883 - 1931 Father (D)
Josephine 1881 - 1979 Mother
(nee: Wlodarek) (D)
Walter no date - 3 Jan 1919 (D)
HUDZINSKI (CHUDZINSKI), Vin-
cent 13 Aug 1887 - 1956 (A)
Bertha 1889 - 1921 (nee:
Smiegielski) (A)
HUDZINSKI, Joanne 17 Aug 1900
- 21 June 1977 Daughter (C)
Frank S 1856 - 3 June 1931
Father (C)
Maryanna 1863 - 1 Jan 1938
Mother (nee: Laskowski) (C)
HUDZINSKI, Walter J 12 Nov
1894 - 12 Feb 1968 Illinois
Cook 9 Ammo Train WWI (F)
Martha C 1897 - 1975 (nee:
Pawlak) (F)
Walter S no date - 1928 Infant
(F)
HUMBERGER, Irene F 1914 -
1964 (G)
Albert 1916 - 1958 (G)
HUNT, Stella 24 Oct 1894 - 8
June 1969 (F)
Arthur P 22 Sept 1893 - 18 Mar
1932 (F)
HYEKIEL, Wladyslaw 1872 - 9
Sept 1938 (A)
(Mary Grzechowiak same lot)
INORAJSKI, Konstanty 17 July
1882 - 21 Oct 1909 (B)
ISBAN, Alex A 1898 - 1900 (C)
Elizabeth 1900 - 1977 (C)
(Jan and Jozefa Lodyga, and
Robakowski same lot)
IZDEPSKI, Stanislaw 1873 - 1949

IZDEPSKI (continued)
(G)
Martha 1877 - 1959 (nee: Borlik)
(G)
JABLONSKI, Jozef 1850 - 27 May
1908 Husband (B)
Wiktorya 1853 - 1929 Wife (B)
JABLONSKI, Walter no date - 6
Aug 1937 (-)
JACHIMIAK, John 1860 - 1926
(E)
Mary 1863 - 1948 (nee:
Kruszewski) (E)
Leo 1893 - 1953 Pvt U S Army
WWI (E)
Bert 29 Mar 1896 - 14 Oct 1978
(E)
JACHIMIAK, Thomas 1854 - 20
Jan 1930 (H)
JACKMOVICH, Joseph S 1900 -
1980 (G)
(Szymon, Alexandria, & Kon-
stanty Lasowicki same lot)
JACKOWIAK, Andrew G 1883 -
1950 (C)
Antonina 1886 - 1971 (nee:
Jurek) (C)
JACKOWIAK, Stanislaw 1861 -
1930 Father (E)
Michalina 1864 - 22 Mar 1936
Mother (nee: Ryska) (E)
Jan J 1892 - 1943 Son WWI (E)
Wladyslaw 1894 - 1952 Son
WWI (E)
JAGLA, Catharine 1959 - 1931
(D)
(Mary Grzegozewski same lot)
JAGLA, Stella H 23 Jan 1895 - 8
Sept 1976 Mother (H)
(Francis and Jadwiga Cyman
same lot)
JAGODETS, Dorothy 1898 - 1972
(F)
(Wit Niedbalski same lot)
JAGODKA, -no name- no dates
(A)
JAGODZINSKI, Hedwige w/o
Alexander 1876 - 1902 (nee:
Bierwagon) (B)
(Mieczyslaw Bierwagon same
lot)
JAGODZINSKI, Marcelli 1860 -

JAGODZINSKI (continued)
1919 Father (E)
Stanislawa 1862 - 1932 Mother
(E)
(Karl Kovacs same lot)
JAGODZINSKI, Stephen h/o Mar-
tha Radecki 1903 - 5 Mar 1933
(PC)
JAHNZ, Frank J 6 Oct 1882 - 14
Jan 1958 (F)
Laura 5 Dec 1892 - 26 Apr 1975
(F)
(Edward C Tobolski same lot)
JAKUBIAK, Micheline 1840 -
1933 (E)
(Piotr Krych same lot)
JAKUBOWICZ, Lewis 1 Aug 1825
- 4 Mar 1913 (A)
JAKUBOWICZ, Wojciech 1897 -
7 Jan 1931 (G)
JAMROZY, Joseph no date - 24
Nov 1980 (C)
JAMROZY, Catharine 1878 -
1965 Mother (A)
Joseph 1876 - 1947 Father (A)
(John W Mathewson same lot)
JANCZAK, Stanislaw J 1882 -
1945 Father (E)
Bernard J 1927 - no date (E)
(Michael Guzicki and Veronica
Korn same lot)
JANDOLA, Marya 22 Feb 1885 -
29 Dec 1935 Wife (D)
(Bronislaw Krotnik, John
Torowicz, and Frank Pawlek
same lot)
JANIAK, Stella 1868 - 1934 (B)
Andrew 1865 - July 1917 (B)
JANIAK, Jan 10 Dec 1888 - 9
July 1953 (D)
JANICKI, Aniela 1868 - 1935
Mother (nee: Podlas) (E)
Marcin 1862 - 16 March 1924
Father (E)
JANICKI, Adalbert no date - 25
Jan 1936 (-)
JANICKI, Casimir 1888 - 1947
(G)
JANISCZAK, Leo no date - 31
Apr 1915 (A)
JANISCZAK, Jozef 1 Jan 1897 -
20 Jan 1968 45 Co Coast Arty

JANISCZAK (continued)
WWI (E)
Reginia 1897 - 1962 (nee:
Bokowski) (E)
Maryanna 1860 - 1957 (nee:
Zalas) (E)
Szczepan 1850 - 2 Aug 1922 (E)
JANISCEWSKI, Nicesor 1893 - 13
July 1918 (A)
Bronislawa 1897 - 1927 (nee:
Kaniewski) (A)
(Vincent K Kaniewski and
Eleanor Brekus same lot)
JANISZEWSKI, Marya -no dates-
Mother (nee: Peczkowski) (E)
Jan -no dates- Father (E)
Alexander 1895 - 1975 Cpl U S
Army WWI (E)
JANISZEWSKI, Roman D 20 Feb
1897 - 18 Aug 1967 Indiana
Pvt Co D 161 Depot Brig
WWI (G)
Wanda 1900 - 1977 (nee:
Smiegielski) (G)
JANKOWIAK, Bernard 5 May
1913 - 27 Sept 1979 (A)
(Walenty and Tekla Michalski
same lot)
JANKOWIAK, Josephine V 1882 -
1955 Mother (A)
(Wawrzyniec and Frank
Mikolajczak same lot)
JANKOWIAK, Pelagia 19 Feb
1878 - 19 Nov 1910 (nee:
Rusiewicz) (B)
Maciej J 1876 - 1935 (B)
JANKOWIAK, Alexander A 20 Apr
1894 - 16 June 1918 "Born in S
B (South Bend, Indiana).
Killed in action in WWI on 16
June 1918" Cpl Co A 3 Div 7
M G Bat Chateau Thierry,
France (E)
Tommy -no dates- (E)
Peter 20 Nov 1834 - 1 Feb 1918
Grandfather (E)
JANKOWIAK, Lawrence no date -
20 Jan 1935 (-)
JANKOWIAK, Francis -no dates-
WW (WW only only on tomb-
stone, no number) Veteran (A)
JANKOWSKI, Frank 1852 - 4

JANKOWSKI (continued)
April 1932 (A)
Marya 1858 - 1916 (nee: Gniot)
(A)
Agnieszka 1815 - 1908 Grand-
mother (A)
(Wladyslawa Nowak & Regina
Tobalski same lot)
JANKOWSKI, Jan 1876 - 1924
Father (C)
Cecylia 1872 - 1947 Mother (C)
(Gertrude Stachurski & Konstan-
cia Nowakowski same lot)
JANKOWSKI, Frank W 1903 -
19-- (H)
Lucille M 1908 - 19-- (H)
JANKOWSKI, Jozefa 1893 - 1973
(nee: Walkowiak) (other hus-
band Antony Niespodziany) (C)
Jozef 11 Feb 1889 - 1942 (C)
(Antony Niespodziany same lot)
JANKOWSKI, Agnes 1864 - 1924
Mother (C)
Martin 1858 - 10 Dec 1915
Father (C)
Sophie 1895 - 1914 (C)
(Katharine Lewandowski, &
Frank, Tillie, & Thomas Niez-
godski same lot)
JANKOWSKI, Helen 1887 - 1917
Mother (nee: Nowak) (D)
Anthony 19 Apr 1886 - 1970
Father (D)
(Stanley & Bernadette Olejniczak
same lot)
JANKOWSKI, Mary 15 Feb 1906 -
19-- (nee: Trytko) (D)
Ignatz 15 Jan 1891 - 7 Oct 1970
WWI Mech Cook Com 6 Div
BN (D)
(Peter Trytko same lot)
JANKOWSKI, Frank no date - 29
July 1927 (-)
JANKOWSKI, Vincent no date -
1920 (-)
JANKOWSKI, Louis M 23 Mar
1895 - 8 June 1980 Pvt U S
Army WWII (E)
(Martha Michalski same lot)
JANKOWSKI, Valentine no date -
24 June 1932 (-)
JANKOWSKI, Matt 1876 - 31 Aug

36

JANKOWSKI (continued)
1935 (B)
JANKOWSKI, George no date - 5
Dec 1923 (-)
JANKOWSKI, J -no dates- (S G
East Fence)
JANKOWSKI, Tomasz 1863 -
1945 (E)
Michalena 1869 - 1925 (nee:
Glon) (E)
JANKOWSKI, William 1880 -
1960 Father (F)
Wanda 1882 - 1967 Mother (F)
Leo 1909 - 1927 Son (F)
JANKOWSKI, Helena 1888 - 1973
(G)
Kazimierz 1888 - 1954 (G)
Klara 1915 - 1925 (G)
JANOWCZYK, Paulina 1868 -
1918 Mother (nee: Ewald) (A)
Joseph 1860 - 5 Feb 1939 Father
(A)
Walter 1899 - 1960 Son (A)
John A 1911 - 1979 Pfc U S
Army WWII (A)
JANOWCZYK, Lucille 1920 -
1977 (A)
Joseph 10 Feb 1887 - 1978
Father (A)
Ludwika 1889 - 1918 Mother
(nee: Tabolski) (A)
Louis no date - 4 June 1918 (A)
JANOWIAK, Franciszek no date -
1 July 1927 "Placowka #125
Polish Vet" (B)
JANOWIAK, Grzegorz 1859 - 16
March 1931 (G)
Maryanna 1859 - 1935 (nee:
Skibinski) (G)
Wincenty 1901 - 1926 (G)
Daniel S s/o Mike & Stella
Janowiak 1921 - 1976 Grand-
son Pfc U S Army WWII (G)
JANOWIAK, Stella T 1887 - 1969
Mother 1 (nee: Leszcz) (G)
Michael M 1885 - 1932 Father
(G)
Stanley L 1919 - 1939 (G)
Bernice 1913 - 1923 (G)
JANOWIAK, Michael no date - 18
Dec 1938 (D)
JANOWIAK, Stella 1873 - 1967

JANOWIAK (continued)
(E)
Valentine 1880 - 1967 (E)
(Michael Przybylski same lot)
JANOWSKI, Vincent no date - 19
Feb 1920 (S G East Fence)
JANUS, Jan no date - 18 July
1942 Indiana 333 Fld Arty 83
Div WWI "Mrs Jan Janus
Died 13 Oct 1929" (E)
JANUSZEWSKI, John no date - 2
March 1931 (E)
JAREMBA, Chrystina 1932 -
1933 (B)
(Stanislaw and Stanislawa
Sniadecki same lot)
JAROCHA, Frank 25 July 1874 -
23 March 1936 "Benefactor of
Little Ones" (H)
JARONIK, Joseph 1867 - 1947 (C)
Victoria 1876 - 1917 (C)
JARONIK, Leokadya 17 Mar 1907
- 22 Dec 1939 Daughter (F)
Eugene 23 Sept 1902 - 12 Dec
1942 Son (F)
Agnieszka 25 Jan 1872 - 13 Dec
1947 Mother (nee: Kopinski)
(F)
Jan 26 Dec 1869 - 5 Feb 1930
Father (F)
JARONIK, Walter A 1901 - 28
Jan 1929 Husband (F)
(Clara Guenther same lot)
JAROSZEWSKI, Jozefa 1835 -
1907 Mother (A)
Frank 1826 - 10 Nov 1918 Father
(A)
(Stanley Graczyk and Patricia
Ann Kazmierczak same lot)
JAROSZEWSKI, Wladyslaw J
1877 - 1946 Father (B)
Maryanna K 1875 - 1963 Mother
(B)
JAROSZEWSKI, Wanda 1897 -
1933 (nee: Pacala) (G)
Vincent 1857 - 29 Aug 1922 (G)
Gabrella 1863 - 1928 (G)
JAROSZEWSKI, Lawrence 1868 -
23 Mar 1932 (G)
JAROSZEWSKI, Francis 20 Sept
1896 - 10 Oct 1923 (nee:
Gornia) (G)

37

JAROSZEWSKI, Bartholomew 1862 - 19 Jan 1938 (PC)
JAROSZEWSKI, Rose K 1907 - 1967 (G)
Casimir J 20 Aug 1896 - 24 June 1967 Indiana S2 U S Navy (G)
JAROSZEWSKI, William J July 1890 - 19-- (G)
Veronica 1891 - 1964 (nee: Giersz) (G)
(Mary Greenwald same lot)
JAROSZEWSKI, Casimir L 1903 - 1969 (H)
Helen 1906 - 19-- (H)
JAROSZEWSKI, Franciszek 28 Sept 1859 - 7 May 1942 (G)
Katarzyna 27 Oct 1868 - 17 Jan 1941 (nee: Makowski) (G)
(Stanley Przybylinski same lot)
JAROSZEWSKI, Martha 25 Jan 1894 - 12 Mar 1973 (G)
(Clara Klysz same lot)
JARZAKOWSKI, Henry 1909 - 18 Mar 1927 (G)
JASICKI, Antoni 1892 - 10 Dec 1915 (C)
(Michael and Jozefa Przybylinski same lot)
JASICKI, Mary 1845 - 10 Nov 1923 (D)
(Ignace and Alice Brambert same lot)
JASICKI, John P 1883 - 19-- (H)
(Anna Sieracki and Frank Kaminski same lot)
JASINSKI, Mary 1919 - 1974 Wife (A)
Joseph P 1865 - 1945 Father (A)
Stella 1877 - 1950 Mother (nee: Piechocki) (A)
Frank C 1898 - 1968 Son (A)
Alex 1902 - 1976 Brother (A)
JASINSKI, Ralph J 22 Jan 1918 - 2 Oct 1978 Tec 5 U S Army WWII (A)
(Eric R Woods same lot)
JASINSKI, Jan 1891 - 1965 Father (C)
Cecylia -no dates- Mother (C)
Jozef 1914 - 1937 Son (C)
Jadwiga 20 July 1917 - 1926 Daughter (C)

JASINSKI, Wawrzyniak 10 Aug 1842 - 28 May 1942 (C)
Anna 1850 - 1912 (C)
(Martha A Taylor and Josephine Witt same lot)
JASINSKI, Jacob July 1851 - 1 Feb 1935 (-)
JASINSKI, Joseph no date - 22 May 1932 (-)
JASKIEWICZ, Helena 4 Feb 1887 - 29 Mar 1956 (A)
Stella 24 Oct 1883 - 7 Aug 1960 (nee: Bonczynski) (A)
Jozef 11 Feb 1880 - 28 Nov 1963 (A)
(Franciszek, Cecylia and Walenty Bonczynski same lot)
JASKIEWICZ, Maryanna 1882 - 1909 (B)
(Ludwika Szulczewski same lot)
JASKOWIAK, Antony M 1907 - 1978 Uncle (H)
Agnes 1865 - 1942 (H)
Hilary 1894 - 1973 (H)
JASNIEWICZ, Jozef 1893 - 1916 (C)
Leon 1889 - 1916 (C)
Babies -no dates- (C)
JASOK, Pawel 26 Nov 1874 - 8 Jan 1938 Father (H)
Marya 1884 - 1974 Mother (H)
JASTRZEBSKI, Vincent 1882 - 1963 (C)
Cecylia 1881 - 1968 (nee: Wroblewski) (C)
Aloysius 1907 - 1968 (C)
Henry 1915 - 1915 (C)
JAWORSKI, Katarzyna 1848 - 1916 Mother (nee: Figorski) (1st husband - Jacob Kubiak)
(Michael Kubiak same lot)
JAWORSKI, Jacob F 1872 - 6 May 1933 Father (B)
Louis S 1911 - 1969 Husband (B)
Eleanor S 1913 - 19-- Wife (B)
Cecylia 1885 - 1932 Mother (nee: Wozniak) (B)
JAWORSKI, Rozalia 1894 - 1918 (C)
(Angela, Maryanna, and Stanislaw Wieczorkowski same lot)
JAWORSKI, Casimir A 1897 -

JAWORSKI (continued)
1965 (E)
Josephine 1897 - 1982 (nee:
Slaby) (E)
Stanley G 20 Nov 1918 - 12 Dec
1918 (E)
JAWORSKI, Albert A 21 Apr 1913
- 7 June 1971 Pfc Co F 413 Inf
Regt WWII (H)
Barbara J 1939 - 1945 (H)
Theresa M 1933 - 1939 (H)
Richard A 1937 - 1938 (H)
JAWORSKI, John F 1945 - 1969
(H)
JAWORSKI, Pelegia 1907 - 1924
(G)
Jadwiga 1904 - 1925 (G)
Jozefa 1874 - 1929 (nee:
Abramowicz) (G)
Franciszek 1865 - 16 Aug 1930
(G)
JEDZEJEWSKI, Bronislawa 1878
- 1928 Mother (nee: Sosinski)
(F)
Jakob 1873 - 29 Aug 1939 Father
(F)
Richard C 19 Oct 1931 - 19 Nov
1931 (F)
Edward D 1902 - 1972 Husband
(F)
Helen M 1905 - 19-- Wife (nee:
Janowiak) (F)
JEDZEJEWSKI, Henrietta E 1921
- 1971 (G)
(James Edward Uminski same
lot)
JEGIER, August J 1878 - 1941
Father (C)
Veronica F 1879 - 1953 Mother
(nee: Mindykowski) (C)
JEGIER, Katarzyna no date - 24
Apr 1928 Mother (nee:
Radomski) (E)
(Harry B & Helen Salomen same
lot)
JENCZAK, Agnes no date - 1920
(C)
(Michael & Victoria Wojcie-
chowski same lot)
JENCZAK, Maryanna 1864 - 1940
(H)
Wojciech 1865 - 1940 (H)

JENCZEWSKI, Frank 1876 - 5
Apr 1938 Father (E)
Anna 1882 - 1953 Mother (E)
Walter 1922 - 1977 U S Army
WWII (E)
Mary Jan 1921 - Apr 1921 (E)
JENCZEWSKI, Frank C 1904 -
1977 (E)
Gladys T 1908 - 1968 "Joined in
Holy Matrimony 8 Feb 1926"
(E)
Irene Ann July 1926 - Nov 1926
"Our Little Angel" (E)
JENCZEWSKI, Theodore 1918 -
1966 (H)
Walter W 1910 - 19-- (H)
Stella 1909 - 17 Oct 1981 (H)
Casimir E "Sonny" 5 March - 22
April 1937 (H)
(Michael Strzelecki same lot)
JENDRZEJEWSKI, Jozef (dates
not legible) (D)
JENDRZEJEWSKI, Jacob 1845 -
1919 (D)
JERZAK, Anthony no date - 29
July 1919 (-)
J E R Z Y K O W S K I (JERZA-
KOWSKI), John 1882 - 15 June
1918 1st Husband, "married
Wladyslawa Kurek" (C)
(Jozef & Wladyslawa Grzelewski
same lot)
JERZYKOWSKI, Edward S 1919 -
1941 (D)
Helena 20 Sept 1891 - 17 Mar
1980 (nee: Ozdych) (D)
Kasimierz W 1888 - 30 Dec 1974
(D)
JERZAKOWSKI, Casimir 1903 -
1970 (G)
Verna 1898 - 1970 (nee:
Lachowski) (G)
Frances 1877 - 1959 Mother
(nee: Chmielewski) (G)
Walter 1874 - 1955 Father (G)
Henrik 1909 - 1927 (G)
Mitchell 1900 - 1923 (G)
JERZYKOWSKI, Michael no date
- 1946 (E)
Tillie 6 Sept 1891 - 1980 (E)
(Joseph S Tobolski same lot)
JEZIORSKI, Szczepan 1863 - 25

JEZIORSKI (continued)
Aug 1920 Father (B)
Jadwiga 1871 - 1946 Mother
(nee: Wacoski) (B)
Joanna 1907 - 1961 Daughter (B)
Rev Louis A 1902 - 1973
"Ordained 18 May 1940" (B)
JEZIORSKI, Angeline M no date -
30 Apr 1904 (E)
Martha M no date - 14 June 1905
(E)
Joseph S 4 July 1894 - 30 Apr
1966 Indiana Pvt 26 Recruit Co
WWI (E)
(Rose Woelfel same lot)
JEZIORSKI, Matt 1898 - 12 June
1980 (E)
Virginia 1922 - 1976 (E)
Victoria 1901 - 19-- (E)
JEZIORSKI, Wincenty (h/o Mary
Kucharski) 1883 - 11 July 1926
Husband (with picture) (F)
JOACHIM, Zofia 1894 - 1937
Mother (H)
Albert 1888 - 1979 Father (H)
JOACHIMIAK, Martin 1886 -
1956 Grandfather (G)
(Walter, Henrietta, Thomas, and
June Marie Labis same lot)
JOACHIMIAK, Tomasz 1854 -
1938 Father (H)
Anna 1858 - 1943 Mother (H)
Kalix 1895 - 1961 Son (H)
Stanley T 26 Apr 1904 - 24 Aug
1968 Indiana Pfc Co C 18 Inf
WWII (H)
JONAS, Stanley T (2nd h/o
Katharine) 1896 - 19-- Father
(E)
Katharine 1886 - 1961 Mother (E)
(1st h/o Katharine - Wojciech
Kusmiez same lot)
JORDANEK, Isadore 1883 - 2
May 1910 (B)
Mrs (no name) 1891 - -no date-
"Born In Galicia" (B)
(Jan Pabis same lot)
JOSWIAK (JOZWIAK), Maryanna
8 Jan 1841 - 17 Oct 1929
Mother (E)
(Thomas Cichos same lot)
JOZWIAK, -no name- -no dates-

JOZWIAK (continued)
(A)
JOZWIAK, Marcin 1849 - 17 July
1917 (B)
Michalina 1851 - 1928 (nee:
Ogorkiewicz) (B)
Carrie F no date - 27 September
1975 (B)
JOZWIAK, Frank J 1883 - 1969
(C)
Catharine 1886 - 19-- (nee:
Grzezinski) (C)
JOZWIAK, Ernest J 1914 - 1978
S/Sgt U S Army WWII (C)
Florence 1916 - 19-- (nee:
Liwosz) (C)
(Stanislaw and Katarzyna Liwosz
same lot)
JOZWIAK, Maryann (2nd w/o
Casimir) 1888 - 19-- Mother
(nee: Polak) (D)
Casimir 1887 - 1963 (D)
Jozefa (1st w/o Casimir) 1891 -
1918 Wife (nee: Modracki) (D)
JOZWIAK, Wladyslaw 1889 - 29
Feb 1924 (E)
Helen 1893 - 1965 (nee: Nitka)
(E)
JOZWIAK, Jennie R 1917 - 19--
(E)
Stanley C 1915 - 19-- (E)
(Joseph J & Mary Kowalewski
same lot)
JOZWIAK, Frank no date - 21
Feb 1939 Indiana Pvt 137 Fld
Arty 38 Div (E)
Clara 1902 - 1936 (E)
JOZWIAK, Harry 1907 - 1941
Husband (F)
Peter 1869 - 1953 Father (F)
Mary 1878 - 1960 Mother (nee:
Cichos) (F)
JOZWIAK, William 1885 - 1943
Father (H)
JURCZYK, Agnieszka 1906 -
1931 (nee: Ewald) (F)
(Michael and Maryanna Ewald
same lot)
JURED, -no name- 1883 - 1908
(A)
JUREK, Joseph 20 Aug 1885 - 20
Nov 1918 (A)

JURGONSKI, Marie 1906 - 1964
(A)
JURGONSKI, Jan 6 Feb 1859 - 16
May 1925 Father (B)
Maryanna 24 June 1868 - 5 Aug
1944 Mother (B)
V Dora 1900 - 1956 Daughter (B)
(Teofil & Salomea Blasczyk
same lot)
JURKIEWICZ, Julianna M
Pacewicz 1864 - 1915 Mother
(D)
(Michael & Josephine Strominski
same lot)
JUSCZAK, Hattie 1891 - 1977
(nee: Klosinski) (PC)
Chester A 1887 - 1948 (PC)
KABZINSKI, Stanislaw 1899 - 25
June 1917 Son "Born in
Poland; veteran of WWI"
"Entered the Army on the 20th
of April 1916; killed in action
on the 25th of June 1917" (E)
Joseph 1869 - 1 Aug 1931 Father
(E)
John J 24 June 1902 - 25 July
1965 (E)
Martha 6 Feb 1902 - 23 Oct 1972
Daughter (E)
KACZMARCZYK, Stanley 1881 -
1959 Father (E)
Anna 1885 - 1950 Mother, with
picture (E)
Evelyn 13 Feb 1922 - 24 Aug
1922 Daughter (E)
KACZMAREK, John L 1892 -
1977 Son (B)
Pelegia 1862 - 1907 Mother (nee:
Wnuk) (B)
Kazimierz 1864 - 1941 Father
(B)
KACZMAREK, Lottie 1884 -
1951 (nee: Marciniak) (C)
John -no dates- (C)
KACZMAREK, Adam 1874 - 1935
(E)
Rozalia 1886 - 1954 (E)
(Sophie Surnecki same lot)
KACZMAREK, Jacob 1859 - 15
Mar 1938 (H)
(Rita Muszynski Caduff & Sophie
Muszynski Merrick same lot)

KACZMAREK, Zofia 1877 - 1949
(H)
Andrew 1867 - 1937 (H)
Bronislaw 1897 - 9 Dec 1938 Il-
linois Pfc 77 Fld Arty 4 Div
(H)
KACZMAREK, Walter no date -
13 June 1919 (-)
KACZMAREK, Frank no date - 9
Jan 1910 (-)
KACZOROWSKI, Wojciech 1839
- 1917 (B)
Maryanna 1848 - 1939 (nee:
Fujawa) (B)
Kazmierz 1890 - 1967 Son (B)
Mieczyslaw M 1875 - 1964 (B)
Zygmont W 1907 - 1940 (B)
Magdolena "w/o Mieczyslaw" 21
May 1876 - 30 May 1911 (nee:
Andrzejewski) (B)
KACZOROWSKI, Mary K 25 Jan
1885 - 24 Mar 1962 Mother
(nee: Burzynski) (F)
Valentine J 25 Jan 1881 - 29 Mar
1963 Father (F)
KADULSKI, Mary 1896 - 1969 (B)
KAFKA, Chester W 1907 - 19--
(E)
Joanna 1907 - 1972 (nee:
Laskowski) (E)
Walter & Richard 21 Oct 1928 -
24 Oct 1928 "Twin Sons" (E)
KAHLLER, Rev Peter H no date
- 8 May 1932 (Fiwek
Mausoleum)
KAJZER, Wojciech 1871 - 1930
(A)
Wiktorya 1877 - 1934 (nee:
Podemski) (A)
Alojzy 1908 - 1 Aug 1927 (A)
KAJZER, Jozefa 7 Feb 1860 - 11
Aug 1938 (B)
Jozef 1857 - 17 Dec 1928 (B)
Krystyna 1833 - 1917 Mother (B)
(Agnieszka Dereszynski, Wawrz-
niec Tafelski, & Zygmont
Kolczynski same lot)
KAJZER, Frank 14 Jan 1868 -
1962 (B)
Mary 27 Oct 1872 - 1953 (nee:
Wegner) (B)
Teresa 1897 - 1920 (nee:

41

KAJZER (continued)
  Kruszka) (B)
KAJZER, Andrzej 1873 - 1951
  Father (B)
  Katarzyna 1872 - 1918 Mother
  (B)
  Jan 1902 - 8 Mar 1923 (B)
  Stanislaw 1907 - 1928 (B)
  Raymond 1923 - 1924 (B)
KAJZER, Sylvester 19 Dec 1898 -
  22 Oct 1975 Cpl U S Army
  WWI (F)
  L Anna 1899 - 1976 (F)
  Evelyn 1919 - 1971 Daughter (F)
KAJZER, Benedict 1914 - 1928
  Son (F)
  John 1881 - 1955 Father (F)
  Hattie 1882 - 1975 Mother (F)
KALAMAJA, Katarzyna 1859 -
  1933 (nee: Kaiser) (B)
  Jozef 1844 - 27 Nov 1913 (B)
  (Martin Kubiak same lot)
KALAMAJA, Leonard J 1884 -
  1951 (G)
  Julia I 1886 - 1967 (G)
  (Josephine Louck same lot)
KALAMAJA, Valentine 1889 - 26
  Dec 1937 Father (H)
  Helen 20 July 1893 - 9 June 1982
  (Nee: Manuszak) (H)
  Harry J 1918 - 1977 Pfc U S
  Army (H)
KALCZYNSKI, Alex 1863 - 19
  Jan 1936 (B)
KALICKI, Marianna w/o Jozef
  1849 - 1937 Mother (D)
  (Elizabeth Was, Mary Putz, and
  Casimir J Putz same lot)
KALINOWSKI, Edward 1908 -
  1924 Son (E)
  Karol 1876 - 1960 Father (E)
  Victoria 1888 - 7 Jan 1981
  Mother (Nee: Dynarski) (E)
KALKA, Stanislaw 1882 - 1969
  Father (A)
  Maryanna 1882 - 1957 Mother
  (Nee: Szotkowski) (A)
  Larry 1913 - 1947 Son (A)
KALKA, Margaret 1844 - 1918
  Mother (C)
  Michael 1876 - 2 Sept 1935 Son
  (C)

KALKA, Frances 1878 - 1964 (D)
  (Joseph Guzicki same lot)
KALKA, Marya 1871 - 1954 (D)
  Jan 1869 - 1941 (D)
KALUZNY, Frank 1878 - 27 July
  1930 (E)
  Victoria 1892 - 1968 (E)
  (Paul J Romanowski, & Theodore
  & Josephine Kosch same lot)
KAMINSKI, Leon 1890 - 19--
  Father (E)
  Clara 1909 - 1955 Daughter (E)
  Lucy 1893 - 1947 Mother (E)
  (Irene Robertson same lot)
KAMINSKI, Stanislaw 1860 - 29
  Apr 1931 (A)
  (Pawel Plonski same lot)
KAMINSKI, Tadeusz 1893 - 16
  Aug 1914 (A)
  Stanislaus 1885 - 17 July 1913
  (A)
  Thaddeus 1911 - 1912 (A)
  Jan 1858 - 1925 Father (A)
  Pelegia 1868 - 1939 (Nee:
  Chrzan) (A)
  (Jozef Rybarkiewicz same lot)
KAMINSKI, Andrzej J 1827 - 19
  Apr 1926 Grandfather (A)
  -no name- 1843 - 1936 Father
  (A)
  -no name- 1856 - 1920 Mother
  (A)
  (Adolph Splitt same lot)
KAMINSKI, Antoni 1866 - 1944
  (B)
  Barbara 1869 - 1935 (B)
  Ignacy 1 June 1892 - 18 June
  1909 (B)
KAMINSKI, Sophie 1891 - 1968
  (Nee: Czewinski) (D)
  Vincent 1888 - 1973 (D)
  Rita 1922 - 1943 (D)
  Gordon 1916 - 1956 (D)
KAMINSKI, Jan F 1878 - 19 Dec
  1942 (E)
  Stanislawa 1885 - 1919 (E)
  (Dorothy Kiska same lot)
KAMINSKI, Jacob no date - 15
  Sept 1911 (-)
KAMINSKI, Walter 1888 - 1965
  Father (F)
  Clara 1895 - 1931 (F)

KAMINSKI (continued)
(Paul Koszewski same lot)
KAMINSKI, Frank 1887 - 1953
(H)
(Anna Sieracki & John P Jasicki
same lot)
KAMINIECKA, Maryanna no date
- 28 Sept 1937 (G)
Casimir 1908 - 1940 (G)
Wojciech 1874 - 1948 (G)
KAMIONKA, Joseph no date - 22
Nov 1928 (E)
KANCZUZEWSKI, Stanley no
date - 17 June 1981 (C)
KANCZUZEWSKI, Alicyza 1916 -
1918 (Note: Obit reads: 19 Aug
1915 - 26 Aug 1917) (C)
Walenty 1886 - 1948 Father (C)
(Madelena Marya Multanski Kolo
same lot)
KANCZUZEWSKI, Joseph Jr 22
Jan 1915 - 14 May 1922 (D)
KANCZUZEWSKI, Walter P 9
May 1922 - 18 Nov 1944 In-
diana Pfc 415 Infantry WWII
(F)
Adam 1880 - 1949 (F)
Teofilia 1882 - 1955 (Nee:
Mindykowski) (F)
KANCZUZEWSKI, Andrew 3 June
1922 - 22 Dec 1922 Son (G)
Mary 1903 - 19-- Mother (Nee:
Olejniczak) (G)
Antony 10 June 1896 - 13 May
1967 Father Indiana Pvt Baker
and Cook School QMC WWI
(G)
(Clem Winkiewicz same lot)
KANIA, Andrew 1884 - 1953
Father (-)
Mary 1882 - 1955 Mother (-)
Martin A 1915 - 1978 Son Sgt U S
Army WWII (-)
KANIEWSKI, Agnes 1854 - 1945
(A)
Antoni 1847 - 11 May 1929 (A)
Antonina 1898 - 1903 (A)
Jan 6 May 1884 - 13 Nov 1907
(A)
KANIEWSKI, Stanislaw 1866 -
1940 Father WWI (A)
Rozalia 1877 - 29 Feb 1964

KANIEWSKI (continued)
Mother (Nee: Markiewicz) (A)
KANIEWSKI, Vincent K 1888 -
1953 (A)
Helen M 1886 - 1975 (Nee:
Nowaczewski) (A)
Edmund 1897 - 1914 (A)
(Nicesor, Bronislawa Janis-
zewski, & Eleanor Brekus
same lot)
KANIEWSKI, Valentine 1892 -
1967 (C)
Mary 1893 - 1956 (Nee:
Grzegorek) (C)
E -no dates- (C)
R -no dates- (C)
(Walenty & Wiktoria Grzegorek
same lot)
KANTOROWSKI, Stella 1899 -
1931 Mother (Nee: Dudek) (C)
Sophie 1920 - 1930 (C)
Walter 1888 - 1979 Father (C)
Joseph 1914 - 1972 (C)
Harry 1916 - 1917 (C)
KAPALCZYNSKI, Stanislaw 1877
- 1950 Father (A)
Augustyna 1880 - 1946 Mother
(Nee: Ewald) (A)
Walter J 5 Sept 1906 - 8 Jan
1969 "Ohio Pfc Co I 395 In-
fantry WWII" (A)
KAPALCZYNSKI, Marcin 21 June
1818 - 25 Jan 1911 (G)
Jan 1843 - 11 Sept 1915 (G)
Marya 1848 - 1928 (G)
KAPALCZYNSKI, Maryanna 1859
- 1928 Mother (F)
KAPALCZYNSKI, Jozef 1857 -
1940 Father (F)
Magdolina 1859 - 1937 Mother
(F)
Joseph 1902 - 1929 Son (F)
(Patricia Niezgodski same lot)
KAPSA, Andrzej J 1846 - 30 Nov
1924 Father (B)
Agnieszka 1848 1924 Mother
(Nee: Szeperski) (B)
(Jozefa & Franciszek Laskowski
same lot)
KAPSA, John 1884 - 27 Sept 1929
Brother WWI (G)
(Adam & Anna Wolkiewicz same

43

KAPSA (continued)
lot)
KAPUSTA, Adam 1896 - 1953
Brother (With Picture as a
Polish Soldier) (D)
(Ignacy & Marta Skwiat same lot)
KARBOWSKI, Bert A 1891 - 1977
(B)
Rose B 1895 - 1975 "Joined in
Holy Matrimony 6 June 1921"
(B)
(Lorraine Rose & Mike Hess
same lot)
KARBOWSKI, Antoni 1856 - 15
Sept 1911 Father (B)
Josephine 1868 - 1945 Mother
(Nee: Schultz) (B)
Joan Betty no date - 19 Aug 1927
(B)
Antony E 1897 - 1967 Son (B)
KARCZEWSKI, John 1887 - 13
Nov 1936 Father (C)
Bernice 1892 - 1975 Mother (C)
(Lillian M Wlodarek & Sue Ann
Audaert same lot)
KARCZEWSKI, Martin J 1912 -
1958 Husband (F)
Jozefa 1905 - 1928 Wife (F)
Pearl 1875 - 1954 Mother (F)
Frank 1875 - 1955 Father (F)
(Leonard Kasprzak same lot)
KARKIEWICZ, Stella 24 Nov
1898 - 25 Dec 1981 Mother
(Nee: Osinski) (C)
John 17 Aug 1895 - 1971 Father
(C)
Regina 15 Sept 1917 - 1935
Daughter (C)
Anna no date - 1918 -age 11
months- (C)
Alfred no date - 1924 -age 5
weeks- (C)
KARMOLINSKI, Blanche 1907 -
19-- Mother (F)
Frank 1904 - 1952 Father (F)
Josephine 1875 - 1936 (with
Picture) (F)
John 1875 - 27 Jan 1929 (with
picture) (F)
KARMOWSKI, Czeslaw 1887 -
1964 Father (C)
KARMOWSKI, Jozefa 1877 -

KARMOWSKI (continued)
1976 Mother (C)
Edmund 1904 - 1915 Son (C)
KARNOFEL, Edward no date - 9
July 1916 (C)
Lawrence no date - 9 Feb 1920
(C)
KARPINSKI, Geneweta -no dates-
(A)
(Jan & Victoria Kuj same lot)
KARPINSKI, Jozef 1892 - 1918
Husband (E)
KARPINSKI, John 6 June 1878 -
18 Apr 1923 (E)
(Jozefa Reskiewicz same lot)
KARPINSKI, Jacob 16 July 1864 -
24 May 1926 (G)
KARPINSKI, ---- no dates Father
(G)
---- no dates Mother (G)
Vincent 7 June 1901 - 18 Aug
1956 "Indiana Pvt - 30 Train
GP - AAF - WWII" (G)
KASCZYNSKI, Franciszek 1915 -
1940 (H)
Hildegard 1921 - 1945 (H)
Catharine 1885 - 1975 Mother (H)
Henry Sr 1886 - 1957 Father (H)
KASIURSKI, Wojciech no date -
30 June 1913 (A)
KASIURSKI, Martha 24 July 1898
- 12 July 1921 "Wife of Jozef
Kasiurski" (D)
(Ignatius & Rose Brzezinski
same lot)
KASNIA, Mamie L 1900 - 1977
(F)
Marion M 11 Mar 1894 - 5 Dec
1946 "Ohio Pfc 312 Guard and
Fire Co QMC - WWI"
KASPRZAK, Henry J 1904 - 1977
(A)
Myrtle 1903 - 19-- (A)
KASPRZAK, Agniszka 1851 -
1927 (A)
Jan 1842 - 22 Jan 1919 (A)
Apolonia 1887 - 1919 (A)
KASPRZAK, Joseph J 1872 -
1952 Father (B)
Mary 1902 - 1941 (B)
Brigada 1909 - 1910 (B)
Bernadyna 1916 - 1917 (B)

KASPRZAK (continued)
Michael 1883 - 8 Jan 1910 (B)
Josephine Jan 1888 - 11 Nov
1918 (Nee: Kruszynski) "Born
in Ohio" Wife (B)
John M 1909 - 1973 Son (B)
Minnie A 1918 - 29 Apr 1981
(Nee: Odusch) (B)
(Domocela Foley same lot)
KASPRZAK, Martha 30 March
1915 - 7 Nov 1915 (C)
Frank J 1889 - 1956 (C)
Josephine 1887 - 1973 (Nee:
Lisek) (C)
KASPRZAK, Felix 27 May 1887 -
23 Apr 1956 "Indiana Pvt Co B
36 Inf WWI" (D)
(Francis & Bernice Hencelewski
same lot) (D)
KASPRZAK, Yolenda 30 Mar 1941
- 18 Dec 1941 Granddaughter
(F)
Leonard 1944 - 1945 Grandson
(F)
(Martin J Karczewski same lot)
KASPRZAK, Josephine 1892 -
1930 Mother (G)
Teofil 1890 - 1952 Father (G)
Bronislawa 1914 - 1922 (G)
Bronislaw 1923 - 1924 (G)
KASPRZYK, Teofil 1871 - 1941
(B)
(Teodozia Kopczynski same lot)
KASPRZYK, Joan 18 Aug 1878 -
1944 (Nee: Hosinski) Mother
"Second wife of Teofil
Kasprzyk" (G)
Matthew J 24 Aug 1916 - 30 June
1960 "Indiana Pfc 483 Medical
Coll Co WWII" (G)
(Esther A Reynolds same lot)
KASURSKI (KASIURSKI), Woj-
ciech 1860 - 30 June 1913
"Age 53 years 3 months 26
days" (A)
KAWSIECKI, Joseph 1887 - 1910
(C)
Aloysius 1918 - 1935 (C)
Heronim Aug 1916 - Sept 1916
(C)
(Michael Nowicki same lot)
KAY, Antonette H 28 Oct 1915 -

KAY (continued)
27 Aug 1973 Mother (A)
(Michael & Helen Pawlowski, &
Frank Dembicki same lot)
KAZMIERCZAK, Patricia Ann
1938 - 1939 (A)
(Frank & Jozefa Jaroszewski &
Stanislaw Graczyk same lot)
KAZMIERCZAK, George B 1874
- 1961 (B)
Frances A 1881 2nd Wife
1957 (Nee: Jankowiak) Wife
(B)
Martha no dates (B)
Clara no dates (B)
Frank no dates (B)
Joseph no date - 18 Jan 1931 (B)
Michael 1903 - 1974 (B)
Petronella no dates (1) w/o
George (B)
KAZMIERCZAK, Jacob 27 June
1878 - 12 Feb 1918 (B)
Casimir no dates (B)
Henry J 1905 - 1974 (B)
Martha 1908 - 19-- (B)
KAZMIERCZAK, Mary 1882 -
1969 (Nee: Niemier) (B)
Andrew 27 Nov 1882 - 1939 (B)
KAZMIERCZAK, John J 1870 -
1946 Father (B)
Marianna 1874 - 1939 (Nee:
Jaworski) Mother (B)
Anna 1897 - 1910 Daughter (B)
KAZMIERCZAK, John 1867 - 21
Jan 1931 Father (B)
Mary 1874 - 1932 (Nee: Kush)
Mother (B)
(Marion Orzechowski same lot)
KAZMIERCZAK, Teofil (Ted)
1897 - 19 Oct 1918 (D)
(John & Mary Gadacz same lot)
KAZMIERCZAK, Harry F 1880 -
1954 (F)
Mary 1884 - 1951 (F)
KAZMIERCZAK, Ernest 1927 -
1929 (F)
KAZMIERCZAK, Joseph P 1893
- 1977 (F)
Joanna 1898 - 1963 (Nee:
Prentkowski) (F)
Walter 1922 - 19-- (F)
(Weronika Prentkowski same lot)

KAZMIERCZAK, John 1861 - 28
Jan 1939 Father (F)
Frances 1861 - 1932 (Nee:
Radzikowski) Mother (F)
KAZMIERCZAK, Theodore 1909
- 1972 (H)
Phyllis 1910 - 19-- (H)
(William Barker same lot)
KAZMIRSKI - KAZMIERSKI,
Rozalia 1883 - 1935 (B)
Antoni 1879 - 1942 (B)
KAZMIRSKI, Michael 1855 - 16
Mar 1926 (B)
---- 1862 - 1944 Mother (B)
Wladyslawa 1884 - 1934 (Nee:
Chmilewski) Wife (B)
Wladyslaw 1885 - 1954 Husband
& Father (B)
Edward no date - 11 Sept 1916
(B)
KAZMIRSKI, Ray 27 Aug 1916 -
15 Oct 1970 "Indiana Tec 5
Medical Dept WWII" (F)
KAZMIRSKI, Jan 1890 - 1966
Father (F)
Eleanora 1891 - 1935 (Nee:
Grzesk) (with picture) Mother
(F)
Jozef J 8 Mar 1919 - 2 Dec 1928
(with picture) (F)
KENCKA, Mary no dates (B)
(Jan & Katarzyna Kruszewski
same lot)
KENDZIORA, Frank 1877 - 1953
Father (A)
Mary 1881 - 1963 Mother (A)
(Michalina Pawlak same lot)
KENDZIORA, Frank 1878 - 1944
(A)
(Konstanty Wiatrowski &
Leonard Szulkowski same lot)
KENDZIORSKI, Teresa 1901 -
1917 (C)
Natali 1900 - 1919 (C)
Genefa 1904 - 1922 (C)
Balbina 1878 - 1936 (Nee:
Gasiorowski) (C)
KENDZIORSKI, Joseph C 16 Nov
1895 - 13 Jan 1968 "Indiana
S/2 US Navy WWI" (D)
Magdaline 1897 - 1976 (Nee:
Banaszak) Mom (D)

KENDZIORSKI (continued)
Gertrude 16 Apr 1922 - 3 Aug
1932 (D)
KENDZIORSKI, Michael no date -
14 July 1936 (F)
Kazimiara 1889 - 1921 (Wife of
Jozef Trok) (F)
Victor 25 Aug 1886 - 5 Oct 1918
"Indiana Pvt Co E 26 Inf 7 Div
WWI Died of Wounds" (F)
Constance P 1831 - 30 Jan 1928
(Nee: Ebel) (F)
KENDZIORSKI, Harry F 1880 -
1954 (F)
Mary 1884 - 1951 (Nee: Barge)
(F)
KENDZIORSKI, Martin 1872 - 5
Mar 1938 Father "Husband of
Balbina Kendziorski) (H)
KIELOCH, Mary 1870 - 1932 (B)
(John Lentych & Antony Wit-
kowski same lot)
KIELOCH, Jacob 1862 - 1949 (D)
KIELTON, Joseph 1896 - 1967
Father (E)
Helen 1897 - 1951 Mother (E)
Melvyn J 1935 - 1968 "MD" Son
(E)
Evelyn 1907 - 1922 (E)
(Jozef & Anna Hanyzewski same
lot)
KIEMNEC, Ignacy no date - 4
July 1924 (-)
KIEMNEC, Szymon - no date - 9
Dec 1911 (A)
Louis L no date - 12 Feb 1925
(A)
KIEMNEC, Malgorzata no dates
(E)
Florian no date - 23 Nov 1928
(E)
(Jozefa & Antoni Robokowski &
Helen Ksycki same lot)
KIEMNEC, Leon 1888 - 1977
Father (G)
Jadwiga 1891 - 1926 Mother (G)
KIEREIN, Joseph A 1899 - 1943
(F)
Severina J 1898 - 19-- (F)
(Frank Niespodziany same lot)
KILINSKI, Jenette 1924 - no date
(D)

KILINSKI (continued)
Marion 1905 - no date (D)
Josephine 1868 - 1952 (D)
Matthew 1867 - 1944 (D)
KILINSKI, Harry 1897 - 1942 (D)
Edward 1922 - 1942 (D)
Theresa 11 Sept 1893 - 27 Mar
1981 (Nee: Mindykowski) (D)
John 1894 - 1932 "Indiana Pvt
52nd Co Trans Corp WWI" (D)
KILMER, Walter 1915 - 1970 (E)
---- 1919 - 1919 Daughter (E)
(Mikolaj & Maryanna Klockowski
same lot)
KINDT, Carl T 1907 - 1967
Father (D)
Thomas C 1940 - 1944 Son (D)
Carl Jr 25 June 1934 - 4 Nov
1934 Son (D)
KISKA (KISZKA), Louis M 1901 -
1958 (B)
Lottie B 1912 - 1966 (#2 Wife)
(B)
KISKA, Dorothy 20 May 1906 - 17
Aug 1934 "Wife of Louis M
Kiszka" (#1 Wife) (E)
(Jan F & Stanislawa Kaminski
same lot)
KISKA, Martin 1844 - 4 May 1924
SG East Fence "Husband of
Marcyanna Buczynski"
KITKOWSKI, Walter 1875 - 1949
(B)
Kate 1880 - 1966 (Nee: Radecki)
(B)
Walter Jr Apr 1909 - 1966 (B)
KITKOWSKI, Franciszek 1880 -
21 Apr 1931 Father (E)
Valaria no dates Mother (E)
KLAYBOR, Michael 1841 - 8 Mar
1923 Father (E)
Casimir 1885 - 1966 (E)
Stella K 1892 - 1971 (Nee:
Laskowski) (E)
KLAYBOR, John 15 June 1891 -
12 June 1929 (C)
(Malgorzata & Tomasz Przybysz
same lot)
KLAYBOR, Michael no date - 24
Aug 1920 (-)
KLAYBOR, Jan F 17 Sept 1876 -
30 Sept 1957 Father (F)

KLAYBOR (continued)
Maryanna M 11 Dec 1880 - 27
Mar 1957 (Nee: Rogalski)
Mother (F)
(Baby - Klemczewski same lot)
KLEIN, J Roman 20 Feb 1876 -
20 May 1935 Husband (C)
Blanche S 24 Jan 1887 - 8 Aug
1954 (Nee: Kazmierski) Wife
(C)
(Helen L Hegedus same lot)
KLEDYNSKI, Adam no date - 26
Sept 1927 (-)
KLEMCZEWSKI, ---- Baby 1948
(C)
(Jan F Klaybor same lot)
KLEMCZEWSKI, ---- 10 Aug
1892 - 19 Nov 1960 "Indiana
Cpl Co F 3 Inf (E)
KLEMCZEWSKI, Jacob 1869 -
1937 Father (H)
Jozefa 1871 - 1944 Mother (H)
KLEMCZUK, Felix 1889 - 1926
(E)
(Frances & Lucas Ambroziak
same lot)
KLEMCZUK, John no date - 15
May 1913
KLIMEK, Rozalie 1867 - 1932
Mother (C)
Thomas 1860 - 1942 Father (C)
Maryanna 1893 - 1915 (C)
KLIMEK, Maryanna 1851 - 1928
(D)
Stanislaw J 1847 - 1931 (D)
KLOCKOWSKI, Mikolaj 1883 -
1950 Father (E)
Maryanna 1888 - 1969 (Nee:
Forecki) Mother (E)
Irene 1917 - 1977 Daughter (E)
---- 1919 - 1919 Daughter (E)
(Walter Kilmer same lot)
KLODZINSKI, Marion 1879 - 1962
(B)
Alexandria 1888 - 1961 (B)
Helen 1912 - 1914 (B)
John 1917 - no date (B)
Casimir 1916 - 1945 (B)
(Edmund A & Stella Szynski
same lot)
KLODZINSKI, Blazy 1874 - 1950
Father (C)

47

KLODZINSKI (continued)
Zofia 1879 - 1969 Mother (C)
(Michael Hanyzewski same lot)
KLOS, Pelegia 1867 - 1942 (F)
Franciszek 1877 - 7 Nov 1927
(F)
(Ignacy & Marcyanna Gorniewicz
same lot)
KLOSINSKI, Janina 1903 - 1942
(B)
(Adam & Josephine Goraczewski,
& Ignacy & Anna Szafranski
same lot)
KLOSINSKI, John T 1894 - 1970
(E)
Marie 1892 - 1957 (E)
KLOSINSKI, Joseph 1866 - 1928
Father (F)
Mary 1868 - 1954 Mother (F)
(Robert Roy Roytek same lot)
KLOSINSKI, Stanley J 1879 -
1936 Husband (F)
Anna 1886 - 1961 (Nee:
Grzegorek) Wife (F)
Aloysius J 1905 - 1944 Husband
(F)
Helen 1905 - 1928 Wife (F)
KLOSINSKI, Walter J 12 June
1905 - 19 Dec 1966 "Indiana
Pvt Co F 333 Inf WWII" (F)
KLOSINSKI, Anastazia 1890 -
1966 (F)
Casimir 1885 - 1941 (F)
KLOSINSKI, Teofil 1879 - 19--
(F)
Katarzyna 1878 - 1942 (F)
KLOSKA, Catharine 1874 - 1955
(C)
Thomas 1872 - 1921 (C)
Alojzy 1903 - 1917 (C)
KLOSKA, Veronica H 1903 - 1968
(F)
John 1900 - 19-- (F)
Joan 1928 - no date (F)
Carolyn Ann 1939 - no date (F)
Sherry L 1959 - 1980 (F)
(Amanda Marie Zemanek same
lot)
KLOSOWSKI, Adam 22 Jan 1932
- no date (D)
Louis 1899 - 1972 (D)
Stella 1899 - 1961 (D)

KLOSOWSKI, Joseph 1866 - 10
Feb 1929 (F)
KLOSOWSKI, John no date - 1953
Father (H)
Mary no date - 1940 Mother (H)
Henry 28 Nov 1896 - 7 Feb 1950
"Indiana Pvt 137 Fld Arty" (H)
KLOSOWSKI, Michael 12 Sept
1895 - 7 Oct 1938 "Veteran of
WWI" (PCI)
KLOTA, Wanda 1900 - 1974
(Nee: Chmiel) (A)
Walter 25 Sept 1898 - 1963 (A)
(Vincent & Stella Chmiel same
lot)
KLOTA, Stanley 25 Sept 1865 -
1944 Father (A)
Katharine 4 March 1870 - 1930
Mother (A)
Marie 25 Aug 1898 - 1971 Daugh-
ter (A)
Clementine 26 Aug 1908 - 1976
Daughter (A)
KLOTA, Stanley 22 Oct 1891 - 15
Aug 1936 (F)
KLUCZYNSKI, Sylvester 10 Oct
1918 (-)
KLUGA, Jan 1875 - 1955 (F)
(Mary Derda same lot)
KLUSINSKI, Frank Sr 1859 - 1941
(H)
Rozalia 1871 - 1949 (H)
KLYSZ, Bert 1880 - 16 Apr 1937
(B)
Mary 1884 - 1942 (B)
(Ludwig Lencki & Evelyn O'Chap
& Patricia May Kozuch same
lot)
KLYSZ, Clara W 20 May 1896 - 2
Jan 1954 (Nee: Jaroszewski)
(G)
(Martha Jaroszewski same lot)
KMIECIAK, John no date - 12
June 1916
KMITTA, Franciszek 1898 - 7
Feb 1922 (C)
(Stefan Wendowski same lot)
KMITTA, Ernest 1822 - 1922
(PCI)
KNAPE, Edward no date - 1942
(PCI)
(Alvin Putrewski & Mary Rose

KNAPE (continued)
Gorney same lot)
K N A P P , Adalbert no date - 12
Oct 1924 (C)
KNAPP, Albert 4 Apr 1890 - 23
Dec 1974 Father "Sgt US
Army" (F)
Theresa 1893 - 1958 Mother (F)
Virginia 1924 - 1926 Daughter
(F)
KOBIERNIAK, Stella 1913 - 1956
Mother (E)
Michael 1900 - 1973 Father (E)
KOBYLAREK, Andrew 1883 - 26
Mar 1939 (F)
----- 1891 - 1945 (F)
Zofia 1913 - 1932 (F)
Olga 1925 - 1927 (F)
Seweryna 1909 - 1927 (F)
KOCHANOWSKI, Kazimierz 29
Mar 1900 - 10 Apr 1922 (A)
Franciszek 1878 - 1940 (A)
Bronislawa 1878 - 1969 (Nee:
Ginter) (A)
KOCHANOWSKI, Anastazia 16
Feb 1858 - 25 Sept 1918 (D)
Piotr 1849 - 1926 Father (D)
Jan Apr 1882 - 1943 Son (D)
K O K O T , Peter 1879 - 10 Aug
1937 Father (G)
Pelegia 1888 - 1929 (Nee:
Rybak) Mother (G)
KOLACZ, Wladyslaw 1887 - 1961
Father (A)
Maryanna 1889 - 1944 (Nee:
Kwestorowski) Mother (A)
Kazimierz 1915 - 1917 (A)
KOLACZ, Jan 1840 - 1917 Father
(A)
Regina 1854 - 1931 Mother (A)
Ralph J 19 Feb 1917 - 2 July
1963 "WWII" (A)
Jan 1891 - 19 Nov 1937 Son (A)
KOLACZ, Leon 1894 - 20 May
1981 (F)
Mary 1896 - 1971 (Nee: Rzepka)
(F)
Albin 1890 - 24 Nov 1932 (F)
Harry no date - 16 Dec 1930 (F)
KOLASSA, Frank 1882 - 1961 (B)
Mary 1875 - 1964 (B)
KOLCZYNSKI, Zigmont 5 Sept

KOLCZYNSKI (continued)
1912 - 11 Feb 1913 (B)
(Jozef & Jozefa Kajzer, & Agnes
Dereszynski , & Wawrzyniec &
Mary Tafelski same lot)
KOLCZYNSKI, Sylvester 1900 -
1917 (B)
Alexander 1863 - 19 Jan 1936 (B)
Catharine 1860 - 1937 (Nee:
Szczypska) (B)
Leo F 1887 - 1961 (B)
KOLCZYNSKI, Casimir 1894 -
1959 Father "Indiana Fireman
1/C US Navy WWI" (E)
Hattie 1905 - 1960 (E)
(Joseph & Rose Pawlicki same
lot)
KOLECKI, Joseph 1849 - 1 Sept
1923 WWI (D)
Cora 1865 - 1945 (Nee:
Kalawaga) (D)
Frank 23 June 1887 - 11 July
1928 (D)
William W 1895 - 1976 "WWI"
(D)
KOLECKI, John no date - 3 May
1913 (D)
KOLECKI, Joseph 1889 - 1971
(F)
Victoria 13 Jan 1891 - 1961
(Nee: Rybicki) (F)
Evelyn M 1918 - 1925 (with
picture) (F)
KOLESIAK, Wanda 1895 - 1926
(Nee: Tobalski) Daughter (A)
(Frank & Agnes Tobalski same
lot)
KOLESIAK, Antony F 8 July 1906
- 5 Sept 1963 "Ohio Cpl 3504
Base Unit AAF WWII" (E)
(Sylvester Wentland same lot)
K O L E S I A K , Adeline E 1923 -
1940 (F)
Sylvester no date - 2 Mar 1941
"Ind Pvt 65 Regt CIC" (F)
Antonina 24 June 1877 - 5 July
1957 (Nee; Bucholtz) Mother
(F)
Frank 4 Oct 1874 - 4 Dec 1929
Father (F)
K O L O , Mary Multanski 1898 -
1919 (C)

KOLO (continued)
(Walenty & Alicya Kanczuc-
zewski same lot)
KOLOCZYK, Joseph 1895 - 1962
Father (F)
Balbina 1887 - 1928 (F)
(Ann Koloczyk Kreciocki same
lot)
KOLSKI, Ludwik 1870 - 1929 (C)
Rozalia 1874 - 1961 (Nee:
Andrzejewski) (C)
(Martha Paege & Michalina
Andrzejewski & Jan Rozplo-
chowski & Klemens Gorac-
zewski same lot)
KOLUPA, Harry 1888 - 1972 (G)
Mary 1895 - 1961 (G)
(Piotr & Marya Majewski same
lot)
KOLUPA, Harriet T Piechorowski
1912 - 1955 Daughter (G)
(Joseph J & Konstancia Piasecki
- Leon Piechorowski same lot)
KOMASINSKI, Jan 1848 - 1915
Father "#2 Husband of Mary"
(D)
Marya A 1850 - 1924 (Nee:
Nowak) Mother "#1 Husband:
Thomas Slott" (D)
Joanna 1879 - 1926 Daughter (D)
Antony 1876 - 1971 Son (D)
(Helen Woltman same lot)
KOMASINSKI, Stanley 1888 -
1975 (E)
Jessie 1887 - 1918 (E)
(Thaddeusz Krempetz same lot)
KOMINKIEWICZ, Joseph 1885 -
1948 (F)
Nellie 1883 - 1980 (F)
KOMINOWSKI, Kazimier no date
- 21 Jan 1924 "Indiana Pfc 369
Bakery Co QMC" (C)
(Stanislaw Michalski same lot)
KOMINOWSKI, Margaret Baby no
dates (F)
(Joseph Wroblewski same lot)
KONSTANTY, Frank 1894 - 1960
Father (D)
Wiktorya 1884 - 1939 Mother (D)
(Jozef Kruk same lot)
KONSTANTY, Jozefa 1902 - 1948
Mother (H)

KONSTANTY (continued)
(Jozef Kuzuch same lot)
KONTNIK, Bronislaw 16 Aug 1874
- 18 July 1921 Husband (D)
(Marya Jandola - John Torwicz -
Franciszek Pawlak same lot)
KOPANSKI, Joseph 1926 - 1931
Son (D)
Vincent 1886 - 1969 (D)
Apolonia 1888 - 1961 (Nee:
Talenkowski) (D)
KOPCZYNSKI, Teodozia 1905 -
1931 (B)
(Teofil Kasprzyk same lot)
KOPCZYNSKI, Stanley 1929 -
1949 Son (D)
Walenty 1885 - 1960 Father (D)
Marta 1890 - 1968 Mother (D)
Alicia 1927 - 1933 Daughter (D)
Benedict 1930 - 1930 Son (D)
KOPCZYNSKI, Anna 1895 - 1969
Mother (E)
(Joe K Sobiecki same lot)
KOPEC, Stefania 1895 - 1953
(Second Wife) (E)
Ignacy 1884 - 1971 (E)
Pelegia 1888 - 1922 (First Wife)
(Nee: Kujawa) (E)
KOPERNIK, Stanley 1873 - 13
Oct 1913 (A)
Frances 1879 - 19-- (Nee:
Kucharski) (A)
KOPERSKI, Stanislaw 27 Apr
1876 - 20 Sept 1916 Husband-
Father (C)
KOPINSKI, Sylvester no date - 21
July 1918 "Indiana Sgt 18 Inf 1
Div WWI" (D)
Wojciech 1865 - 1947 Father (D)
Antonina 1866 - 1945 Mother (D)
Joseph 19 Mar 1896 - 2 Aug 1955
"Indiana Cpl 39 Inf WWI" (D)
KORDELEWICZ, Antoni no date
- 7 Apr 1930 (-)
KORLOWICZ, Martha 1884 -
1952 (E)
Andrew 1884 - 1956 (E)
KORLOWICZ, Amelia 1890 -
19-- (E)
Dominic 1882 - 1972 (E)
Veronica 1829 - 1930 (Age 101)
(E)

KORLOWICZ (continued)
Sophie 1922 - 1924 (E)
KORN, Veronica Janczak 1888 -
1977 (Nee: Guzicki) Mother (F)
(Michael Guzicki & Stanislaw
Janczak same lot)
KORPAL, Jan 1877 - 1942 (A)
Stanislawa 1880 - 1942 (Nee:
Jankowski) (A)
Ernest 1924 - 1942 (A)
(All three murdered by intruder)
KORPAL, Charles Valentine 1853
- 7 Nov 1932 (B)
Catharine 1852 - 1931 (Nee:
Gonia) (B)
Clement L 1911 - 1976 (B)
KORPAL, Aloysius V 1909 - 1936
(B)
Cecylia 1883 - 1940 Mother
(Nee: Hosinski) (B)
Lott 1874 - 1952 "WWI" (B)
KORYTKOWSKI, ---- 1906 -
1957 (E)
KOSCH, Josephine 1910 - 19--
(E)
Theodore 1908 - 19-- (E)
(Frank Kaluzny & Paul C
Romanowski same lot)
KOSIAK, Franciszek 1858 - 25
June 1927 (C)
Karolina 1870 - 1921 Mother (C)
(William Stanislaw Dopieralski
same lot)
KOSIK, ---- no dates (D)
KOSIK, Katarzyna 1879 - 1968
Mother (H)
Wincenty 1877 - 1964 Father (H)
KOSIK, Antony S 1941 - 1943 (H)
Joan 1919 - 1945 Mother (H)
KOSINSKI, John no date - 30 July
1927 (-)
KOSMALSKI, Helen 1885 - 1973
(H)
Bronislaw 1884 - 1941 (H)
KOSTRUV, Steve no date - 6 Nov
1929 "Indiana Pvt 336 Inf 34
Div WWI" (D)
(Stanislaw Bolka same lot)
KOSZEWSKI, Peter 1869 - 1940
Father (B)
Theodora 1879 - 1924 (Nee:
Kalamaja) Mother (B)

KOSZEWSKI (continued)
Leon 1913 - 1924 (B)
Kazimierz 1900 - 1924 (B)
Antonina 1923 - 1923 (B)
Gertruda 1918 - 1923 (B)
KOSZEWSKI, Paul 1897 - 1927
(F)
(Walter & Clara Kaminski same
lot)
KOTERAS, Jan 17 Nov 1896 - 12
Jan 1920 "Indiana Pfc 46 Inf 9
Div WWI" (E)
Delores Marie 1932 - 1935 (E)
Stanley 1902 - 1950 (E)
Jadwiga 1901 - 1929 (E)
KOTERAS, Casimir 1853 - 1925
Father (F)
Mary 1859 - 1925 Mother (F)
Peter 11 July 1894 - 19 Nov 1944
"Indiana Pvt 22 Co Coast
Arty" (F)
KOTERAS, Lottie 1894 - 2 Dec
1935 "Indiana Pfc 12 Cav
WWI" (H)
Michael 1859 - 25 Jan 1937
Father (H)
Wiktorya 1867 - 1933 Mother (H)
Jozef 1887 - 1951 Son (H)
KOTOLINSKI, Maryanna 1908 -
1911 Daughter (A)
Antony 1866 - 1946 Father (A)
Veronica 1880 - 1950 (Nee:
Wojtalawicz) Mother (A)
Regina 1901 - 1955 Daughter (A)
Helen 1912 - 1968 Daughter (A)
John 1853 - 19 Aug 1932 (A)
Michalena 1846 - 1926 (Nee:
Herman) (A)
KOVACH, Karon M 1955 - 1957
(C)
(Antonina & Adalbert Guzicki &
Leonard Lukasiak same lot)
KOVACS, Karl 1913 - 1942 (E)
(Marcelli & Stanislawa Jagod-
zinski same lot)
KOWALEWSKI, Vincent 1897 -
1975 (E)
Julia 1900 - 19-- (E)
Jozef 1866 - 1942 Father (E)
Agnieszka 1865 - 1920 (Nee:
Jasinski) Mother (E)
KOWALEWSKI, Joseph J Jr 1890

51

KOWALEWSKI (continued)
- 1966 (E)
Mary A 1893 - 1972 (Nee:
Poturalski) (E)
(Stanley C Jozwiak same lot)
KOWALEK, Jan 1891 - 29 July
1928 (F)
Antoni 1890 - 1944 (F)
KOWALSKI, Stephen 30 Aug 1890
- 6 Feb 1912 (A)
Joanna Ludwika Aug 1898 - 1918
(A)
Franciszek X Oct 1844 - 11 July
1929 (A)
Paulina B Oct 1856 - 1942
Mother (A)
KOWALSKI, Fred A 1894 - 1975
"Son of Franciszek X &
Paulina Kowalski" (A)
Agnes 1895 - 19-- (A)
KOWALSKI, Leonard S 1880 -
1966 Father "Son of Francis-
zek X & Paulina Kowalski" (B)
Joan F 1886 - 1976 (Nee:
Hazinski) (B)
Nicholas Baby no date - 5 May
1910 (B)
KOWALSKI, F H 1845 - 17 Dec
1907 (Mausoleum) (B)
Katarzyna Sept 1848 - no date
(Nee: Andrzejewski) (B)
"FH Kowalski one of the Or-
ganizers of the St Joseph
Cemetery. Mausoleum built by
Katharine in memory of her
husband"
KOWALSKI, Pelegia 1885 - 1924
(B)
---- 1853 - 1930 Mother (B)
---- 1845 - 1920 Father (B)
(Walenty Pietroszewski same
lot)
KOWALSKI, Simon 1885 - 1939
Father (C)
Stella 1878 - 1951 (Nee:
Lemanski) Mother (C)
Martin F 1877 - 1929 (C)
KOWALSKI, Ignacy 1848 - 25
May 1913 (C)
Petronella 1854 - 1933 Mother
(C)
KOWALSKI, Frank 1883 - 29

KOWALSKI (continued)
March 1928 Father (-)
Anna 1892 - 19-- (Nee:
Grabarek) (-)
KOWALSKI, Franciszek 16 Apr
1863 - 8 Oct 1925 (F)
KOWALSKI, Joan Mae 1934 -
1946 (G)
KOZACH, Bertha no dates (C)
(Maryanna Wojciechowski same
lot)
KOZAKIEWICZ, Allen no dates
(G)
Wilbert no dates (G)
(John Skowronski & John Strojny
same lot)
KOZLOWSKI, Julian 1884 - 1918
(C)
(Antoni & Amelia Bobowski
same lot)
KOZLOWSKI, Bert Sr 1917 - 1961
(G)
Maciej 1885 - 1931 (G)
KOZLOWSKI, Symeon 1879 -
1924 Father (G)
Alexandria Lasowicki 1888 -
1939 Mother (G)
(Konstanty Lasowicki & Joseph S
Jackmovich same lot)
KOZUCH, Patricia May 1943 -
1944 Daughter (B)
(Bert Klysz & Ludwik Lencki &
Evelyn O'Chap same lot)
KOZUCH, Joseph 1920 - 15 Jan
1937 (H)
Joseph 1900 - 1939 Father (H)
(Jozefa Konstanty same lot)
KRAKOWSKI, Frank 1889 - 1955
(A)
(Antony Stachowiak same lot)
KRAKOWSKI, Adalbert 1881 -
1961 Father (B)
Sally 1886 - 1961 Mother (Nee:
Czerniak) (B)
Joseph 1838 - 16 Nov 1912
Grandfather (B)
Harriet no dates (B)
Regina no dates (B)
Joseph no dates (B)
Alice no dates (B)
(Helen Barczykowski same lot)
KRAKOWSKI, Florentyna Paw-

52

KRAKOWSKI (continued)
lowski 1910 - 1927 Daughter
(D)
(Franciszek & Malgorzata
Nowrocki same lot)
KRAMASZEWSKI, Pelegia 1871
- 1957 Mother (B)
Konstanty 1864 - 1936 Father (B)
(Allan Michael Maciejewski
same lot)
KRANIEWSKI, Stanley no date -
15 Feb 1918 (-)
KRANTZ, Jan 1866 - 1953 (C)
Bronislawa 1876 - 1926 (C)
Stefan 1894 - 1922 "USN Baker
USA Kaiserene Augusta
Victoria"
(Richard W Deka same lot)
KRASINSKI, John 1869 - 1950 (F)
Josephine 1877 - 1949 (F)
Andrew 24 Sept 1886 - 2 Oct
1932 (D)
KRAWCZYK, Clement M 20 Aug
1920 - 2 March 1944 Son
"Indiana Tec 5 1st Armd Regt
1st Ammo Div" (D)
Anna no dates Mother (Nee:
Wrobel) (D)
Michael K 1872 - 1938 Father
(D)
Walter no dates Son (D)
KRAWIEC, Joseph 1889 - 1963
(D)
Anna 1895 - 19-- (Nee: Lis) (D)
Genevieve no date - 1986 Daugh-
ter (D)
KRECIOCH, Michael 1880 - 1948
(H)
Balbina 1883 - 1964 (H)
Jean M 1927 - 1974 (H)
KRECIOZCK, Anna Koloczych
1912 - 1940 Sister (F)
(Joseph & Balbina Koloczyk
same lot)
KRECMER, Stefan 1897 - 1977
"Pvt USA WWI" (B)
Peter P 30 Aug 1898 - 26 Mar
1974 "Indiana Sp4 USA WWI &
WWII" (B)
Walter no dates (B)
Franciszek 22 Dec 1883 - no
date Son (B)

KRECMER (continued)
Michalia no dates Mother (Nee:
Jedraczkiewicz) (B)
Piotr no date - 14 Feb 1935
Father (B)
Boleslawa no dates Daughter (B)
(Veronica D Ryan same lot)
KRECMER, Marcin 1854 - 9 Jan
1926 (D)
Wojciech 1885 - 1920 (D)
Franciszka 12 Apr 1857 - 31 May
1917 (Nee: Rozplochowski) (D)
William 3 Aug 1880 - 12 June
1937 (D)
KREMPETZ, Thaddeus 1917 -
19-- (E)
Evelyn 1917 - 19-- (E)
(Stanley & Jessie Komasinski
same lot)
KRILL, Christine Deanna no
dates Baby (F)
Michael Allen no dates Baby (F)
Wm Michael no dates Baby (F)
(Steve & Clara Wegenka same
lot)
KRISTOFZSKI, Stephen A 1911 -
1976 (H)
Stella A 1920 - 19-- "Married 22
Oct 1930" (H)
Stephen A 1950 - 19-- Son (H)
Stephen Albert no date - 1945 (H)
(David Norbert Roets same lot)
KROJNIEWSKI, Antonina 1882 -
1955 (B)
Mikolaj 1884 - 1954 (B)
Stanislaw 1879 - 5 Feb 1912 (B)
Marya no dates "Daughter of
Stanislaw" (B)
KROL, Ignatius 25 July 1878 - 19
Feb 1948 (C)
Stella 12 Dec 1889 - 20 Feb 1948
(C)
Bernice 1916 - 1917 Daughter (C)
Joseph T 1912 - 1964 (C)
KROL, Marcyanna 1870 - 5 Mar
1958 (Nee: Gorecka) (C)
Michael 1870 - 20 Feb 1933 (C)
(Irene Golubski same lot)
KROL, Stanislaw 1859 - 4 Dec
1930 (D)
Teofilia 1868 - 1948 (D)
Martha S 1880 - 1 May 1960

KROL (continued)
(Nee: Niedbalski) (D)
John Louis 1870 - 27 June 1931
(D)
K R O L, Stanislawa 1880 - 1967
Wife-Mother (D)
W l a d y s l a w   1 8 8 4   -   1 9 7 3
Husband-Father (D)
Zofia 1888 - 1920 Wife-Mother
(Nee: Szynski) (D)
KROLL, Esther 1916 - 1958 (Nee:
Reiter) (E)
(Julius & Agnes Reiter same lot)
KROMKOWSKI, Heronim 1917 -
1925 Son (B)
Jan 1875 - 28 Feb 1935 Father
(B)
Katarzyna 1878 - 1962 Mother
(Nee: Czerniak) (B)
(Antonina Czerniak same lot)
KROMKOWSKI, Chester 1928 -
1968 (With picture) Son (F)
Boleslaw 1891 - 1964 (With
Picture) Father (F)
Klara 1898 - 1946 (With Picture)
Mother (F)
Edward 1914 - 1941 (With
Picture) Son (F)
KROMKOWSKI, Stanley F 1906 -
19-- (F)
Robert 18 Aug 1928 - 1 Mar 1929
(F)
Josephine M 1906 - 1974 (Nee:
Wroblewski) (F)
KROTNIK, Bronislaw 16 Aug 1874
- 18 July 1921 Husband (D)
Mary Jadala 22 Feb 1885 - 29
Dec 1935 Wife (D)
(John Torowicz & Franciszek
Pawlak same lot)
KRUK, Jozef 1882 - 11 May 1918
(D)
(Frank-Victoria Konstanty &
Katharine Sobecki same lot)
KRUK, Anna Vargo 1887 - 1947
(Nee: Wisniewski) "First Hus-
band Jozef Kruk" (A)
KRUK, Jan F 1900 - 26 Oct 1925
WWI (B)
Jan 1870 - 1912 Father (B)
Apolonia 1875 - 1916 (Nee:
Strychalski) Mother (B)

KRUK (continued)
Sylvester 1906 - 1909 (B)
Tekla 1914 - 1916 (B)
KRUK, Mary 8 Apr 1900 - 11 Feb
1982 (Nee: Babicz) (G)
Joseph 18 Dec 1893 - 24 Apr
1931 (G)
KRUPNIK, Stanley 1873 - 3 Jan
1938 (PC1)
KRUSINSKI, Frank S 1893 - 19--
(F)
Mary A 1892 - 1977 (F)
Leonard F 1918 - 1936 (F)
KRUSKA (KRUSZKA), Weronika
1854 - 1918 (A)
(Lukasz Michalski & Tekla Hoj-
nacki same lot)
K R U S K A (KRUSZKA), Helen C
1898 - 19-- (Nee: Korpal)
Mother (D)
Stanley W 1894 - 1977 Father
(D)
Edmund L 1917 - 1923 (D)
KRUSNIAK, Franciszek 1875 - 26
Mar 1917 (C)
Kadzia 1914 - 1918 (C)
Michael 1884 - 1927 (C)
Jan C 1904 - 1938 (C)
KRUSZEWSKI, Antony 1852 - 14
Oct 1924 (A)
Julianna 1854 - 1918 (A)
Sophia 1889 - 1956 (Nee:
Otolski)
Leo H 1890 - 1951 (A)
KRUSZEWSKI, Frances 30 Nov
1900 - 1948 "Wife of Casimir
Kruszewski" (A)
(Mary Podolak same lot)
KRUSZEWSKI, Jan Jr 1892 -
1912 (B)
Katarzyna 1860 - 1922 (B)
Jan 1859 - 25 Oct 1923 (B)
Agnieszka 1833 - 1920 (B)
(Mary Kencka same lot)
KRUSZEWSKI, Leo 1913 - 21
July 1924 (B)
Kazimier 1900 - 23 Apr 1924 (B)
KRUSZEWSKI, George B 1886 -
1962 (B)
Blanche G 1888 - 1977 (Nee:
Kazmierczak) (B)
KRUSZEWSKI, Antony J 1890 - 6

54

KRUSZEWSKI (continued)
May 1928 Father (F)
KRUSZEWSKI, Joseph 1864 -
1937 (B)
KRUSZYNA, Michael 27 Aug 1863
- 28 Nov 1906 "Husband of
Valaria Staskiewicz Arendt"
(A)
KRUSZYNSKI, Michael K 19 Jan
1883 - 2 Nov 1908 (A)
KRUSZYNSKI, Casimir no date -
9 March 1924 (-)
KRUSZYNSKI, Mihala 19 Sept
1833 - 2 Nov 1908 (A)
KRUSZYNSKI, Jozef 1866 - 4 Nov
1922 (E)
Zofia 1868 - 1950 (E)
Laura 12 June 1896 - 2 Nov 1973
(Nee: Michalski) (E)
Walter 18 June 1894 - 24 May
1955 "Illinois Sgt Co H 60 Inf
WWI" (E)
Bernice 1901 - 1973 (E)
KRYANA, Walter no date - 25
June 1916
KRYCH, Valentine Jr 9 Dec 1899
- 29 May 1927 "Husband of
Mary Haus - Pvt Provost Co
59th Inf" (B)
Walenty Feb 1868 - 1955 Father
(B)
Katarzyna Dec 1863 - 14 Oct
1914 (Nee: Grzeskowiak)
Mother (B)
KRYCH, Piotr 1888 - 1942 (E)
Jozefa 1893 - 19-- (E)
Henrietta 1919 - 1920 (E)
Jan 1931 - 13 Sept 1931 (E)
(Micheline Jakubiak same lot)
KRYZA, John 1857 - 1931 (E)
Agnes 1857 - 1925 (E)
KRZEMIN, John no date - 8 Oct
1918 "Indiana Pvt 336 Inf" (D)
KRZYMIS, Adam 4 Dec 1881 - 16
June 1973 Father (A)
Rozalia 15 June 1883 - 14 Feb
1935 Mother (A)
Mieczyslaw Franciszek 22 Aug
1907 - 16 Oct 1907 (A)
KRZYZANIAK, ---- 15 June 1855
- 17 June 1911 Father (B)
Sylvester dates not legible

KRZYZANIAK (continued)
"Indiana Pvt USA" (B)
Walter 11 May 1891 - 27 May
1968 "Pvt Indiana Btry D 8th
Fld Arty" (B)
KRZYZANIAK, Joseph T 1893 -
1960 (E)
Agnes P 1902 - 1970 (E)
Agnes A 1903 - 19-- (E)
Leokadya 1898 - 1924 (Nee:
Hanyzewski) (E)
KRZYZANIAK, Klotylda Helena
no dates (F)
John 16 June 1894 - 23 Feb 1966
"Indiana Pvt Co K 1st Pioneer
Inf WWI" (F)
KRZYZANOWSKI, Franciszka
1898 - 1940 (C)
(Joseph & Pelegia Luzny same
lot)
KRZYZEWSKI, Wanda 1887 -
1923 (E)
Alex 1881 - 1958 (E)
John M 1912 - 1945 Died at Sea
"WWII S2c USN" (E)
KSYCKI, Jozefa 1862 - 1927
Mother (E)
Antoni 1862 - 1924 Father (E)
Edward K 1921 - 1923 (E)
(Peter & Helen Robakowski same
lot)
KUBACKI, Rev John F "Born USA
of Polish Parents" 20 Nov
1860 Died 23 July 1951 - Or-
dained Catholic Priest of the
Diocese of Fort Wayne Indiana
19 June 1894 - Organizer and
first Pastor of St Adalberts
Parish of Poles in South Bend
Indiana 1 July 1910 - Removed
2 Feb 1920 - Appointed Pastor
of St Patrick Parish - Walker-
ton Indiana 1 Feb 1927" (E)
KUBERSKI, Katarzyna 1882 -
1977 (With Picture) Mother (C)
Wladyslaw 1877 - 1940 (With
Picture) Father (C)
Wanda 1909 - 1917 (C)
Waclaw 1908 - 1908 (C)
KUBIAK, Michael 1839 - 25 Feb
1913 Father (A)
Jozefa 1840 - 1913 Mother (A)

KUBIAK (continued)
Jakob 1884 - 15 May 1912
Brother (A)
KUBIAK, John 10 Aug 1871 - 2
Jan 1915 (A)
Teresa 22 Aug 1877 - 1 Mar 1907
(Nee: Witucki) Wife (A)
Tadeusz 30 Oct 1901 - Nov 1906
Son (A)
KUBIAK, Jozefa 1873 - 1941 (A)
Michael 1868 - 1941 (A)
Michalena 1868 - 1943 (Nee:
Mleczek) (A)
(Katarzyna Jaworski same lot)
KUBIAK, Martin 20 Sept 1893 -
26 Mar 1968 "Indiana Pvt
USMC WWI" (B)
(Jozef & Katarzyna Kalamaja
same lot)
KUBIAK, Maryanna J 10 July
1882 - 3 Dec 1939 (C)
Franciszek 1887 - 16 Apr 1904
(C)
Maryanna 1858 - 1939 Mother (C)
Wojciech 1849 - 1919 Father (C)
Helen M 1912 - 1913 (C)
Stanley 1924 - 1924 (C)
Ruth G 1924 - 1927 (C)
Stanley J 13 Aug 1899 - 16 Sept
1967 "Indiana F3 USN" (C)
Genevieve 8 Dec 1896 - 10 Aug
1977 (C)
KUBIAK, Raymond E 5 Dec 1916
- 20 Feb 1960 "Indiana Ammo
2 USNR WWII" (G)
KUBIAK, Sylvester F 1898 - 1976
(D)
(Frances Makowski same lot)
KUBIAK, Nancy Brownell 21 July
1943 - 13 Aug 1972 (With
Picture) (D)
(John J Pinkowski same lot)
KUBIAK, Frances 1867 - 1937
(Nee: Nowak) (F)
Stanley 1865 - 1946 (F)
Carol 1910 - 25 Dec 1938 (F)
KUBISIAK, Leo 1887 - 1975 (D)
(Henry Hahn & Milton Davis
same lot)
KUCHARSKI, Richard G 1907 - 2
July 1934 (A)
Marta 30 Mar 1886 - Oct 1912

KUCHARSKI (continued)
(Married Russell Alger Bell -
1911) (A)
KUCHARSKI, Anna 1873 - 1920
(Nee: Broczinski) Mother (D)
Frank 1866 - 1958 Father (D)
KUCHARSKI, Frank Walter Jr 3
Dec 1897 - 4 Oct 1930 "Indi-
ana Fireman 2C USN WWI"
(F)
Pelegia 1898 - 1926 Wife (F)
KUCHARSKI, John 1840 - 19 Apr
1920 (-)
KUCHOWICZ, Henry C 1918 -
1979 "Pfc USA WWII" (B)
Wladyslawa 1890 - 1951 Mother
(B)
Jan 1887 - 1960 Father (B)
Edward 1916 - 1942 Son (B)
KUCZMANSKI, ---- 3 May 1907
- 15 Feb 1973 "Pennsylvania
Sgt USA" (H)
Stanislaw 1880 - 1971 Father (H)
Agnieszka 7 Apr 1884 - 24 June
1937 (Nee: Hes) Mother (H)
KUCZMANSKI, Jakub 1878 -
1960 Father (C)
Pelegia 1879 - 1925 (Nee:
Herman) Mother (C)
Piotr 28 June 1890 - 20 Apr 1919
WWI (C)
Wladyslaw 11 Oct 1876 - 21 Aug
1924 Brother (C)
Michael no date - 7 Nov 1920 (C)
KUCZWARA, Ignacy 1862 - 1943
(A)
Stanislawa 1870 - 1951 (Nee:
Kapsa) (A)
Antonette no date - 1963 (A)
KUJAWA, Jan 1852 - 1925 (B)
Jozefa 1854 - 1940 (B)
KUJAWA, Mary 1902 - 1934
"Married to Steve Kujawa"
Wife-Mother (D)
(Arthur - Agnes - Herbert &
Jozef Ewald same lot)
KUJAWA, Steve 8 Aug 1899 - 24
May 1936 (A)
KUJAWSKI, Walentyna 1898 -
1918 (Nee: Markiewicz) "Wife
of Walter Kujawski" (A)
(Stanislaw & Peter Markiewicz

56

KUJAWSKI (continued)
same lot)
KUJAWSKI, Walter J 1918 - 1957
Son (D)
Walter S 1886 - 1962 Father (D)
Agnes 1881 - 1943 (Nee: Miller)
Mother (D)
KUJAWSKI, Antony 1866 - 1930
(D)
Mary 1865 - 1954 (D)
Steve 25 Dec 1897 - 4 Oct 1962
"Indiana Pvt 3 Co Coast Arty
WWI" (D)
KUJAWSKI, Joseph 1903 - 1961
(E)
Jennie 1904 - 19-- (E)
KUJAWSKI, Antony 1877 - 1966
Father (F)
KUJAWSKI, Agnieszka 1861 -
1927 (E)
Joseph 1885 - 13 Feb 1932 (E)
Leo 1891 - 1950 (E)
KUJAWSKI, Lawrence no date -
29 May 1924 (-)
KUJAWSKI, Frank 27 Dec 1896 -
9 Oct 1971 "Pvt Co E 46 Inf
Indiana WWI" (F)
Alex W 21 June 1911 - 26 Mar
1948 "Indiana Pvt 275 Inf
WWII" (F)
(Tomasz Sawicki same lot)
KUJAWSKI, Jozefa 1880 - 1962
(Nee Przybysz) (F)
John 16 Apr 1880 - 1950 (F)
(Al J Leda same lot)
KUKLA, Terry 30 June 1954 - 4
May 1976 Son (D)
Natalie 1898 - 1918 (Nee: Paege)
"Wife of Frank J Kukla" (D)
Norbert Alan 19 Sept 1942 - 20
Jan 1943 (D)
KUKLA, Casimir 1900 - 19-- (E)
Sophie 1897 - 1968 (Nee:
Winkowski) (E)
(Edwin Winkowski & Wladyslaw
J Laskowski same lot)
KULESIA, Aloysius A 2 Apr 1902
- 5 Jan 1967 "Indiana Pvt Co
M 11 Inf" (F)
Theodore 1904 - 1960 (F)
Rose 1881 - 1968 (F)
Frank J 1880 - 1961 (F)

KULIBERDA, Franciszka 1842 -
1926 Mother (C)
Franciszek 1866 - 1914 Son (C)
(John Markiewicz & Stella Long
same lot)
KULWICKI, Helena no dates
Mother (A)
Stanislaw no date - 21 Dec 1914
Son (A)
KULWICKI, Shirley Ann 26 Mar
1943 - 27 Feb 1944 Daughter
(A)
Mary 1882 - 1929 (Nee: Chrzan)
(A)
Frank 1871 - 1946 (A)
KULWICKI, Jozefa 19 Mar 1888 -
1952 (F)
Wladyslaw 15 Aug 1874 - 1960
(F)
Marta 1918 - 1925 Daughter (F)
KURASZKIEWICZ, Kate 1846 -
1924 Mother (A)
Marcin 1846 - 18 Feb 1928
Father (A)
(Stella Beczkiewicz same lot)
KURCZEWSKI, Jozefa 1864 -
1937 (B)
Antoni 1863 - 10 Mar 1936 (B)
KURDYS, Martin F 1879 - 19--
(E)
Lillian M 1878 - 1963 (Nee:
Niezgodski) (E)
Jan 1853 - 1919 (E)
Franciszka 1860 - 1942 (Nee:
Nowakowski)
KURLANSKI, Stanley 1883 - 1961
(G)
Lottie 1888 - 1930 (G)
KUROWSKI, Joseph 1886 - 1957
(C)
Katarzyna 1891 - 19-- (Nee:
Bazan) (C)
(Joseph Dziubinski same lot)
KURTIS, Joseph 1901 - 1909 (F)
Ronald 17 Mar 1926 - 13 Apr
1926 (F)
(Walter P Kanczuzewski same
lot)
KURTKOWSKI, Joseph no date -
27 Feb 1939 (H)
KUS, Wiktorya no dates (A)
Virginia no dates (A)

KUS (continued)
Jan 1879 – no date (A)
Pelegia 1879 – no date (Nee: Slott) (A)
(Genewefa Karpinski same lot)
KUS, Stanley no date – 13 Jan 1917 (-)
KUSCH, Steve 13 Mar 1891 – 5 May 1951 "Indiana Pvt 5 Eng 7 Div WWI" (H)
KUSCH, Michael Patrick 2 July 1945 – 14 July 1945 (H)
KUSH, Joseph 1884 – 1969 (A)
Stella 1887 – 1919 (Nee: Rzepka) First Wife (A)
KUSH, Teofilia 1884 – 1956 Mother "First Wife of Wladyslaw Liszewski – Second Wife of Joseph Kush" (B)
KUSH, Jacob May 1840 – 16 Oct 1911 (-)
KUSH, John 1873 – 1942 Father (E)
Agnes 1879 – 1941 Mother (E)
Leona M 1905 – 1921 (E)
(Margaret Twardowski same lot)
KUSMIEZ, Wojciech 10 Apr 1889 – 26 Jan 1927 "First Husband of Katharine– Indiana Pvt QM Corp" (E)
Katharine 1886 – 1961 Mother (E)
(Stanley J Jonas – second Husband of Katharine same lot)
KUSPA, Blanche J 6 Mar 1902 – 28 June 1944 (A)
(Jozef Gawronski & Jean Tobolski same lot)
KUSPA, Stanley 1878 – 1954 (A)
Maryanna 1884 – 1975 (A)
KUSPA, Vincent 1907 – 1950 (E)
(Josephine Wojtysiak same lot)
KWASNESKI, Bert J 1903 – 1958 WWII (C)
Stella 1905 – 1976 (C)
Gladys 26 Sept 1917 – 29 Sept 1917 (C)
(Peter & Josephine Dyskiewicz same lot)
KWASNIEWSKI, Aloysius no date – 30 June 1925 (A)
Joseph 1887 – 1910 (A)
Antony 1857 – 1918 (A)

KWASNIEWSKI (continued)
(Mike Nowicki same lot)
KWASNIEWSKI, Jan M 1870 – 1932 Father (E)
Prakseda 1871 – 1934 Mother (E)
KWESTOROWSKI, Joseph Jr 1888 – 1974 Father (E)
Joanna C 6 Aug 1895 – 18 Aug 1954 (Nee: Glon) Mother (E)
Theresa 1926 – 1970 Daughter (E)
KWESTOROWSKI, Jozef 19 Mar 1860 – 3 June 1926 (A)
Franciszka 1867 – 1952 (A)
KWIATEK, Louise 1877 – 1955 Mother (H)
Frank 1878 – 1946 Father (H)
KWIATKOWSKI, Mary 1895 – 19-- (H)
Peter 1892 – 1954 (H)
Joseph A 1923 – 1939 (H)
Christina 1920 – 1924 (H)
KWIATKOWSKI, Frank 1880 – 1958 (B)
Rose 1884 – 1923 (Nee: Rengielski) (B)
KWIATKOWSKI, Mary 1875 – 1942 (D)
John 1873 – 1935 (D)
Vincent 10 Jan 1896 – 17 Oct 1969 "Indiana Pvt 2 Co Div Bn WWI" (D)
(Peter Flowers same lot)
KWIATKOWSKI, Adam 1880 – 1959 Father (F)
Rose 1882 – 1958 Mother (F)
Lawrence A 6 March 1910 – 29 Aug 1927 Son (F)
KWIECINSKI, Antoni 1857 – 1918 Father (D)
Maryanna 1867 – 1925 Mother (D)
Thomas J 3 Nov 1899 – 28 Feb 1981 "Pvt USA" (D)
Rose 8 Mar 1907 – 14 Dec 1976 (D)
KWIERAN, Alexander no date – 21 Mar 1939 (C)
KWILINSKI, Stanislawa 1887 – 1923 (D)
KWILINSKI, Apolonia 1867 – 1917 (Nee: Laskowski) (D)
KWILINSKI, Vincent no date – 9

KWILINSKI (continued)
Jan 1932 (D)
KWITEK, John 1886 - 1965 Husband (C)
Maryanna 5 July 1883 - no date (Nee: Paczesny) Wife (C)
Frances 1899 - 1979 (C)
LABIS, Joseph 1900 - 1964 (G)
Stella 1902 - 19-- (G)
Robert 1933 - 1937 Son (G)
(Casimir & Josephine Rybacki same lot)
LABIS, Walter 1905 - 1966 (G)
Henrietts 1911 - 1950 (G)
Thomas 23 June 1943 - 23 Nov 1943 Son (G)
June Marie 1 Apr 1942 - 24 Apr 1942 Daughter (G)
(Martin Joachmiak same lot)
LABUZIENSKI, Franciszek A 1874 - 23 Aug 1932 Husband-Father (A)
Edward no dates (A)
LACH, John no date - 15 Jan 1939 (PC1)
LADEWSKI, Kazimierz S 1 Jan 1883 - 10 Sept 1978 (C)
Stella 1887 - 13 Apr 1955 (Nee: Szulczewski) (C)
Theodore 1923 - 1930 (C)
Stephania 1919 - 1974 (C)
LADEWSKI, Adam 1854 - 1931 Father (G)
Julianna 1853 - 1938 (Nee: Jagodzinski) Mother (G)
Stanislaw 1890 - 1960 Son (G)
LAGNER (LANGER), Anna 1879 - 1955 (Nee: Sobecki) Mother (A)
Leon 1865 - 1938 Father (A)
Klemens Jr 1913 - 7 June 1931 Son (A)
Wladyslawa 1900 - 1915 Daughter (A)
LAGNER (LANGER), Sophie Tomal 8 June 1902 - 8 June 1906 (C)
(Matthew & Stella Luczkowski same lot)
LAGOCKI, Antoni 1873 - 1934 Father (G)
Helena 1872 - 1957 (Nee: Stefanski) Mother (G)

LAGOCKI, Konstancya 1872 - 1959 (G)
Antoni 1867 - 1949 (G)
LAKOMSKI, John 1888 - 1929 (B)
(Clifford Roberts same lot)
LAMENSKI, Wawrzyniec 1870 - 1942 (A)
Jozefa 1867 - 1944 (A)
Chester no date - 25 Jan 1941 "Pfc WWII USRC" (A)
Steven 1900 - 16 June 1932 "Pvt Inf 2 Div WWI" (A)
LANCTAT, Edgar 1903 - 1925 (E)
(Sylvester & Helen Gorka same lot)
LAPCZYNSKI, Stanley F 1885 - 1973 (A)
Frances 1890 - 1976 (Nee: Rengielski) (A)
Stanley Jr no dates (A)
Angela no dates (A)
Lorraine no dates (A)
LAPCZYNSKI, John J 1889 - 1972 (C)
Mary H 1883 - 1961 (Nee: Nowak) (C)
LAPCZYNSKI, Michael 1850 - 12 Jan 1941 Father (C)
Maryanna 1853 - 2 Jan 1945 (Nee: Switalski) Mother (C)
LAPKIEWICZ, Ignacy 1888 - 1962 (C)
Helena 1893 - 1957 (Nee: Hoffman) (C)
Alojzy 9 May 1915 - 14 May 1915 (C)
Henrietta 16 May 1920 - 25 Aug 1920 (C)
LASKOWSKI, Jozef 1809 - 22 Apr 1914 (Age 105) Husband-Father (A)
Marcyanna 1840 - 1935 (Nee: Paszkiet) Second Wife (A)
(Veronica Laskowski Piechoski same lot)
LASKOWSKI, Franciszek 1873 - 1928 (B)
Jozefa 15 Sept 1875 - 7 Dec 1958 (Nee: Kapsa) (B)
(Andrzej Kapsa same lot)
LASKOWSKI, Szczepan 1847 - 1 Apr 1909 Father (B)

LASKOWSKI (continued)
Agnieszka 1863 - 1941 (Nee:
Walorski) Mother (B)
(Katarzyna Walorski same lot)
LASKOWSKI, John 1860 - 3 Nov
1929 Father (B)
Catharine 15 June 1869 - 30 Nov
1932 (Nee: Przestwor) Mother
(B)
Michael Aug 1888 - 15 Oct 1915
Son (B)
Genevieve 1900 - 10 March 1920
(B)
LASKOWSKI, Wojciech (George)
1854 - 1945 (Son of Jozef)
Father (D)
Maryanna 1857 - 1941 (Nee:
Zell) Mother (D)
(Frank & Hattie Laskowski
Stachowiak same lot)
LASKOWSKI, Bronislaw 1909 -
1932 Father-Husband (D)
LASKOWSKI, Vernon no date - 3
Jan 1922 (D)
LASKOWSKI, Antonette 1874 -
1960 (Nee: Jablonski) "Wife of
John Laskowski" (H)
LASKOWSKI, Wladyslaw J 1889
- 28 Aug 1969 Husband "Son of
Wojciech & Maryanna Las-
kowski" (E)
Seweryna R 1899 - 5 Jan 1975
(Nee: Winkowski) Wife (E)
Maryanna 1918 - 1975 Daughter
(E)
(Edwin Winkowski - Casimir &
Sophie Kukla same lot)
LASKOWSKI, Bert 1905 - 1975
"Son of Walenty Laskowski &
Jozefa Laskowski Stajbach"
(Jozefa same lot) (H)
LASKOWSKI, Will 14 Feb 1881 -
28 Feb 1934 "WWI Vet" (-)
LASOWICKI, Konstanty 1883 -
1954 (G)
(Szymon Kozlowski - Alexandria
Lasowicki Kozlowski & Joseph
Jackmovich same lot)
LATKOWSKI, Joseph no date - 4
Dec 1936 (A)
LATKOWSKI, Marcelli 1863 -
1946 Father (A)

LATKOWSKI (continued)
Magdalena 1869 - 1948 (Nee:
Kurasz) Mother (A)
(Frank & Veronica Marcell same
lot)
LATOSINSKI, Joseph 1853 - 12
Feb 1937 Father (A)
Michalina 1867 - 1945 (Nee:
Tawicki) Mother (A)
LATOWSKI, Marcin 1849 - 13
Mar 1914 (B)
Rozalia 1851 - 1912 (Nee:
Plucinski) (B)
LATOWSKI, Bert 4 Oct 1897 -
1957 (F)
Frank 26 Nov 1862 - 1942 (F)
Frances 11 Mar 1867 - 2 Aug
1946 (Nee: Michalski) (F)
LATOWSKI, Theresa M Aug 1925
- Feb 1926 (F)
Josephine H Mar 1922 - Sept
1922 (F)
Barbara M 1891 - 1946 (Nee:
Niezgodski) (F)
Stanley 11 Apr 1888 - 11 Jan
1967 "Indiana S2 USN" (F)
LATOWSKI, Adrain J 1917 - 29
June 1935 (PC1)
LEBIEDZINSKI, Franciszek 1878
- 1967 Father (F)
Adamina 1882 - 1950 Mother (F)
Frank no date - 13 Feb 1931
"Indiana Pvt US Coast Arty
Corps" (F)
LECHTANSKI, Antoni 1875 - 20
Mar 1928 Father (A)
Michael 26 Sept 1916 - 13 Feb
1959 "Indiana Pvt USA WWII"
(A)
George no date - 30 June 1913
(A)
(Jan Pietrzak same lot)
LECHTANSKI, Frances 1879 -
1928 Mother (F)
Joseph 1879 - 20 Mar 1939
Father (F)
Mary 1908 - 1972 Daughter (F)
LECHTANSKI, Elfreda Butts
1917 - 1968 (G)
(George & Pearl Niespodziany
same lot)
LECHTANSKI, Gloria A 1941 -

60

LECHTANSKI (continued)
19-- (H)
Euguene R 1937 - 19-- (H)
Victoria 1913 - 19-- (Nee:
Przybylski) (H)
Joseph S 1907 - 1978 (H)
Dorothy 21 Dec 1933 - 8 Jan
1965 Infant (H)
LEDA, Henry 23 Mar 1906 - 23
Jan 1965 "Indiana BMC USN
WWII" (A)
(Rudolph Fujawa & Anna Fujawa
same lot)
LEDA, Stanislawa 1872 - 11 Feb
1918 (Nee: Makowski) Mother
(A)
Wiktorya 1907 - 1916 (A)
Martin 15 Oct 1862 - 17 June
1926 "Indiana Pfc 2 Bn US
Guards WWI" (A)
(Joseph Mikolajczak same lot)
LEDA, Joseph 1866 - 24 Mar
1936 Father (A)
Elizabeth 1874 - 1944 (Nee:
Sawinski) Mother (A)
(Harriet Grontkowski same lot)
LEDA, Stanley no date - 29 Jan
1918 (-)
LEDA, Wojciech 5 Apr 1897 - 23
May 1936 (A)
Stanley 8 May 1864 - 19 Dec
1927 Father (A)
LEDA, Antoni 22 Apr 1886 - 29
Jan 1918 (C)
Stanislawa 17 Sept 1884 - 31
May 1920 (Nee: Michor) (C)
(Frank Wroblewski same lot)
LEDA, Andrzej 1880 - 1921 (C)
(Steve & Antonina Przestwor
same lot)
LEDA, Wojciech 1871 - 16 Feb
1915 (C)
(Henrietta - Frank - Mary -
Joseph & Rose Walorski -
Michael - Apolonia Lodyga
same lot)
LEDA, Al J 2 June 1903 - 21 July
1971 "Indiana Pfc Btry B 16
Fld Arty" (F)
(Jozefa & John Kujawski same
lot)
LEERS, Marie M 1907 - 1943 (C)

LEE VAN, Frank 1907 - 1951 (F)
Gertrude 1910 - 19-- (F)
LEHMAN, Viola G 1942 - 1979
(G)
(Joseph S & Clara D Spychalski
same lot)
LEKARCZYK, Walter S 1907 -
1976 (H)
Louise A 1912 - 1970 (H)
Stanislaw 25 Apr 1879 - 1950 (H)
Marya 7 Apr 1885 - 1938 (H)
LEMANSKI, Michael 1866 - 1931
(B)
Frances 17 Aug 1869 - 5 Feb
1957 (Nee: Halas) (B)
William 1898 - 1977 "Mec USA
WWI" (B)
LENCKI, Ludwig 1852 - 1940
Grandfather (B)
(Evelyn O'Chap & Patricia May
Kozuch & Bert Klysz same lot)
LENCZKOWSKI, Mary 1886 -
1968 (D)
Joseph 1883 - 1947 (D)
LENETTY, Henrietta 1924 - 1938
(H)
Antony 1883 - 1944 Father (H)
Valaria 1887 - 1959 (H)
Joseph M 19 Mar 1911 - 23 Mar
1956 "Indiana Sgt USAAF
WWII" (H)
LENTYCH, Mary 1883 - 1944
(Nee: Tobolski) Mother (B)
Florentine 1909 - 1961 Daughter
(B)
Jan 1879 - 1940 Father (B)
LENTYCH, Jan 4 July 1841 - 5
Oct 1913 (B)
(Antony Witkowski & Marie
Kielock same lot)
LENTYCH, Theresa 1914 - 1970
(E)
Bernard J 1914 - 1974 (E)
(John W Staszewski same lot)
LEONARD, Genevieve no dates
(A)
(Isadore Van Hoke & Franciszek
Markiewicz same lot)
LEPKOWSKI, Clement 1919 -
1940 Son (H)
Mary 1884 - 1966 (Nee:
Jankowski) Mother (H)

LEPKOWSKI (continued)
Walter 1885 - 1967 Father (H)
LESEWSKI, Adam no date - 11 July 1931 (G)
LESICKI, Albert 1840 - 8 Aug 1911 (A)
Malgorzata 13 July 1855 - 10 Jan 1936 (Nee: Piasecki) (A)
Antonina 1885 - 1909 (A)
Wawrzyniec 1830 - 12 Dec 1914 (A)
LESICKI, Mary 1885 - 1920 (Nee: Zakowski) (E)
Theodore 1905 - 23 Feb 1930 (E)
Edward 1907 - 1924 (E)
Joseph 1878 - 1931 (E)
LESINSKI, J no dates (H)
LESNIEWICZ, Henry K 1902 - 1972 (F)
Jeanette H 1901 - 19-- (F)
LESNIEWSKI, Joseph 1891 - 1963 (D)
Stella 1895 - 1963 (Nee: Michalski) (D)
(Walter Przestwor & Jozef Michalski same lot)
LESZCZYNSKI, Karol W 1893 - 1965 (A)
Stanislawa 1895 - 19-- "Joined in Holy Matrimony 17 May 1915" (A)
LESZCZYNSKI, Genewefa 1879 - 1934 (C)
Wouchiech 1876 - 1957 (C)
Stanley G 1902 - 1977 (C)
LESZCZYNSKI, Edward 1905 - 2 Nov 1930 Father (D)
LE VAN (Name changed: was Lewandowski), Charles 1904 - 1977 AMM 1 USN WWII (B)
Blanche L 1913 - 1972 (B)
(Michael & Anastazya Lewandowski same lot)
LE VAN, John no dates (E)
LEWANDOWSKI, Michael 1865 - 1941 Father (B)
Anastazya 1869 - 1954 Mother (B)
(Charles & Blanche Le Van same lot)
LEWANDOWSKI, Katharine 1887 - 1930 (C)

LEWANDOWSKI (continued)
(Martin - Sophia Jankowski & Frank - Tillie Niezgodski same lot)
LEWANDOWSKI, Michael 1872 - 1957 (C)
Valaria 1880 - 1972 (Nee: Rakowski) (C)
Casimir no dates (C)
Edward no dates (C)
Joseph 1911 - 1973 (C)
Roman 1902 - 1959 (C)
LEWANDOWSKI, Jozef 1861 - 19-- (D)
Michalena 1863 - 1912 (D)
Maryanna 1868 - 1920 (D)
Stanley no dates (D)
LEWIECKI, Franciszek 9 Mar 1897 - 5 May 1928 Father (E)
(Antonina V Terlicki same lot)
LEWINSKI, Lillian 1896 - 19-- (A)
Aloysius 1899 - 1976 (A)
(Pawel - Franciszka Wegner same lot)
LEWINSKI, Adolph J 1893 - 1979 Father (B)
Tekla 1897 - 1942 (Nee: Kaczmarek) Mother (B)
Leonard A 1924 - 1980 Son "Husband of Alice - Father of Jane & Julee" (B)
LEWINSKI, Lottie G 1893 - 1970 (Nee: Gonsiorowski) "First Husband Antony Laskowski" (C)
LEWINSKI, Anna 1875 - 1961 (Nee: Stasinski) (F)
Sam 1874 - 1 June 1928 (F)
LEWINSKI, Hilarya 1903 - 1925 (Nee: Wroblewski) (F)
Edward J 11 Apr 1897 - 22 Nov 1965 "Indiana Pvt USA WWI" (F)
LIBERTOWSKI, Antoni 1880 - 1940 Father (H)
Helena 1883 - 1944 Mother (H)
LIBERTOWSKI, Wladyslawa 1908 - 1942 (H)
Stanley 1909 - 1960 (H)
LIPINSKI, (Mausoleum) I no date - 1925 (E)

LIPINSKI, Lawrence no date - 1926 (E)
LIPINSKI, Anna no date - 22 Nov 1926 Grandmother (F)
(Julianna Grocki same lot)
LIPOWSKI, Eleanora 1900 - 1975 (E)
Alojzy 1887 - 1949 (Polish Veteran) (E)
Edward 1921 - 1921 (E)
Anna 1923 - 1926 (E)
LISEK, Michael 1857 - 1934 Father (C)
Mary 1863 - 1933 (C)
Frank 1881 - 1947 (C)
Stanley 5 Apr 1895 - 16 June 1963 "Kentucky Pfc 323 Aero Sq WWI" (C)
LISEK, Stephen F 1886 - 1965 (C)
Hattie 1891 - 1975 (Nee: Kalamaja) (C)
Jan no date - 1903 age two weeks (C)
Joseph 1918 - 1923 (C)
Theodore J Sr 8 Apr 1911 - 5 Feb 1971 "Indiana Pfc 564 Ord Trk Maint Co WWII" (C)
LISEK, Szeczepan 1837 - 19-- (C)
LISEK, Josephine 1885 - 1936 (Nee: Witkowski) "Wife of Frank Lisek" (D)
(Katharine Nijak same lot)
LISEK, Jozef 1915 - 1930 (With Picture) Son-Brother (F)
Stanislawa 1884 - 1949 (With Picture) Wife-Mother (F)
Jan 1883 - 1963 (With Picture) Husband-Father (F)
Leon 1910 - 19-- Son-Brother (F)
(Joseph & John Taberski - Mary Ann Miller same lot)
LISENKO, John F 1893 - 1974 (F)
Lillian M 1900 - 19-- (Nee: Wasikowski) (F)
Daniel 26 Sept 1930 - 6 Feb 1932 Baby (F)
Eugene 25 Aug 1927 - 12 Jan 1928 Baby (F)
LISIECKI, Walenty 9 Jan 1865 - 8 Oct 1948 Father (B)

LISIECKI (continued)
Maryanna 22 Jan 1871 - 1 Apr 1946 Mother (B)
Georgianna G 12 Sept 1930 - 28 Apr 1933 (B)
LISIECKI, Ray 1898 - 1938 (F)
(Christopher Fox same lot)
LISIECKI, Napomycena 1854 - 1950 Mother (F)
(Robert D Niespodzinany same lot)
LISZEWSKI, John 1839 - 3 Jan 1914 (A)
Kate 1841 - 1927 (Nee: Laskowski) (A)
Sylvestor H 15 Nov 1898 - 8 Oct 1967 "Indiana Pfc Co C 66 Coast Arty WWI" (A)
LISZEWSKI, Jacob no date - 1 Mar 1939 (A)
Ignacy 1865 - 1915 (A)
Veronica 1867 - 1938 (Nee: Wojciechowski) (A)
Leonard 6 Mar 1895 - 25 Mar 1939 "Co I 77 Inf USA" (A)
(Jozefa Wojciechowski same lot)
LISZEWSKI, John 1875 -1923 (B)
Mary 1874 - 1910 (Nee: Rybarkiewicz) (B)
(Mary E Pennfield same lot)
LISZEWSKI, Wladyslaw 1878 - 9 Dec 1919 (B)
Marta 1912 - 1918 (B)
Helenka 25 Aug 1909 - 30 Aug 1909 (B)
Thomas E no date - 1949 (B)
(Teofilia Kush- Nee: Wroblewski w/o Wladyslaw same lot)
LISZEWSKI, Walter 1893 - 1941 Father (D)
Regina 10 Oct 1921 - 15 Nov 1921 (D)
Anna no dates (Nee: Zakrzewski) Mother (D)
Blondine 1930 - 1950 (D)
Patty 1927 - 1977 (D)
Bridget no dates (D)
Paula Patty no date - 1950 (D)
LISZEWSKI, Sophie 1906-1960 (F)
(Frederich Cook same lot)
LITKA, Sabina 1897 - 1977 (Nee:

LITKA (continued)
Walorski) (H)
Casimir 1897 - 1973 (H)
Katarzyna 1866 - 1936 (H)
LIWOSZ, Stanislaus 1863 - 1916 (C)
Katarzyna 1862 - 1918 (C)
(Ernest & Florence Jozwiak same lot)
LODYGA, Jan Dec 1842 - 15 Nov 1924 (C)
Jozefa Apr 1846 - 1916 (Nee: Wroblewski) (C)
(Alex A Isban & Robakowski same lot)
LODYGA, Rose 1891 - 1958 (H)
Joseph 1877 - 1943 Father (H)
Elizabeth Ann no date - 1965 Daughter (H)
(Kenneth Chudzicki same lot)
LODYGA, Michael Sept 1864 - 1939 Father (C)
Apolonia Aug 1873 - 1959 (Nee: Leda) Mother (C)
(Wojciech Leda - Henrietta - Mary - Jozef & Rose Walorski same lot)
LONG, Stella 1880 - 1931 (With Picture) (C)
(Franciszek & Franciszka Kuleberda same lot)
LOOMIS, Helen 1902 - no date (F)
Cecylia no date - 1973 (F)
LOPEZ, Ramiro no dates (D)
Maria no dates (D)
LOPINSKI, Stanley 1882 - 1957 Father (B)
Josephine 1884 - 1957 Mother (B)
Mary 1908 - 1910 Baby (B)
LORENCE, Teofil no date - 22 Dec 1916 (B)
LORENCE, Peter J 1913-19-- (F)
Irene B 1918 - 1974 (F)
LOSECKI, John 1894 - 1953 Father (F)
Maryanna 1894 - 1952 (Nee: Dyszkiewicz) Mother (F)
Katarzyna 1867 - 1947 Mother (F)
Jacob S 1865 - 1934 (F)

LOUCK, Josephine 1900 - 1974 (G)
(Leonard J & Julia I Kalamajski same lot)
LOVAS, Joseph 1892 - 19-- (G)
Sophia 1897 - 1977 (G)
LUBELSKI, Stanley 1891 - 1964 (With Picture) (C)
Agnes 1895 - 1941 (With Picture) (C)
Irene no date - 1915 (C)
Stanley J Jr 30 Oct 1929 - 13 Dec 1968 "California AS USN" (C)
Thaddeus S 20 Mar 1929 - 21 Mar 1975 (With Picture) Dad (C)
LUBINSKI, Bernice 2 Sept 1897 - 1 Mar 1982 (Nee: Trojanowski) (D)
Karl 27 Nov 1895 - 16 Nov 1971 "Indiana Pvt Co I 337 Inf WWI" (D)
LUC, Sophie 1892 - 1966 (Nee: Stachowiak) (D)
Stanley 1889 - 1968 (D)
Anna 1892 - 1918 (D)
LUCAS, Edgar 18-- - 1936 (PC1)
LUCHOWSKI, Felix 1883 - 1950 (B)
Johanna 1890 - 1937 (B)
LUCZKOWSKI, Cecylia J 30 Sept 1894 - 26 June 1963 (Nee: Kujawa) (B)
Vincent 20 May 1895 - 24 Feb 1971 "Pvt Co B 9 Ammo Train WWI" (B)
LUCZKOWSKI, Raymond 1923 - 1925 (B)
(Wojciech Bonek - Jozef Strozewski - Susan C Wiltroit same lot)
LUCZKOWSKI, Anna B 1897 - 1971 (C)
Stanley J 12 Nov 1893 - 1967 (C)
Richard H 1926 - 1937 (C)
Annabelle 3 Apr 1918 - 4 Apr 1918 (C)
(Tadeusz Michalski (Baby) same lot)
LUCZKOWSKI, Matthew 1862 - 24 July 1938 (C)

64

LUCZKOWSKI (continued)
Stella 1865 - 1922 (C)
Stella 1891 - 1916 Daughter (C)
Frank 1900 - 1925 (C)
(Sophie Langner Tomal same lot)
LUCZKOWSKI, John 1887 - 1935
Father (E)
Cecylia 1893 - 1978 Mother (E)
LUCZKOWSKI, Edward C 29
March 1920 - 14 July 1944
"Indiana Pvt 12 Inf 4 Div
WWII" (F)
Vern Jr 1929 - 1929 (F)
Vern S Sr 23 Dec 1895 - 30 Oct
1974 "Pvt USA WWI" (F)
Theresa A 25 Aug 1896 - 8 Feb
1981 (Nee: Moskwinski) (F)
(Casmir Moskwinski same lot)
LUCZYK, Stanislaw 1866 - 12
Oct 1918 (A)
Mary 1860 - 1948 (A)
Jan 1896 - 12 Apr 1912 (A)
LUCZYNSKI, Janina 1906-1924
(D)
Anna 1880 - 1921 (D)
Wladyslaw 27 June 1915 - 28
June 1915 (D)
Stanley no date - 1933 (D)
LUCZYNSKI, Irena 1913-1942 (D)
Dorota 1919 - 1940 (D)
Maximillian 1885 - 1932 (D)
Wladyslawa 1885 - 1919 (D)
Alicya no date - 17 Sept 1917 (D)
LUCZYNSKI, Maryanna 26 Mar
1871 - 5 Oct 1922 (Nee:
Jasinski) (F)
Anna 1885 - 1974 (F)
LUDWIKOWSKI, Frank 4 Aug
1882 - 23 Aug 1935 (H)
Catharine 1880 - 1948 (Nee:
Andrysiak) Mother (H)
Esther M 1918 - 1973 (H)
LUKASIAK, Andrew no dates (C)
Leonard 1909 - 19-- (C)
Helen 1912 - 19-- (C)
Phyllis no date - 1941 Infant (C)
(Adalbert - Antonina Guzicki &
Karen M Kovach same lot)
LUKASIEWICZ, Frances 1844 -
1936 (H)
Albert 1857 - 1941 (H)
(Leon & Josephine Sciba same

LUKASIEWICZ (continued)
lot)
LUKASIEWICZ, Stanley 1868 -
1934 (A)
Michaline 1877 - 1956 (A)
Walter 1893 - 1980 (A)
LUKASZEWSKI, Antony 20 Sept
1891 - 1 Feb 1947 "Indiana
Pvt 20 QM Labor Regt" (D)
LUKASZEWSKI, Nancy 6 Feb
1889 - 20 Mar 1942 (F)
Martin 20 Oct 1881 - 16 May
1964 (F)
LUKOWSKI, Valentine no date -
1912 (-)
LUPA, Casimir no dates (A)
Andrew no dates (A)
Josephine no dates (A)
Mary 1877 - 1951 Mother (A)
Andrew 1875 - 1952 Father (A)
LUPA, Stanley 1879 - 1914 (C)
Alice no date - 1 May 1914 (C)
(Joseph Brusick & Vincent Grud-
zicki same lot)
LUSAK, Thomas no date - 3 Apr
1917 (C)
LUZNY, Joseph 1893 - Jan 1918
(C)
Pelegia Sniadecki Luzny no
dates (C)
Franciszka Krzyzanowski Luzny
1898 - 1940 Wife (C)
LYCZYNSKI, James J 1955 -
1971 (A)
(Jakob Swiatowy same lot)
LYCZYNSKI, Andrew 30 Oct 1865
- 1956 (A)
Blanche (Pelegia) 11 Dec 1870 -
1953 (Nee: Wlodarek) (A)
LYCZYNSKI, Julianna 1875 - 4
May 1941 (Nee: Wlodarek) (A)
Stanislaw 1874 - 8 March 1928
(A)
Teodor 1905 - 1905 (A)
Kazimierz 1901 - 1908 (A)
Wiktor 1916 - 1917 (A)
LYCZYNSKI, Jozef 1880 - 1935
Father (B)
Helen 1885 - 1979 (Nee:
Piekarski) Mother (B)
Alex J 2 June 1913 - 26 Feb
1975 Son "Pvt USA" (B)

65

LYCZYNSKI, Franciszek 1883 - 19 Nov 1948 (C)
Jadwiga 1882 - 8 July 1968 (Nee: Wlodarek) (C)
Brian Patrick 15 Dec 1977 - 16 Dec 1977 (C)
(Wiktoria Rybak same lot)
LYCZYNSKI, Jacob 1888 - 1925 (B)
LYKOWSKI, Martin 1859 - 13 Dec 1914 (D)
MACHALSKI, Helen 1912 - 19-- (H)
Edward L 1913 - 19-- (H)
Henry Sr 1886 - 1949 (H)
Blanche 1890 - 1938 (Nee: Skwarcan) (H)
MACHOWIAK, John 1886 - 1970 (D)
Carrie 1886 - 1970 (D)
Mieczyslaw 1915 - 1916 (D)
MACIEJEWSKI, Bartlomiej 1833 - 14 Apr 1914 Husband (A)
Regina 1834 - no date Wife (A)
Wincenty Dec 1863 - 17 Sept 1928 Father-Son (A)
Stanislawa May 1867 - no date Mother (A)
Vincent no dates Son (A)
Edmund M Oct 1899 - 1976 (A)
Myrtle E 21 Dec 1902 - 14 Feb 1982 (Nee: Kowalewski) (A)
MACIEJEWSKI, Marcin 31 Oct 1871 - 25 Sept 1939 Father (B)
Regina 1908 - 1975 (B)
MACIEJEWSKI, Allen Michael no date - 1946 Baby (B)
(Konstanty & Pelegia Kramaszewski same lot)
MACIEJEWSKI, Krystina 1846 - 20 May 1925 (Nee: Olejniczak) Grandmother (C)
Marcin 1875 - 1943 Father (C)
Franciszka 1882 - 1957 (Nee: Stachowiak) Mother (C)
Pelegia 1908 - 1968 Daughter (C)
MACIEJEWSKI, Helena 1882 - 1954 Mother (F)
Wojciech 1879 - 1965 Father (F)
MACIEJEWSKI, Frances 1829 - 1920 Grandmother (E)

MACIEJEWSKI (continued) (Martin & Anna Obarski same lot)
MACIULSKI, Anna 1873 - 1941 (C)
Jozef 1869 - 1922 Father (C)
MACIULSKI, Peter 1862 - 1939 (F)
MACIULSKI, Betty Jane 1927 - 1976 Mom (E)
MACIULSKI, Ike W 27 Jan 1900 - 13 Jan 1964 "Indiana S2 USNRF WWI" (F)
Genevieve 1902 - 19-- (F)
MACKOWIAK, Jennie 1896 - 19-- (Nee: Chrzan) Mother (D)
Joseph A 1892 - 1970 Father (D)
Mary T no dates Daughter (D)
MACKOWIAK, Stanislaw 1902 - 10 Oct 1918 (D)
Ludwik 1900 - 1918 (D)
Marcin 1859 - 1945 Father (D)
Jozefa 1864 - 1950 Mother (D)
MACKOWIAK, ---- no date - 15 Mar 1921 (-)
MACKOWSKI, Adam no dates (-)
MACKOWSKI, Martin no dates (A)
John 1877 - 1924 (A)
(Franciszek & Bertha Wroblewski same lot)
MACKOWSKI, Frank 1873 - 1958 (A)
Sophie 1893 - 1918 (Nee: Rozwarski) (A)
Jacob 1830 - 24 Mar 1915 Father (A)
Antonette 1836 - 1912 (A)
MACKOWSKI, Frank 1878 - 1944 Father (A)
Victoria 1881 - 1914 (Nee: Splawski) Mother (A)
Maryanna 1889 - 1943 (Nee: Lusa) Mother (A)
MACKOWSKI, Paul A 1911 - 1972 (A)
Bernice J 1912 - 19-- (A)
Wladyslaw 1886 - 1923 (A)
MACKOWSKI, Stanley L 1904 - 1970 (B)
Helen C 1907 - 19-- (B)
Wanda 1908 - 1965 (B)

MACKOWSKI (continued)
John 24 Jan 1944 - 25 Jan 1944
(B)
MACULSKI, Maryanna 1872 -
1934 Mother (F)
Piotr 1862 - 1929 Father (F)
MADEJ, Magdelena 1885 - 1954
(E)
Matthew 1883 - 1960 Father (E)
(Walter Regulinski same lot)
MAEYENS, Elizabeth no date -
29 Nov 1972 Baby (D)
MAGDALINSKI, Joseph 1885 - 5
Feb 1931 Father (A)
Jozefa 1886 - 1935 (Nee:
Buczkiewicz) Mother (A)
MAGDALINSKI, Frank no dates
(-)
MAGIERA, Stanley 1863 - 29 Jan
1919 (D)
Weronica 1872 - 1944 (D)
MAIS, Dorothy 1896 - 19-- Wife
(D)
Peter J 1883 - 1965 Husband (D)
MAJEWSKI, Roman F 23 Jan
1909 - 19-- (H)
Clara 22 Oct 1909 - 19-- (H)
Jacquilene 1940 - 1941 (H)
MAJEWSKI, Helen 1895 - 1929
(A)
(Franciszek & Stanislawa
Taberski same lot)
MAJEWSKI, Paul 1870 - 1928
(B)
Cecylia 1877 - 1925 (Nee:
Jackowiak) (B)
MAJEWSKI, Peter 7 Mar 1854 -
1920 (G)
Mary 1862 - 1947 (G)
(Harry & Mary Kolupa same lot)
MAKIELSKI, John no date - 26
Feb 1926 (-)
MAKIELSKI, Frank no date -
1937 (PC1)
(Nettie Niezgodski same lot)
MAKIELSKI, Vicotria D Dec 1885
- 1961 (Nee: Stachowiak)
Mother (F)
Stanley T 1886 - 1922 Father (F)
(Bartholomew J Stachowiak same
lot)
MAKOSKI, Leon 1886 - 1920 (E)

MAKOSKI (continued)
(Jan & Maryanna Michalski same
lot)
MAKOWSKI, Ralph J 25 Mar
1916 - 18 Mar 1967 "SSgt Ohio
59 Air Depot WWII" (A)
Jozefa 1888 - 1949 (A)
Ignacy 1879 - 1965 (A)
MAKOWSKI, Franciszka 1885 -
1941 (Nee: Kolecki) Mother (D)
Steven Francis 1906 - 3 Dec
1933 (D)
John no date - 31 Dec 1915 (D)
(Sylvester F Kubiak same lot)
MAKOWSKI, Lawrence 1838 - no
date (-)
MAKOWSKI, Jozefa 1849 - 1937
Mother (F)
(Wladyslaw & Eleanor Plonski
same lot)
MALEOKA, Marcyanna 1847 - 4
Mar 1913 (A)
MALICKI, Casimir 1875 - 1949
Father (C)
Rose 1879 - 1959 (Nee:
Andrysiak) Mother (C)
John K 1910 - 1916 (C)
(Agnes Witkowski same lot)
MALICKI, Leo 1899 - 1974 Son
(C)
Josephine 1873 - 1953 (Nee:
Kimnicz) Mother (C)
Joseph 1871 - 1915 Father (C)
Clem 1909 - 1966 Son (C)
MALICKI, Leokadya 1898 - 1934
Daughter (E)
Marya 1866 - 1943 (Nee: Pier-
zorowski) Mother (E)
Stanislaw 1867 - 1929 Father (E)
MALICKI, Peter J 1860 - 1929
Father (F)
Antonia 1864 - 1936 Mother (F)
Louise F 1897 - 1954 (F)
Edward P 16 Mar 1909 - 18 Aug
1963 "Ohio Pfc Btry B 764 Fld
Arty Bn WWII" (F)
MALICKI, Lawrence no date -
1930 (C)
MALKOWSKI, Walter 1908 -
1969 Son (B)
Jan 1 Sept 1867 - 1957 Father
(B)

MALKOWSKI (continued)
Maryanna 14 Sept 1873 - 21 Mar
1921 Mother (B)
Antonie no dates Son (B)
Jozef no dates Son (B)
MALKOWSKI, Stanislaw 1890 -
1917 (C)
(Michael & Anna Hudak, Cecylia
Rybicki & Theresa Miller
same lot)
MALKOWSKI, Stanislaw 13 Apr
1873 - 13 Feb 1919 "Married
to Antonina Borlik" (E)
MALKOWSKI, Roman no date -
21 June 1928 (-)
Leon no dates (-)
MANKOWSKI, Ronald 16 June
1951 - 23 July 1960 (G)
MANKOWSKI, Ignatius F 1885 -
1934 Father (D)
Antonette R 1880 - 1972 (Nee:
Bennett) Mother (D)
Cecylia 1921 - 1932 Daughter (D)
MANTYCK, Leo no dates "Indi-
ana Pfc QM Corps WWII" (D)
Catharine 1864 - 1934 Mother (D)
Alexander no date - 20 July 1923
(D)
MANUSZAK, John no date - 14
May 1925 (A)
MANUSZAK, Maryanna 1844 -
1914 Mother (B)
Franciszek 1848 - 1933 Father
(B)
(Jozefa, Raymond & Edward No-
wak same lot)
MANUSZAK, Gladys G 1914 -
19-- (G)
Casimir S 1912 - 1980 (G)
Stanislaw 1873 - 12 Mar 1939
Father (G)
Helena 1875 - 1966 (Nee:
Piechorowski) Mother (G)
(Stella Rajter & John Nowa-
kowski same lot)
MARCELL, Frank 1886 - 1967
(A)
Veronika E 1896 - 19-- (Nee:
Latkowski) (A)
(Marcelli Latkowski same lot)
MARCINKOWSKI, John M 1892 -
13 Mar 1971 (C)

MARCINKOWSKI (continued)
Mary 1896 - 7 Feb 1979 (Nee:
Niemier) (C)
(George & Victoria Niemier same
lot)
MARCINKOWSKI, Helena 1896 -
1923 Daughter (E)
Jozefa 1862 - 1918 Mother (E)
Marcin 1857 - 1941 Father (E)
Steven 12 Dec 1886 - 3 Nov 1962
"Indiana Pvt 5 Co Ord Rep
Shop Det WWI" (E)
MARCINKOWSKI, Valentine no
dates (-0
MARCINIAK, C no dates (C)
Stanley no date - 20 Jan 1937 (C)
MARKIEWICZ, Peter 28 June
1891 - 25 Oct 1954 "SSgt Fld
Arty WWI & WWII" (A)
Stanislaw 1863 - 1941 (A)
Antonina 1867 - 1908 (A)
(Walentyna Kujawski same lot)
MARKIEWICZ, Franciszek 12
Nov 1834 - 30 Apr 1912 (A)
Katarzyna 1837 - 1909 (A)
(Isadore & Helen Van Hoke -
Genevieve Leonard same lot)
MARKIEWICZ, Jan S 1870 -
1961 Father (C)
Maryanna 1877 - 1942 (Nee:
Kitkowski) Mother (C)
MARKIEWICZ, John 16 Feb 1924
- 16 Sept 1925 Baby (C)
(Franciszek & Franciszka Kuli-
berda same lot)
MARKIEWICZ, Frank M 1888 -
1976 (C)
Victoria 1893 - 1971 (Nee:
Chmiel) (C)
Esther no date - 1906 Baby (C)
(Joseph A Walowski same lot)
MARKIEWICZ, Leon no date -
15 Jan 1924 (F)
Frank J 17 Mar 1896 - 1 Oct
1947 "Indiana Cpl 164 Inf 41
Div WWI" (F)
(Michael & Pearl Muszynski
same lot)
MARKIEWICZ, Michael 1873 -
1946 Father (F)
Marya 1878 - 1957 (Nee: Dus-
zynski) Mother (F)

MARKIEWICZ (continued)
Regina 1903 - 1978 (F)
Kazimierz 1900 - 1928 (F)
MARNOCHA, Lottie 1891 - 1970
(Nee: Jagla) (G)
Frank 1887 - 1955 (G)
MARNOCHA, Michael 29 Dec
1861 - 31 Aug 1918 (B)
Edward J 1913 - 1942 Son (B)
Henrietta M 1915 - 1937 Daughter (B)
Marta 1912 - 1927 (B)
Mary M 1889 - 1955 (Nee:
Durski) (B)
Stanley J 1883 - 1961 (B)
MARSHAL, Stefan 1885 - 1974
(A)
Wladyslawa 1888 - 1951 (Nee:
Julkowski) (A)
Stefania 1914 - 1920 (A)
MARSHAL, William 1883 - 1951
(F)
Anastazia Feb 1887 - 1970 (Nee:
Wroblewski) (F)
(Maryanna & Orville Badora
same lot)
MARSZAL, Adalbert 1852 - 1
Mar 1921 (A)
Agnes 1856 - 1942 (Nee: Polega)
(A)
MARSZALKOWSKI, Joseph 1883
- 1930 (D)
Evelyn J 13 June 1927 - 17 Dec
1975 Daughter (D)
MARSZALKOWSKI, Casimir F 6
Mar 1893 - 14 July 1964
"Indiana Mech Co G 307 Inf
WWI" (G)
Tadeusz 1 Jan 1902 - 14 July
1935 (G)
Franciszek J 1869 - 1933 Husband, Father (G)
MARSZALKOWSKI, Ann 1900 -
1965 (G)
MARTINCZAK or MAR-
TYNCZAK, Bronislawa 1900 -
1917 (D)
MARTINEZ, Rodolfo no date - 1
July 1954 (D)
MARZEC, Genowefa B 1884 -
1965 (F)
Andrzej G 1880 - 1954 (F)

MARZEC (continued)
Francis T 1922 - 1928 (F)
MASON, Warren J 1917 - 1978
(C)
Clementine M 1915 - 19-- (C)
MATELA, Michael 1866 - 21
June 1938 Father (H)
Stella 1899 - 1938 (H)
Joseph 22 Feb 1895 - 2 Jan 1954
"Indiana Pvt Btry E 323 Fld
Arty WWI" (H)
(Verna Seymour same lot)
MATHEWSON, John W 13 Aug
1915 - 16 July 1968 "Indiana
Em3 USNR WWII" (A)
(Jozef & Catharine Jamrozy
same lot)
MATERNOWSKI, Charles B 1892
- 1975 Father (F)
Stella 1895 - 1952 (Nee:
Kalamaja) Mother (F)
Pamela A no date - 8 March
1956 (F)
(Marcin & Agnes Grzeskowiak
same lot)
MATUSZEK, Andrzej 12 Sept
1830 - 9 May 1909 (D)
MATUSZEWSKI, Feliks 8 Dec
1889 - 3 Nov 1962 (C)
Mary 21 June 1895 - 15 Sept
1980 (Nee: Dankowski) (C)
MAZGAJCZYK, Frances 1886 -
1976 (D)
John F 1890 - 1954 (D)
McCAULEY, Edward H 1881 -
1952 (B)
Katharine 1878 - 1951 (Nee:
Piotrowski) (B)
(Walter Torzewski same lot)
McCLURE, Michael 1 Feb 1964 -
20 Apr 1964 Baby (D)
(John Schultz same lot)
McKIEL, Joseph T 1892 - 1942
(E)
Stephanie 1897 - 19-- (E)
Joseph no date - 1918 Baby (E)
Armand D no date - 1917 (E)
MEJER, Carrie P 2 Mar 1909 - 2
June 1969 Mother (A)
(Teodore - Katharine Ewald &
Mikolaj Urbanski same lot)
MEJER, Theodore 1891 - 27 Jan

MEJER (continued)
1937 (C)
MEJER, Alexander 1877 - 1957
Father (H)
Marya 1880 - 1935 (Nee:
Grocholski) Wife (H)
Alexandria 20 Sept 1860 - 9 Feb
1937 Mother (H)
(Jozefa Grochulski same lot)
MEJER, Clem R 15 Nov 1921 -
26 Dec 1960 "Indiana MSgt Hq
492 Port Bn TC WWII" (H)
Michael L 1884 - 1953 Father
(H)
MEJER, Cecylia 1884 - 1977
(Nee: Kluszynski) Mother (H)
Damazy J 1909 - 1954 (H)
MELCZEREK, Aloysius no dates
(G)
MELEROWICZ, Jozefa G June
1870 - 15 July 1940 Mother (D)
MELLER, Walenty 1875 - 1942
(B)
Jozefa 1880 - 1977 Mother (B)
(Anna Bentkowski same lot)
MELTON, Gladys A 9 June 1905
- 20 May 1974 (C)
(Joseph Torszewski same lot)
MELVIN, Edward E 1 July 1926 -
23 Dec 1945 "Indiana Pfc 27
Inf WWI" (G)
MENDLIKOWSKI, Jacob no date
- 27 Nov 1916 (-)
MERRICK, Sophie Muszynski
1922 - 1955 (With Picture)
Daughter, Mother (H)
(Jakub Kaczmarek & Rita Mus-
zynski Radoff same lot)
MEZYKOWSKI, John 1882 - 1918
(C)
Rose 1884 - 1915 (Nee: Lisek)
(C)
Pearl 1915 - 1918 (C)
(Tony & Sophie Szymkowiak
same lot)
MEZYKOWSKI, Boleslaw 1878 -
1949 (C)
Teofilia 1878 - 1966 (C)
MEZYKOWSKI, Joseph no date -
14 Sept 1924 (-)
MICHALSKI, Maryanna 1825 -
1918 (A)

MICHALSKI (continued)
Jakob 1815 - 24 Jan 1918 (A)
Valentine 1867 - 1950 (A)
Mary 1869 - 1955 (Nee:
Wroblewski) (A)
MICHALSKI, Walenty 8 Feb
1865 - 10 Apr 1928 WWI (A)
---- no date - 1911 Daughter (A)
Catharine 6 Nov 1877 - 4 Apr
1937 (Nee: Jendrzejewski) (A)
MICHALSKI, Walenty 1880 -
1943 Father (A)
Tekla 1885 - 1939 (Nee:
Mikolajczak) Mother (A)
Leon 1907 - 1907 Son (A)
(Bernard Jankowiak same lot)
MICHALSKI, Lukasz 1876 - 29
Sept 1929 (A)
Marya 1909 - 1930 Daughter (A)
(Weronika Kruszka & Tekla Hoj-
nacki same lot)
MICHALSKI, Wojciech 1846 - 6
May 1928 (A)
Konstancya 1853 - 1929 (A)
(Vincent & Elizabeth Grabarek
same lot)
MICHALSKI, Jozef 1846 - 1915
Father (C)
Apolonia 1854 - 1927 Mother (C)
Wladyslaw 1899 - 1948 Son (C)
MICHALSKI, Stanislaw 1914 -
1935 (C)
(Kasimir Kominowski same lot)
MICHALSKI, Jacob 1857 - 1915
Father (C)
Maryanna 1865 - 1934 (Nee:
Gruszynski) Mother (C)
Wincenty 1886 - 1944 Son (C)
Antonina 1887 - 1954 Daughter
(C)
MICHALSKI, Tadeusa 7 Feb
1918 - 26 Feb 1918 (C)
(Stanley J & Anna Luczkowski
same lot)
MICHALSKI, Frank J 1899 -
1973 (D)
Frank W 1897 - 1933 (D)
William no date - 18 Aug 1933
"Indiana S1c USNRF" (D)
MICHALSKI, Jozef 1898 - 1928
Father (D)
Jadwiga 1894 - 1929 Mother (D)

MICHALSKI (continued)
(Walter Przestwor & Jozef Lesniewicz same lot)
MICHALSKI, John no dates (D)
MICHALSKI, Jan 1856 - 1930 (E)
Maryanna 1856 - 1933 (Nee: Makowski) (E)
(Leon Makoski same lot)
MICHALSKI, Ladyslaw 26 Jan 1893 - 9 Nov 1938 "Indiana Cook 22 Eng" (E)
MICHALSKI, Martha M 1898 - 1959 Sister (E)
(Louis Jankowski same lot)
MICHALSKI, Edward 6 July 1906 - 1930 (PC1)
MICHALSKI, Casimir no dates (E)
Walter 26 June 1893 - 9 Nov 1935 (E)
MICHALSKI, Michalena 1892 - 1979 (Nee: Zawisza) Mother (F)
Stanislaw 1882 - 1945 Father (F)
MICHALSKI, Wojciech 1867 - 1928 (F)
Stephen 1902 - 1941 (F)
Frances 1875 - 1952 (Nee: Bladecki) (F)
Joseph B 1904 - 1976 (F)
MICHALSKI, Stanley 1879 - 13 Apr 1937 (PC1)
MICHALSKI, James E 2 Feb 1926 - 4 Feb 1956 "Indiana Sp3 511 ABN Sig Co" (F)
Vincent 1893 - 1941 Father (F)
Rita no date - 28 Oct 1927 Baby (F)
MICHOWSKI, Helen 1895 - 1964 (Nee: Bojewicz) (E)
Chester 1891 - 1979 (E)
MIELCAREK, Gene (Eugene) 1912 - 5 Jan 1955 (G)
Mary 1882 - 1968 (Nee: Cencelewski) Mother (G)
Adam 1886 - 1943 Father (G)
Alojzy 1909 - 1930 Son (G)
MIKOLAJCZAK, Wawrzyniec 19 July 1846 - 18 Nov 1914 (A)
Frank 21 Oct 1888 - 6 Nov 1918 "Indiana Pvt 26 Inf 1 Div" (A)
(Josephine Jankowiak same lot)

MIKOLAJCZAK, Joseph no dates (A)
(Stanislawa Leda same lot)
MIKOLAJCZAK, Agnieszka Magdelena 1870 - 1931 (Nee: Niemier) (B)
Andrzsj 1864 - 1944 Father (B)
Piotr 1909 - 1912 (B)
MIKOLAJCZAK, Tomasz 21 Dec 1863 - 1935 Father (E)
Jozefa 9 Feb 1865 - 1923 Mother (E)
Victoria 21 Dec 1890 - 1960 (E)
Bernice 1 Nov 1897 - 1962 (E)
MIKOLAJEWSKI, Jozef 1852 - 20 Dec 1925 (F)
Apolonia 1862 - 1934 (Nee: Lasecki) (F)
(Thaddeus Blomberg same lot)
MIKOLAJEWSKI, Casimir 1885 - 1946 Father (PC1)
Catharine 1886 - 1968 (Nee: Jedrzejewski) Mother
(Elizabeth & Joseph Snyder same lot)
MIKULA, Weronica 1915 - 1957 (C)
(Alex - Wincenty - Katarzyna Strzelicki same lot)
MIKULA, Jakob 25 July 1885 - 27 Nov 1918 (E)
Jozef 5 Jan 1893 - 26 June 1923 (E)
Maryann 29 Jan 1870 - 26 May 1949 Mother (E)
Nikodem 1909 - 1942 Son (E)
MILEWSKI, Anna 1879 - 1951 Mother (A)
Clement 20 Sept 1906 - 3 Apr 1964 (A)
Alex B 3 Feb 1901 - 4 Nov 1961 (A)
MILEWSKI, Anna 1848 - 1933 (A)
Florentina 1898 - 1920 (A)
Al 1908 - 1943 (A)
Frank 1873 - 1952 (A)
Antoncttc 1874 1959 (Nee: Andrysiak) (A)
MILEWSKI, Matthew 29 Aug 1847 - 19-- (A)
MILEWSKI, Harry L 1904 - 1979

MILEWSKI (continued)
(F)
Anna R 1906 - 19-- (Nee: Kruk)
(F)
MILIK, John 1885 - 1914 (D)
MILLER, Frank E 1885 - 1968
(A)
Monica S 1888 - 1965 (Nee:
Strantz) (A)
Agnes 1847 - 1928 (Nee: Kus)
(A)
George A 1845 - 1916 (A)
MILLER, Theresa 1914 - 1920
(C)
(Michael & Anna Hudak, Stanis-
law Malkowski, & Cecylia
Rybicki same lot)
MILLER, Mary Ann 4 Sept 1943 -
6 Sept 1943 Granddaughter (C)
(John & Rozalia Kwitek same
lot)
MILLER, Everette Jr 14 July
1924 - 4 Dec 1927 (F)
(Clementine Fischer same lot)
MILLER, Mary Ann 27 Apr 1945
- 27 Apr 1945 Baby F)
(John & Stanislawa Lisek same
lot)
MILOSERNY, ---- 1855 - 1933
Mother (A)
Franciszek 1859 - 27 Dec 1918
(A)
Stefan 1892 - 1 Dec 1918 (A)
MINCINSKI, Jan 1889 - 1950 (B)
Franciszka 1891 - 1945 (Nee:
Niespodziany) (B)
Ludwik 1849 - 6 Feb 1920 (B)
Jozefa 1858 - 1924 (B)
MINCINSKI, Walter 1888 - 9
June 1920 (B)
MINDYKOWSKI, Steve 1871 - 1
Feb 1939 (A)
Louis 1887 - 1927 WWI (A)
Frank 1847 - 4 Sept 1926 Father
(A)
---- 1850 - 1920 Mother (A)
MINDYKOWSKI, Frank 1875 -
1948 (A)
Salomea 1883 - 1960 (Nee:
Bartol) (A)
Leon 1905 - 1914 (A)
MINDYKOWSKI, Bert F no date -

MINDYKOWSKI (continued)
4 Sept 1941 "Indiana Pvt 55
Regt CAC WWII" (B)
Frances Sept 1876 - 1944 (Nee:
Paszkiet) (B)
Ladislaus 1873 - 1919 Father (B)
Maria no dates Mother (B)
Jakob no dates Father (B)
Juliusz no dates (B)
MINDYKOWSKI, Matthew 23 Dec
1900 - 1980 (D)
Cecylia 1908 - 19-- (Nee:
Wentland) (D)
(Vincent & Jozefa Witczak same
lot)
MINDYKOWSKI, Frank 1871 -
1922 (-)
MIROCHA, Antony 1872 - 1928
(F)
Katharine 1884 - 1965 (F)
Alice T 1917 - 1955 (F)
MISCEWICZ, Eleanor 1890 -
1961 Mother (A)
Casimir 1885 - 1972 Father (A)
Eva M 1914 - 1974 (A)
MITCHELL, James no date - 8
Apr 1981 (G)
MNICHOWSKI, Helen 1886 -
1967 (G)
Stanley 1887 - 1971 (G)
Agnieszka 1892 - 1931 Mother
(G)
Klemens 1910 - 1929 (G)
MOCZYDKOWSKI, Hendryk 1900
- 1940 (F)
(Kasper & Boleslawa Wisniewski
same lot)
MODRACKI, Tomasz 1859 - 1923
(B)
Maria 1859 - 1932 (B)
Casimir 8 Feb 1897 - 9 Dec 1968
"Indiana Pvt USA WWI" (B)
MODRACKI, Joseph 1885 - 1960
Father (E)
Frances 1889 - 1949 (Nee:
Ziolkowski) Mother (E)
Alojzy 1916 - 1920 (E)
MODZELEWSKI, ---- no dates
WWI (E)
MOLENDA, Margaret 1880 - 1958
(F)
Peter 1876 - 6 Dec 1928 (F)

MOLENDA, Marian no date - 30
Mar 1935 (PC1)
MOLENDA, Walenty 1879 - 1927
Father (F)
Anna 1886 - 1965 (F)
Henry E 1913 - 1972 (F)
MOLENDA, Frank J Jr 29 Sept
1895 - 11 Sept 1967 Husband
"Indiana Pvt USA WWI" (G)
Stanislawa 1909 - 1936 Daughter
(G)
Andrzej 1860 - 1941 Father (G)
Bronislawa 1863 - 1946 Mother
(G)
Anna 22 May 1903 - 12 Nov 1980
(Nee: Przybylski) Wife (G)
MOLENDA, Stephen M 1909 -
1972 (G)
Helen J 1916 - 19-- (G)
(Alexander & Helen Cholaj same
lot)
MONCZKO, Stanislaw 1869 -
1933 Husband-Father (D)
Katarzyna 1876 - 1955 Mother
(D)
(Zofia & Konstanty Cierniak
same lot)
MOORE, Myron O 1902 - 1977
(A)
(Stella Chrzan same lot)
MORMAN, Michalena 1888 -
1946 Mother (H)
Julius no date - 27 Apr 1937 (H)
MOSKWINSKI, Margaret 22 Feb
1923 - 17 Apr 1923 (A)
MOSKWINSKI, Patricia Ann 8
Jan 1947 - 5 Jan 1952 (B)
(Ludwik & Anna Mucha same lot)
MOSKWINSKI, Henry A 1902 -
1973 (B)
Martha E 20 Nov 1905 - 28 Apr
1939 (Nee: Jeziorski) (B)
MOSKWINSKI, Mateusz 1862 -
1938 Father (C)
Rozalia 1870 - 1926 Mother (C)
---- Infant Daughter of S & M
Moskwinski 20 Apr 1925 - 29
Apr 1925 (C)
Teresa 2 Oct 1899 - 23 Sept 1916
(C)
MOSKWINSKI, Adam 1891 - 1928
(F)

MOSKWINSKI (continued)
Apolonia 1904 - 1929 (F)
MOSKWINSKI, John J 1865 - 14
Nov 1933 (F)
Marie M 1906 - 1924 (F)
Anna 26 July 1869 - 16 Feb 1951
(Nee: Kruk) Mother (F)
MOSKWINSKI, Casimir 1 Mar
1894 - 19 Aug 1955 "Indiana
Pvt Co B 36 Inf WWI" (F)
(Vern S & Teresa Luczkowski
same lot)
MOSKWINSKI, Constance 1874 -
7 Mar 1957 (Nee: Cyranowski)
(G)
Louis 1919 - 19-- (G)
Antony 1870 - 25 Mar 1936 (G)
Rev Casimir 1907 - 1972 (G)
MROCZKIEWICZ, Wiktorya 1843
- 1916 "Wife of Leon Mrocz-
kiewicz" (B)
(Marcin Szcesny & Prakseda
Witkowski same lot)
MROCZKIEWICZ, Frank F no
date - 21 June 1915 (C)
MROCZKIEWICZ, Antoni P 1916
- 1918 (D)
(Marie J Wozniak same lot)
MROCZKIEWICZ, Martha Barry
3 Mar 1904 - 16 Feb 1979 (D)
Irene 1908 - 1915 (D)
Praxida 20 July 1872 - 7 Dec
1943 (Nee: Izdepski) (D)
Antony 15 Jan 1870 - 8 Mar 1954
(D)
MROZ, Edward 1912 - 1914 (C)
John 4 Apr 1874 - 1931 Father
(C)
Rozalla 1884 - 1949 Mother (C)
Casimir 1906 - 6 Sept 1935 (C)
Ervin 21 Mar 1921 - 9 June 1946
"Indiana Tec 5 583 Sig Bn
WWII" (C)
MROZEK, Walter 18 June 1895 -
4 Dec 1939 "Illinois Sgt 320
Repair Unit Mtc" (H)
MROZINSKI, Franciszek 1884 -
1972 Son (F)
Maryanna 1888 - 10 Oct 1948
(Nee: Szymczak) Wife (F)
Marcin 1860 - 1935 Father (F)
Antonina 1856 - 1926 (Nee:

73

MROZINSKI (continued)
Koniecka) Mother (F)
MUCHA, Andrew no date - 20
March 1924 (-)
MUCHA, Ludwick M 1863 - 13
Sept 1924 Father (B)
Anna 1860 - 1917 (Nee: Stopka)
Mother (B)
Stanley 1892 - 1941 Son (B)
(Patricia Moskwinski same lot)
MUCHLICKI, Michalena 1849 -
1914 (C)
Kazimierz 1854 - no date (C)
(Joseph & Frances Strauss same
lot)
MULTANSKI, Magdalina 1901 -
1919 (C)
Mary Kolo 1898 - 1919 (C)
(Walenty & Alicya Kanczczewski
same lot)
MURAWSKI, Hazel 1918 - 19--
(Nee: Stull) Wife (F)
Irwin C Sr 1910 - 1980 Husband
(F)
Hattie 6 Oct 1883 - 10 Nov 1980
(F)
Stanislaw 1878 - 1929 (F)
MUSZYNSKI, F 1844 - 1935
Grandmother (D)
(Aloysius & Harriet Chrapek
same lot)
MUSZYNSKI, Rita Caduff 1933 -
1973 (With Picture) Daughter-
Wife, Mother (H)
Sophie Merrick 1922 - 1955
(With Picture) Daughter-Wife-
Mother (H)
(Jakub Kaczmarek same lot)
MUSZYNSKI, Stanley no dates
(D)
MUSZYNSKI, Michael 1880 -
1948 Father (F)
Pearl 1873 - 12 Jan 1945 (Nee:
Kuliberski) Mother (F)
Agnes 1913 - 1926 Daughter (F)
(Frank J Markiewicz same lot)
MYSLIWSKI, Joseph 1885 - 1929
(E)
(Michael Pinkowski same lot)
MYSZAK, Lynn Ann July 1954 -
Oct 1954 (D)
Ralph no dates (D)

MYSZAK (continued)
Patricia no dates (D)
(Michael & Cheryl Rafalski same
lot)
MYSZAK, Antoni 1867 - 1915 (C)
Maryanna 1863 - 1936 (Nee:
Nowak) Mother (C)
MYTYK, Walenty 1891 - 1953
(D)
(Wojciech & Ludwika Wojcik
same lot)
NADOLSKI, Joseph P 25 Jan 1899
- 20 Nov 1974 "Pvt USA
WWI" (F)
(Alexander & Bernice
Dombrowski same lot)
NAJAK, William J 1919 - 1967
Son (E)
Jakob 1882 - 1959 Father (E)
Marta 1883 - 1945 Mother (E)
Franciszek 1914 - 1925 Son (E)
NAJDEK, Pelegia 1893 - 1976
"Pearl Najdek Snyder" Mother
(C)
Roman F 1914 - 1914 (C)
Tadeusz A 1912 - 1915 (C)
NAJDEK, Lawrence no date - 16
Mar 1914 (-)
NALAZEK, Ferdyand 1897 - 1925
WWI (G)
Leon 1889 - 1929 WWI (G)
Jan 1866 - 1928 Father (G)
Raymond 1899 - 1963 (G)
NALEPA, Ignacy no date - 28 Jan
1912 (-)
NAPIERALSKI, Walter 16 Sept
1896 - 7 Feb 1964 "Indiana
Pvt Base Hosp 125 WWI" (F)
Lillian V no date - 27 Nov 1901
(F)
NAPIERALSKI, ---- no dates (F)
(Agnes Gadacz same lot)
NASH, Steven 1912 - 1951 (D)
(John & Josephine Nasztka same
lot)
NASH, Edgar R no date - 4 Sept
1925 WW1 (F)
NASZTKA, John 1889 - 1955 (D)
Josephine 1891 - 1931 (D)
(Stephen Nash same lot)
NAVE, Marjorie 29 Apr 1927 - 1
May 1927 (D)

NAVE (continued)
(Jozef Pinkowski same lot)
NAWROCKI, Florentina no dates
(D)
Franciszek no dates (D)
Franciszka no dates (D)
NEJMAN, Nell E 1886 - 1969
Mother (E)
Frank 1896 - 1966 Father (E)
NEMETH, Zigmond 1897 - 1956
(D)
(Edward Chrzan same lot)
NESPO (NIESPODZIANY),
Michael 8 Sept 1900 - 9 Jan
1980 Pvt USA (B)
Bertha 1909 - 19-- (B)
NICENSKI, Wladyslaw 1888 -
1930 Father (D)
(Joseph Nowak same lot)
NIEDBALA, Wojciech 1871 -
1953 Father (H)
Jozefa 1878 - 1966 Mother (H)
NIEDBALSKI, Helena 24 Sept
1893 - 1 Apr 1939 (Nee:
Witucki) (B)
(Sophie Witucki, & Casimir &
Catharine Balka same lot)
NIEDBALSKI, Kazimierz 1889 -
1962 Father (E)
Rose 1894 - 1942 (Nee:
Wierzbicki) Mother (E)
NIEDBALSKI, Wm M 15 June
1895 - 1 July 1929 "Indiana
Pvt 14 Ord Guard Co" (F)
(Dorothy Jagodits same lot)
NIEDBALSKI, Stanislaw no dates
(PC1)
Wladyslawa no dates (Nee:
Wegner) (PC1)
NIEDBALSKI, Donald 27 Apr 1932
- 30 Aug 1950 Son "Indiana Sgt
USAF Korea" (H)
Witt 1891 - 1962 "Married to
Helen Witucki" Father (H)
Jack 1924 - 1941 Son (H)
NIEDOSIK, Lucien 1911 - 1955
(D)
Cecylia 1914 - 1955 (D)
Jerome 1940 - 1955 (D)
NIEDZWIADEK, Edwin J 15 Apr
1929 - 20 Apr 1947 "Indiana
Pvt USMC" (E)

NIEDZWIADEK (continued)
Wanda no dates (E)
Wojciech 1881 - 1963 Father (E)
Jozefa 1887 - 1965 Mother (E)
NIEMIER, George 1871 - 1940
Father (C)
Victoria 1877 - 1963 (Nee: Hess)
(C)
(John & Mary Marcinkowski
same lot)
NIEMIER, Walenty 1867 - 1918
Father (D)
Zofia 1890 - 1924 (Nee:
Wojtaliewicz) (D)
Michael I 1890 - 1957 (D)
Stanislawa 1867 - 1941 Mother
(D)
NIEMIER, Jacob J 1859 - 1926
Father (E)
Katharine L 1862 - 1944 (Nee:
Plencner) Mother (E)
Lottie 1908 - 1965 (E)
NIEMIER, Melchior S 1894 -
1980 "Cmdr USN WWI" (E)
(Wiktorya & Agnieszka Smigiel-
ski same lot)
NIEMIER, Antonette 1887 - 1971
(Nee: Jachimiak) (E)
Albert 3 Apr 1886 - 1 Mar 1956
"Indiana Cox USN" (E)
NIESPODZIANY, Joseph 1846 -
1915 (A)
Maryanna 1851 - 1907 (Nee:
Duszynski) (A)
NIESPODZIANY, S T 8 May 1905
- 2 May 1918 (B)
NIESPODZIANY, Maryanna 1865
- 1920 Mother (B)
Joseph 1866 - 1936 Father (B)
NIESPODZIANY, Stella May 1874
- 19-- (Nee: Pietrzyk) (B)
Alex "Firpo" 1905 - 1978 (B)
Helen 1906 - 1980 (B)
Ignatius July 1869 - 19-- "Step-
brother to Szymon Paszkiet"
(B)
NIESPODZIANY, Josephine 1893
- 1973 (Nee: Walkowiak) Wife
(C)
Antony 1888 - 1965 2nd Husband
(C)
(Jozef Jankowski 1st Husband

NIESPODZIANY (continued)
same lot)
NIESPODZIANY, John 1887 -
1940 (D)
Pelegia 1888 - 1933 (Nee:
Dalkowski) (D)
NIESPODZIANY, Paul 5 Jan 1877
- 30 Nov 1920 Father (D)
Mary 6 Sept 1878 - 8 Apr 19--
(Nee: Szymkowiak) (D)
(Dorothy Stachowicz same lot)
NIESPODZIANY, Pearl 1886 -
1973 (Nee: Szymkowiak)
Mother (G)
George 1884 - 1972 Father (G)
(Elfreda Butts Lechtanski same
lot)
NIESPODZIANY, Mary 6 Dec
1894 - 20 Dec 1966 (E)
(Genofa Ruszkowski same lot)
NIESPODZIANY, Stanislaw 28
Apr 1877 - 3 June 1931 (D)
Maryanna 22 Aug 1872 - no date
(D)
NIESPODZIANY, Robert D 12 Jan
1935 - 9 Aug 1962 "Illinois
Sp4 Co B 15 Eng Bn" (F)
NIESPODZIANY, Michael 1880 -
1956 (With Picture) (F)
Joanna Kolacz 1883 - 1937 (With
Picture) (F)
(Virginia De Shong same lot)
NIESPODZIANY, Frank 1872 -
1943 Father (F)
Victoria 1876 - 1962 (Nee:
Kurek) (F)
NIESPODZIANY, Helen no date -
1942 (Nee: Kreczmer) (1st
Husband Theodore Bilinski
same lot) (F)
NIESPODZIANY, Jan 1910 - 7
Mar 1928 Son (F)
Marcin 1865 - 2 July 1940 Father
(F)
Michalina 1875 - 8 Oct 1961 (F)
Genevieve 7 Jan 1929 - 9 Jan
1929 (F)
Stephen P 1898 - 1964 Father (F)
Stella 1907 - 1933 Wife (F)
NIEZGODSKI, Nettie 1872 - 19--
(PC1)
(Frank Makielski same lot)

NIEZGODSKI, Franciszka 1898 -
1924 "Wife of Stanley Niez-
godski" (A)
(Jakub Tylka same lot)
NIEZGODSKI, Thomas 4 Oct 1915
- 2 Nov 1915 (C)
Frank V 1882 - 1967 (C)
Tillie L 1890 - 19-- (Nee:
Jankowski) (C)
(Katharine Lewandowski, & Mar-
tin & Sophie Jankowski same
lot)
NIEZGODSKI, Joseph 1874 - 22
Dec 1923 (D)
Agnes H 27 Nov 1878 - 27 Nov
1954 (D)
Gertrude J 1910 - 1931 (D)
(Irene Verbeke same lot)
NIEZGODSKI, Ludwik 18 Aug
1861 - 1933 (E)
Jozefa 1867 - 1924 (Nee: Sass)
(E)
Antonina 1863 - 1954 2nd Wife
(E)
(Konstanty Bajdek & Franciszka
Przeradzka same lot)
NIEZGODSKI, Nicholas 1902 -
1959 (F)
Antonina 1867 - 1948 (F)
John 1859 - 1943 (F)
NIEZGODSKI, Marion V 2 July
1894 - 12 Jan 1929 WWI (F)
Mary J 1893 - 1977 (F)
NIEZGODSKI, Patricia 1931 -
1934 (F)
(Jozef & Magdalena Kapalczyn-
ski same lot)
NIEZGODSKI, Paul 1840 - 28 Oct
1917 (-)
NIJAK, Katharine 1860 - 1926 (D)
(Josephine Lisek same lot)
NIJAK, Valentine no date - 5
June 1917 (-)
NIJAK, William 1919 - 1967 Son
(E)
Jakob 1882 - 1957 Father (E)
Martha 1883 - 1945 (Nee:
Harmacinski) Mother (E)
Franciszek 1914 - 1925 Son (E)
NIJAK, Clement 1912 - 1969 (F)
Anna 1915 - 1964 Mother (F)
(Eugene Herman same lot)

NOWACKI, Stella 1889 - 1962 (A)
Walter 1884 - 1968 (A)
Henry 1928 - 19-- (A)
Mary 1931 - 19-- (A)
NOWACKI, Katarzyna 1851 - 11
Nov 1911 (B)
Franciszka 1916 - 1924 (B)
Teodor 1913 - 28 June 1934 Son
(B)
Stanislaw 1925 - 1931 Son (B)
NOWACKI, Christine no dates (C)
(Pawel & Leokadya Bikowski
same lot)
NOWACKI, John 1853 - 2 Sept
1931 (A)
NOWACKI, Balbina 1885 - 1915
(Nee: Kolacz) Mother (A)
Boleslaw 1912 - 27 Nov 1937
(With Picture) Son (A)
Joseph 1917 - 1942 (With
Picture) Son (A)
Florian 1882 - 1953 Father (A)
NOWACKI, Estera 19 Aug 1918 -
15 May 1919 (E)
Anna 1901 - 19-- Mother (E)
Frank K 1894 - 1963 Father
"Indiana 3 Regt FA Repl Depot
WWI" (E)
NOWACZEWSKI, Szczepan 1862
- 25 Oct 1937 Father (B)
Michalina 1864 - 1953 Mother
(B)
Jan 1882 - 1938 (B)
(F Bryski same lot)
NOWACZEWSKI, Walenty 1870 -
2 July 1927 Father (F)
Anna 1870 - 1958 Mother (F)
NOWACZEWSKI, Sylvester M
1900 - 1969 (H)
Felice M 1904 - 1974 (H)
NOWAK, Wladyslawa 1884 -
1911 (Nee: Jankowski) (A)
Hildegard no date - Feb 1911 (A)
(Frank & Mary Jankowski, &
Regina Tobalski same lot)
NOWAK, Jacob 1872 - 1957 (B)
Pauline 1874 - 1959 (Nee:
Peroska) (B)
Clara D 7 Apr 1904 - 3 Jan 1974
(B)
Sylvester 1903 - 1908 (B)
Jozef 1915 - 1915 (B)

NOWAK, Edward J 1914 - 1961
Brother (G)
Chester J 1908 - 1975 Brother
(G)
NOWAK, Katarzyna 1863 - 1940
(H)
Franciszek 1858 - 1937 Father
(H)
Laura no date - 1969 (H)
NOWAK, Michael 22 Oct 1844 -
10 Dec 1906 (B)
Bert 24 Oct 1897 - 9 Apr 1922
"Kentucky Mech Co F 8 Inf
WWI" (B)
NOWAK, Raymond 1918 - 1918
Son (B)
Jozefa 1896 - 1935 (Nee:
Manuszak) Mother (B)
Edward T 1 July 1891 - 26 Oct
1957 "Ind Cpl USA WWI" (B)
(Franciszek & Maryanna Manus-
zak same lot)
NOWAK, Alexander 8 July 1894 -
23 July 1963 "Ind Pfc USA
WWI" (B)
(Steve & Konstancia Nowakowski
same lot)
NOWAK, Jan 1841 - 1919 (C)
Jozefa 1830 - 1914 (C)
Giny no date - 31 July 1916 (C)
NOWAK, Antonette 1882 - 1976
(C)
Joseph 1883 - 1920 (C)
(Edmund & Violet Opaczewski
same lot)
NOWAK, Joseph 1876 - 1916
First Husband Father (C)
Jozefa 1882 - 1949 Mother (C)
(Stanislaw Gilas - 2nd Husband -
same lot)
NOWAK, Jan 1891 - 1930 Hus-
band "Married Helen Bonek"
(D)
(Theresa Brodowski same lot)
NOWAK, John 1824 - 1 Aug 1927
"Wife Kunegunda" (C)
NOWAK, Jozef 1902 - 1965 (D)
Carrie 1902 - 1944 (D)
(Thomas & Veronica Rozwarski
same lot)
NOWAK, Stefan dates not legible
(D)

NOWAK, Maryanna 1873 - 1930 (Nee: Kush) (D)

Jozef 1873 - 1946 (D)

Andrew B 18 Mar 1915 - 20 Feb 1944 "Indiana TSgt 44 AAF Bomb Group WWII" (D)

NOWAK, Stanley 1899 - 1931 (D)

Martin J 1869 - 1953 Father (D)

Bertha F 1875 - 1964 Mother (D)

NOWAK, Frank J 8 Apr 1882 - 2 June 1945 "Indiana Farrier Trp Gp GI Cav" (E)

Mary G 6 June 1890 - 22 Sept 1973 (E)

Mary Martha 17 Jan 1919 - 13 Feb 1919 (E)

Beata Jane 12 Sept 1926 - 26 Feb 1927 (E)

NOWAK, Jozef Stanley 19 Oct 1907 - 24 Dec 1979 Son "TSgt USA WWII" (E)

Magdelena 1873 - 1956 (E)

Jozef W 1871 - 1950 Father (E)

Katarzyna 1905 - 1918 Daughter (E)

NOWAK, Mary 1875 - 1922 (E)

(Stephen Szymkowiak same lot)

NOWAK, John Jr 1897 - 1955 Son (H)

John 1855 - 22 June 1937 Father (H)

Agnes 1868 - 1943 (Nee: Michalski) Mother (H)

Ksawry 1894 - 12 Sept 1936 "Indiana Pvt 9 Ammo Div" (H)

NOWAK, Frank C 1889 - 1974 (F)

Josephine 1891 - 1976 (Nee: Mikula) (F)

Robert 1930 - 1940 Son (F)

NOWAK, Jozef 1883 - 28 Jan 1927 (F)

(Alex P Hoffman same lot)

NOWAK, Frank no date - 18 May 1934 (A)

John no date - 27 Sept 1917 (A)

NOWAK, Joseph 11 Mar 1873 - 3 Feb 1920 (C)

Jacob no date - 9 Nov 1912 (C)

NOWAK, Jacob no date - 26 Jan 1924 (-)

Zygmond no date - 17 Oct 1925 (-)

NOWAK, Joseph 1876 - 30 July 1916 (C)

NOWAK, Michael 1856 - 10 Dec 1906 (B)

·Michael no date - 22 Jan 1923 (B)

NOWAKOWSKI, Louis J 14 Apr 1899 - 7 Sept 1958 "Indiana Co B 9 Inf Tng Bn" (G)

Chester 20 July 1892 - 6 July 1948 "Indiana Sgt Co I 7 Inf WWI PH & OLC" (G)

(Richard J Wrzesien same lot)

NOWAKOWSKI, John 26 July 1896 - 20 Aug 1971 "Indiana Cpl 163 Depot Brig" (B)

(Bernard & Bernice Nowicki same lot)

NOWAKOWSKI, John no date - 12 Sept 1937 "Ohio Cpl 20 Eng" (G)

(Stanislaw & Helena Manuszak, & Stella Rajter same lot)

NOWAKOWSKI, John J Jr 2 Nov 1901 - 13 Oct 1977 "Pfc USA" (B)

Harriet R 1902 - 19-- (Nee: Futa) (B)

(Walenty & Mary Futa same lot)

NOWAKOWSKI, Konstancia 1872 - 21 March 1911 Mother (B)

Steve 1869 - 14 Apr 1930 Father (B)

(Alexander Nowak same lot)

NOWAKOWSKI, Konstancia 8 Mar 1902 - 1 Apr 1975 (Nee: Jankowski - Divorced from Frank Nowakowski) (C)

(Jan & Cecylia Jankowski, & Gertruda Stachurski same lot)

NOWAKOWSKI, Katharzyna 22 Oct 1884 - 1954 (Nee: Paruzynski) Wife (E)

Edward Jan 1889 - 1968 Husband (E)

(Maryanna Szymarek - daughter of Frank & Mary Szymarek same lot)

NOWAKOWSKI, John 14 Dec 1889 - 11 Sept 1932 (G)

John no date - 27 Jan 1915 (G)

NOWASTOWSKI, Joseph 16 Mar

NOWASTOWSKI (continued)
1881 - 2 Sept 1952 Grandfather
(D)
(Jan Janiak, Mary Szako Horvath,
Stanley F Zalas, & Victor
Putrzewski same lot)
NOWASTOWSKI, Pearl 1887 -
1968 (Nee: Stachowiak) Mother
(F)
(Frank & Martha Banaszak same
lot)
NOWICKI, Michael 1865 - 1953
Husband-Father (A)
Bronislaw 1901 - 1971 (A)
Franciszka 1866 - 1942 (Nee:
Mroczkiewski) Wife, Mother
(A)
Antonina 1896 - 1912 (A)
NOWICKI, Jacob 1 July 1875 -
1950 Father (A)
Magdolina 25 Apr 1871 - 1955
(Nee: Jendrzejewski) Mother
(A)
Stanislaw 1902 - 1915 Son (A)
Stella 1890 - 1939 (A)
NOWICKI, Jan 1853 - 2 Sept 1931
(A)
Elzbieta 1860 - 1927 (A)
Ignacy 1879 - 31 Oct 1910 (A)
Jadwiga 1890 - 1912 (A)
NOWICKI, Joseph 1867 - 1947
(A)
Marcyanna 1869 - 1952 (Nee:
Wlodarek) Mother (A)
NOWICKI, Julianna no dates (B)
(Andrzej & Maryanna Grzes-
kowiak same lot)
NOWICKI, Frances 1845 - 1930
(B)
(Andrew & Agnes Borkowski
same lot)
NOWICKI, Bernard F 1916 - 1942
(B)
Bernice 1911 - 1937 (B)
Leo M 1905 - 22 May 1938 (B)
(Jack Nowakowski same lot)
NOWICKI, Michael 1892 - 1917
(C)
(Joseph Kwasniewski same lot)
NOWICKI, Clara 1914 - 1970
Daughter (D)
Jozef 1908 - 20 Dec 1920 (With

NOWICKI (continued)
Picture) Son (D)
Marta 1888 - 1936 (Nee:
Makowski) (D)
John 1882 - 1971 Father (D)
NOWICKI, Georgiana 1930 - 1936
(E)
George 1909 - 1974 (E)
Mamie no date - 12 Mar 1910 (E)
NOWICKI, Clara 1907 - 1972
Daughter (F)
Klemens 1912 - 1942 Son (F)
Helen M 1891 - 1960 (Nee:
Wierbicki) Mother (F)
Jan 1885 - 29 April 1930 Father
(F)
(John William Casner same lot)
NOWICKI, John C 19 May 1894 -
19 Mar 1968 "Indiana Pvt 309
Trench Mortar Bn WWI" (F)
Eleanor 1900 - 1960 (F)
Laura 1901 - 1928 (F)
NOWICKI, William 1894 - 22
Feb 1932 (PC1)
NOWICKI, Michael 1852 - 15
Sept 1927 (D)
Frances 1864 - 1924 (D)
NOWINSKI, Albin S 1893 - 1919
WWI (A)
(Frank R Wesolowski - Jan &
Julia Elantowski same lot)
NOWINSKI, Czeslaw 30 July 1906
- 1925 (B)
Zygfried Frank July 1921 date
buried "Indiana S2c USN" (B)
Franciszka 1914 - 1919 (B)
Klementina 1901 - 1909 (B)
Seweryn 1904 - 1904 (B)
Franciszek 1909 - 1909 (B)
Frank 1873 - 1939 "Spanish
American War Co A" (B)
Julia 1882 - 1934 (Nee:
Gierzynski) Mother (B)
NOWINSKI, Clement J 1889 -
1959 Uncle (F)
Matt 8 Dec 1894 - 15 Mar 1927
"USN WWI" (F)
NOZYKOWSKI, Frank J 2 Oct
1920 - 19 Dec 1944 "Indiana
Pvt Med Depot WWI & WWII"
(B).
Mary 1889 - 1964 (B)

NOZYKOWSKI (continued)
Joseph 1886 - 1924 (B)
NYCZ, Henry 1909 - 1972 Son (G)
Helena 1878 - 1965 Mother (G)
Jozef 1868 - 1930 Father (G)
OBARSKI, Martin 1854 - 1935
Father (E)
Anna 1860 - 1937 Mother (E)
Alex 1900 - 19-- Son (E)
(Frances Maciejewski same lot)
O'CHAP, Arthur no dates (G)
Lucille 1927 - 1968 (G)
Joseph 1899 - 1965 (G)
Bernice 1903 - 19-- (G)
Mary no dates Baby (G)
Adeline Baby no dates (G)
O'Chap, Evelyn 1921 - 1969
Daughter (B)
(Patricia May Kozuch - Ludwig
Lencki & Bert Klysz same lot)
O'CHAP, Phillip no dates (PC1)
ODYNSKI, John F 1904 - 1976 (A)
Josephine 1913 - 19-- (Nee:
Michalski) (A)
ODYNSKI, Mary 1885 - 1921
(Nee: Terkowski) (C)
Joseph 1877 - 24 Dec 1922 (C)
Walter 1902 - 6 Jan 1921 (C)
ODYNSKI, Norman S 1932 - 1974
Son (D)
Bert 1897 - 12 Feb 1938 WWI
Father (D)
Eugene 4 Apr 1931 - 8 Dec 1936
(D)
ODYNSKI, Frank Nov 1840 - 19
Mar 1925 (A)
OGNISCZAK, Andrew no date -
1938 Father (A)
OGORKIEWICZ, Jan 1862 - 1939
Father (B)
Magdelena 1873 - 1947 (Nee:
Filipiak) Mother (B)
Sylvester no date - 14 Oct 1939
"Indiana WWI" (B)
OKOMOWSKI, Louis no dates (A)
OLAWSKI, Maryanna 16 Aug 1877
- 14 May 1913 Wife (B)
OLEJNICZAK, Waclaw 1883 -
1934 (C)
(Ignacy & Maryanna Banicki
same lot)
OLEJNICZAK, Andrew K 1874 -

OLEJNICZAK (continued)
1938 (A)
Mary C 1885 - 1961 (Nee:
Bergal) Mother (A)
OLEJNICZAK, Teresa 1900 -
1962 (Nee: Zamiatowski)
"Wife of John Olejniczak" (B)
(Wawrzyniec & Helena
Zamiatowski same lot)
OLEJNICZAK, Jacob 27 June
1883 - Dec 194- (not legible)
"Indiana Pfc Btry F 21 Fld
Arty WWI" (C)
Mary 1892 - 1970 (Nee: Botka)
(C)
Ignacy 1885 - 1932 (C)
OLEJNICZAK, Raymond 1915 -
1954 Husband (C)
Emilia 1912 - 1917 (C)
John F 1879 - 29 Mar 1918 (C)
OLEJNICZAK, Stanley 5 Sept
1907 - 15 May 1982 (D)
Bernadette 1910 - 10 Mar 1978
(D)
(Helen & Antony Jankowski same
lot)
OLEJNICZAK, ---- 1875 - 1939
Mother (D)
---- 1868 - 1943 Father (D)
OLEJNICZAK, Thomas 1854 - 3
Feb 1938 (PC1)
OLEJNICZAK, Casimir no date -
30 Dec 1923 (-)
Boleslaw no date - 21 Aug 1915
(-)
OLEJNICZAK, Roman no dates
(C)
M J no dates (C)
OLEWNIK, Jadwiga 1880 - 1927
(F)
(Stanislaw & Stanislawa
Bentkowski same lot)
OLEWNIK, Valentine no date - 2
Nov 1927 (East Fence)
OLSOWSKI, Jozef 1878 - 1956
Father (F)
Rozalia 1882 - 1941 Mother (F)
(Stanley & Lillian Zdoniak same
lot)
OLSZEWSKI, Joseph S 1892 -
1979 (F)
Victoria 1885 - 1972 (F)

OLSZEWSKI (continued)
(Bartholomew Rembleski & Stanislaus Wietrzynski same lot)
OLSZEWSKI, Peter no date - 1920 (A)
Sylvester no dates (A)
OLSZEWSKI, Adam 1874 - 22 July 1936 (H)
Josephine 1878 - 1942 (H)
Alex 1909 - 1980 (H)
Anne 1908 - 19-- (H)
ONIEWSKI, Helen 1912 - 1950 (F)
OPACZEWSKI, Stanislaw 7 Apr 1874 - 1954 Father (G)
Franciszka 29 June 1877 - 1948 Mother (G)
Pelegia 1899 - 1924 Daughter (G)
OPACZEWSKI, Eugene R 6 June 1929 - 14 Aug 1972 "Indiana Co C 712 Mil Pol BAN Korea" (B)
Lucille 1930 - 19-- (B)
OPACZEWSKI, Edmund 25 Oct 1907 - 1970 (C)
Violet 1909 - 19-- (C)
(Antonette & Joseph Nowak same lot)
OPACZEWSKI, Andrzej 1868 - 1933 (D)
Katarzyna 1874 - 1944 (D)
Stanley M 1900 - 1969 (D)
ORLOWSKI, Martin 1888 - 1972 (D)
Hattie 11 Jan 1896 - 3 July 1980 (Nee: Przybylski) (D)
ORLOWSKI, John no date - 3 Jan 1937 WWI (D)
Walter no dates (D)
ORLOWSKI, Joseph J 11 Dec 1925 - 16 Oct 1970 "Indiana Tec 5 Co H 8 Armd Inf 20 Inf Div WWII" ORNAT (D)
Theresa 1897 - 1934 (Nee: Michalski) "Wife of George Ornat" (D)
ORSTYNOWICZ, Maryanna 1881 - 1957 (Nee: Bladecki) Mother, 2nd wife (B)
Mateusz 1881 - 1955 Father (B)
Ludwig 1906 - 20 May 1925 Son (B)

ORSTYNOWICZ (continued)
Julianna 1879 - 1910 First Wife (B)
ORSZULAK, Andrew 1889 - 1945 (D)
Benedict 14 Nov 1922 - 9 May 1946 "Pfc 1297 Mil Pol Bn" (D)
(Agnieszka Rybarkiewicz same lot)
ORZECHOWSKI, John 1865 - 2 Aug 1937 (A)
Maryanna 1888 - 1929 (A)
John 27 May 1888 - 16 Feb 1966 "Indiana Pvt Fld Arty WWI" (A)
Casimir 1902 - 1941 (A)
Joseph S 7 June 1895 - 28 Jan 1955 "Indiana Mech Btry F 16 FA 4 Div PH WWI" (A)
ORZECHOWSKI, Marion 1896 - 1979 "Pfc USA" (B)
(John & Mary Kazmierczak same lot)
OSCARD, Anthony 1878 - 1934 Father (G)
Jadwiga 1880 - 1955 Mother (G)
OSMANSKI, Pelegia 1881 - 1959 (Nee: Lodyga) (B)
Jan 1881 - 1960 Father (B)
Edward J 26 Apr 1918 - 8 July 1969 "Indiana 1Sgt Co C 10 Armd Inf WWII" (B)
(Teodor Szymanski same lot)
OSMANSKI, Theodosia 1918 - 1939 Wife (D)
(Maryanna & Wawrzyniec Grembowicz same lot)
OSOWSKI, Boleslaw 25 Apr 1908 - no date (G)
Joseph 18 Mar 1923 - 26 Oct 1930 (G)
Leokadya no date - 1912 (G)
Czeslaw no date - 1912 (G)
(Paul & Bernice Eitler same lot)
OSOWSKI, Virginia Sue 26 May 1948 - 21 July 1951 (E)
OTOLSKI, John 1902 - 10 Dec 1921 (C)
OTOLSKI, Martha 1917 - 1939 Daughter (F)
John 1883 - 13 July 1933 Father

OTOLSKI (continued)
(F)
Marion 1919 - 1936 Son (F)
Marian 1886 - 1963 (Nee:
Rakowski) Mother (F)
OTOLSKI, Lottie 18 Apr 1914 -
19-- (H)
Clement 25 July 1908 - 20 Oct
1960 (H)
OTOLSKI, Matthew 1863 - 1956
Father (G)
Paulina 1864 - 1924 Mother (G)
William M 4 Sept 1892 - 3 Oct
1958 Indiana Pvt Ord Depot
WWI (G)
OTOLSKI, Michael 1913 - 1945
Husband (G)
Joseph 1876 - 1945 Father (G)
Josephine 1880 - 1938 (Nee:
Robakowski) Mother (G)
Tillie 1900 - 1922 (G)
OTOLSKI, John J 1881 - 1921 (G)
Blanche 1882 - 1970 (Nee:
Urbanski) (G)
OTOLSKI, Joseph F 12 Dec 1892
- 30 Apr 1971 (G)
(Wladyslaw Hes same lot)
OZDYCH, Andrzej 1864 - 1919
(D)
Antonina 1870 - 1917 (Nee:
Kapalczynski) (D)
PABIS, Jan 12 Dec 1878 - 29 July
1911 (B)
(Isadore Jordanek same lot)
PACALA, Thomas 1865 - 1949
(C)
Frances 1874 - 1961 (C)
Harry J Sr 12 May 1910 - 16 Nov
1979 (C)
(Andrew C Potts same lot)
PACAYTES, Stanislaw 13 Sept
1891 - 7 Aug 1962 "Indiana
Pvt Co C 158 Depot Brigade
WWI" (-)
(Petronella & Michael Bobrowski
same lot)
PACEWICZ, Julianna M 1864 -
1915 (Nee: Jurkiewicz) Mother
(D)
PACHOLSKI, Cecylia 1894 -
1940 (C)
(Michael, Edward, & Robert

PACHOLSKI (continued)
Szynkowiak same lot)
PACZESNY, Antonina 1854 -
1914 Mother (A)
Martin J 1897 - 1976 "Cpl USA
WWI" (A)
Joseph 1851 - 30 Apr 1931
Father (A)
PACZESNY, Jakub 1 Aug 1889 -
18 Sept 1932 (D)
John H 1864 - 1941 (D)
Rose 1868 - 1951 (D)
PACZKOWSKI, Alexander 1894 -
1912 (B)
Frances 1844 - 1908 (B)
PACZKOWSKI, Ignatius 1887 -
1971 Father (C)
Anna 1888 - 1969 (Nee: Dietz)
Mother (C)
Marya 1908 - 19-- Daughter (C)
Richard no dates (C)
Benedict no dates (C)
Hildegard no dates (C)
Esther no date - 6 June 1915 (C)
PACZKOWSKI, Marya 1880 -
1945 (Nee: Wieczorek) (D)
Joseph W 1877 - 1956 (D)
Frank no dates (D)
Virginia 8 Mar 1902 - 4 Sept
1924 (D)
(Lucya Pawlak same lot)
PACZKOWSKI, Julian 1883 -
1951 Father (E)
Helen 1884 - 1933 Mother (E)
Stanley & Erwin Twins 1920 -
1923 (E)
PACZKOWSKI, Diane no dates
(H)
PAEGE, Rudolph 1857 - 1932
Father (D)
Mary 1857 - 1924 Mother (D)
Leo R 27 Oct 1898 - 28 July
1917 "Indiana Pvt 23 Inf Div"
(D)
(Dallas Feldmier same lot)
PAEGE, Martha 4 Mar 1887 - 11
Oct 1918 (C)
Helen 1916 - 1918 Daughter (C)
(Wawrzyniec & Michalena Andr-
zejewski same lot)
PAGLICKI, Frank 1864 - 1929 (F)
PAHOLSKI, Edward 1905 - 1963

PAHOLSKI (continued)
Father (D)
Betty J 1928 - 1931 Baby (D)
PAJAKOWSKI, Helen 1893 - 1927
Wife (F)
Stefan W 1887 - 1958 Husband
(F)
PAJAKOWSKI, Roman R 1921 -
1975 Husband, Father (B)
PAJAKOWSKI, Maryanna 1880 -
1959 (B)
Walenty 1875 - 1953 (B)
Stanislawa 1880 - 1910 (B)
Maryanna 28 Nov 1893 - 28 Mar
1910 (B)
PALICKI, Eliguisz 1899 - 1911
(A)
Felix 1901 - 28 Apr 1917 (A)
Jozef Sept 1868 - 1956 Father
(A)
Prakseda Sept 1876 - 1935
Mother (A)
PALICKI, Marya 1880 - 1933
(Nee: Jerzekowski) (D)
Frank 1870 - 1950 Father (D)
Roman 25 July 1905 - 13 Mar
1950 "Indiana Pvt 8 Svc Cmd
WWII" (D)
Thaddeus J 1914 - 1976 "Sgt
USA WWII" (D)
PALICKI, Valentine 28 Oct 1895
- 6 June 1979 (-)
Katharine 1866 - 1942 Mother (-)
Frank 1864 - 1929 Father (-)
PALKA, Clem F 1916 - 1940 (H)
Frances no dates (Nee: Nowak)
Mother "Wife of Steve Palka"
(H)
PALKA, Evelyn 1916 - 1916 (A)
Arthur 1918 - 1918 (A)
Mary 1895 - 1963 (Nee: Gonsio-
rowski) (A)
Leo F Jan 1895 - 1959 (A)
(Antony Gonsiorowski same lot)
PALKA, Marcin May 1849 - 1942
Father (C)
Malgorzata July 1858 - 1920
Mother (C)
Jozef Jan 1889 - 1918 Son (C)
PALKA, Chester 1921 - 16 May
1935 (PC1)
PALKOWSKI, Katarzyna 1891 -

PALKOWSKI (continued)
1924 (Nee: Chudzicki) (F)
John Jr 1892 - 1947 (F)
Chesterine 1904 - 13 Oct 1979
(Nee: Stefanski) (F)
Leon 1902 - 25 July 1933 (F)
PALOMA, Rogiella no date - 2
June 1980 (D)
Angie no dates "Born San Juan"
(D)
(Mary Filipiak, Esther Rodri-
guez, & Ramiro & Maria Lopez
same lot)
PALUSZEWSKI, Wiktorya 1884 -
1966 Mother (C)
Michael 1883 - 1954 Father (C)
(Wladzia Cassler same lot)
PANICKI, Franciszek 1852 - 1941
Father (F)
Agnieszka 1862 - 1927 (Nee:
Paszkiet) Mother (F)
(Franciszka Paszkiet & Aunt
same lot)
PAPAI, Florence 1910 - 1943 (E)
PAPCZYNSKI, Alexander Sr 14
Nov 1895 - 1947 Husband,
Father (G)
(Genevieve Wroblewski Papc-
zynski Slessman same lot)
PAPCZYNSKI, Stella K 1902 -
1981 (Nee: Grackowski) (G)
Frank no date - 17 Sept 1939
"Indiana Pfc 37 Fld Arty 13
Div" (G)
PAPROCKI, Tekla 1810 - 1910
Age 100 Grandmother (B)
Franciszek 1864 - 26 Jan 1927
Father (B)
Jozefa 1874 - 1937 (Nee: Sojka)
Mother (B)
PARAFANOWICZ, Euralia 1889 -
1966 (F)
Romuald 1878 - 10 Nov 1925 (F)
(Helen Urbanski same lot)
PARIS, Clara 1891 - 1945 (Nee:
Hojnacki) (E)
Stanislaw 1879 - 1949 Father (E)
Marya 1880 - 1939 (Nee: Stas-
zewski) Mother (E)
(Boleslaw Hojnacki & Walenty
Staszewski same lot)
PASELL, Paul F no dates (F)

PASZKIET, Franciska 1849 -
1927 Aunt (F)
(Franciszek & Agnes Panicki
same lot)
PASZKIET, Paul 29 June 1875 -
28 Nov 1950 "Born in Szubin,
Bydgoszcz, Poland" (D)
Pelegia (Pearl) no date - 1924
(Nee: Szynski) Wife (Pearl
died in Logansport, Indiana,
interrment unknown)
PASZKIET, Stanislaw Apr 1896 -
15 Dec 1918 Son "Pvt Btry E
146 Fld Arty Died in Verdan,
France WWI" (D)
Ludwika July 1873 - 15 Jan 1947
(Nee: Wendowski) Mother (D)
Szymon 2 Oct 1870 - 10 Jan 1943
Father (D)
PASZKIET, Bertha 25 Sept 1889 -
17 Sept 1975 (Nee: Gorski) (E)
John 26 June 1886 - 21 April
1967 (E)
PASZKIET, ---- no date - 1935
Child (H)
(Adam - Frances - Peter - Stella
Cygart & Fritz Brian same lot)
PASZKIEWICZ, Stefan 1892 - 6
Apr 1912 (B)
Stanislaw 1893 - 2 Jan 1919 (B)
Sylvester 1895 - 1909 (B)
Stanislawa 1893 - 1909 (B)
PASZKIEWICZ, Konstancya 1845
- 1918 (D)
(Piotr & Konstancya Dankowski -
Regina Piechowiak same lot)
PASKIEWICZ, Antony no date - 8
Dec 1932 (D)
PATTERSON, Bernice R 1909 -
19-- (Nee: Piotrowski) (B)
Leroy E 1906 - 1979 (B)
(Wladyslaw & Valentine
Piotrowski same lot)
PATURALSKI, Antony no dates (-
)
PAULINSKI, Tomasz 21 Mar 1866
- 1923 (C)
Maryanna 1877 - 1964 (C)
PAWALOWSKI or PAWLOWSKI,
Jadwiga no dates (Nee:
Budzianowski) (C)
Tadeusz no dates (C)

PAWALOWSKI (continued)
Anastazia no dates (C)
PAWELSKI, Charles T 1896 -
1979 (G)
Veronica A 1902 - 1943 (G)
PAWELSKI, Maryann no date -
23 Feb 1930 (Nee: Jankowski)
(C)
Hypolet no date - 23 Dec 1930
(C)
(Frank & Anna Spilski same lot)
PAWELSKI, Florentya Krakowski
1910 - 1927 Daughter (D)
(Bernice & Frances Hencelewski,
Felex Kasprzak, & Malgorzata
& Franciszek Nawrocki same
lot)
PAWLAK, Jan 1854 - 1943
Father (F)
Anna 1854 - 1925 Wife (F)
Stella 1896 - 19-- (F)
PAWLAK, Emilia 1852 - 1934
(G)
(Wladyslaw, Wojciech, & Stanis-
lawa Pendzinski same lot)
PAWLAK, Michalena 1842 - 1915
Grandmother (A)
(Frank & Mary Kendziora same
lot)
PAWLAK, Wojciech 30 Jan 1861
- 3 Dec 1929 (A)
John 1900 - 1951 (A)
Valentina 1862 - 1940 Mother (A)
(Helena Gorny same lot)
PAWLAK, Franciszek 10 Aug
1886 - 23 Jan 1932 Brother (D)
(Bronislaw Krotnik, & Marya
Jandala & John Torowicz same
lot)
PAWLAK, Lucya 1902 - 1927
(Nee: Paczkowski) Mother (D)
(Joseph & Mary Paczkowski
same lot)
PAWLAK, Joseph no date - 28
Feb 1923 (-)
PAWLAK, Lawrence 6 May 1888
- 4 June 1926 (East Fence)
PAWLAK, Michael no date - 13
Dec 1933 (D)
PAWLICKI, Joseph 1860 - 1923
(E)
Rosa 1866 - 1927 (E)

PAWLICKI (continued)
(Casimir & Hattie Kolczynski same lot)
PAWLIKOWSKI, Piotr 28 Sept 1889 - 4 Aug 1918 (D)
PAWLOWSKI, Helen 1892 - 1974 (With Picture) (A)
Michael 1886 - 1957 (With Picture) (A)
(Frank Dembicki & Antonette H Kay same lot)
PAWLOWSKI, Anastasia Budcznowski no dates (C)
PAWLOWSKI, William 1894 - 1934 (F)
(Alex & Stella Dubicki, & Sharon J Tucker same lot)
PECKOWSKI, Lucian 7 Jan 1894 - 18 July 1960 "Indiana Btry D 12 Fld Arty WWI SS PH" (F)
Teresa 1893 - 1933 Mother (F)
PEJZA, Stanley 1874 - 17 Nov 1929 Father (A)
Constance 1876 - 1952 Mother (A)
Franciszka 1902 - 1924 (A)
(Maryanna Slot same lot)
PEJZA, Wladyslaw 1876 - 24 Aug 1924 Father (D)
Jozefa 1874 - 1942 Mother (D)
Stanley 1916 - 1961 Son (D)
Alex B 24 Mar 1912 - 22 Sept 1971 "Indiana Pfc Co B 116 Med Bn WWII" (D)
PENAR, Jan 1889 - 1926 (F)
PENDZINSKI, Wojciech 1887 - 1966 Father (G)
Stanislawa 1881 - 1935 Mother (G)
Wladyslawa 1907 - 1945 Son (G)
(Emilia Pawlak, & Frank & Frances Wruble same lot)
PENKALA, Mary 1888 - 1928 (F)
Alex 1883 - 1963 (F)
PENKALA, Clem J 1918 - 19-- (D)
Loretta T 1917 - 1980 (D)
PENNFIELD, Mary E 1898 - 1922 (B)
(John & Mary Liszewski same lot)

PERZAK, Mary 1888 - 1957
Mother (F)
Andrew no date - 3 June 1927 (F)
(Lee W Teghon same lot)
PIASECKI, Jan 11 Aug 1911 - 12 Aug 1934 Husband (PC1)
(Wladyslawa & Stanislaw Piechorowski same lot)
PIASECKI, Joseph J 1893 - 1965 Father (G)
Konstancia 1890 - 1939 (Nee: Janowiak) Mother (G)
(Leon Piechorowski & Harriet T Kolupa Piechorowski same lot)
PIASECKI, Helen 1872 - 1930 (Nee: Sawicki) (A)
Martin 1857 - 24 Dec 1924 Father (A)
Theodore 1913 - 1917 (A)
PIASECKI, George no date - 20 Sept 1913 (-)
PIATEK, Anna 1887 - 1923 Mother (G)
Sophia 1914 - 1953 Wife (G)
PIATEK, Adalbert no date - 22 Jan 1925 (-)
PIECHOCKI or PIECHOSKI, Jozef Mar 1837 - 12 Jan 1929 Father (A)
Anna May 1840 - (Nee: Strachonowski) Mother (A)
PIECHOCKI, Marcin 1837 - 30 Apr 1921 Grandfather (B)
(Jan & Antonina Hechlinski same lot)
PIECHOCKI, Peter 1873 - 2 May 1935 (C)
Mary 1886 - 1969 (Nee: Wroblewski) Mother (C)
John 1883 - 1943 Father (C)
(Mary Wroblewski, Edward Wroble, Maryanna Saunders, & David Lee Carroll same lot)
PIECHOCKI, Adalbert 1891 - 1964 (G)
Martha 1891 - 1969 (G)
PIECHOCKI or PIECHOCKI, Adam 1870 - 1939 (F)
Wiktorya 1880 - 1967 (F)
PIECHOROWSKI, Jan 1848 - 1926 Father (G)
Emilia 1852 - 1938 (Nee:

PIECHOROWSKI (continued)
Chmielewski) Mother (G)
Rozalia 1888 - 1965 (G)
Ludwik 1888 - 1972 (G)
PIECHOROWSKI, Bert 1918 -
1967 Son (PC1)
Wladyslawa 1888 - 1955 (Nee:
Nowaczyk) Mother (PC1)
Stanislaw 1880 - 10 Nov 1930
Father (PC1)
(Jan Piasecki same lot)
PIECHOROWSKI, Leon 1885 -
1920 Father "Married to
'Gusty' Konstancya Janowski"
(G)
Harriet T Kolupa 1912 - 1955
Daughter (G)
(Joseph J & Konstancia Janowski
Piechorowski Piasecki same
lot)
PIECHOSKI, Veronica 27 Jan
1888 - 7 June 1976 (Nee:
Laskowski) (A)
(Jozef & Marcyanna Laskowski
(parents) same lot)
PIECHOSKI (Name changed to
Pierce), Sam 29 June 1889 -
10 May 1949 "Husband of
Veronica Laskowski Piechoski
(Divorced)" (-)
PIECHOSKI or Joseph 1900 -
1972 (F)
Harriet 1899 - 1969 (F)
PIECHOWIAK, Regina 1905 -
1930 Wife "Wife of Joseph
Piechowiak" (D)
(Konstancia Paszkiewicz, &
Piotr & Konstancia Dankowski
same lot)
PIECHOWIAK, W no dates (D)
V no dates (D)
A no dates (D)
PIECHOWICZ, Barbara Ann no
date - 1944 (G)
(Ignatius & Carrie Hanyzewski
same lot)
PIECHOWICZ, Anton 1871 - 12
Jan 1913 (A)
Anna 1874 - 1953 Mother (A)
Henrietta 1913 - 19-- (A)
Alexander 1905 - 1946 (A)
PIECUCH, Clemens 1868 - 1939

PIECUCH (continued)
Father (A)
Anna 1871 - 1927 Mother (A)
Franciszek 1892 - 1918 Son (A)
PIEKARSKI, Walter 1886 - 1961
Father (A)
Adella 1892 - 1952 Mother (A)
Josephine 1928 - 1963 (A)
John 10 Feb 1927 - 10 Mar 1927
(A)
Carrie 6 Feb 1912 - 24 Feb 1912
(A)
Genevieve 19 June 1913 - 19 Aug
1913 (A)
PIELACH, Stanley 30 Apr 1888 -
8 Nov 1965 (D)
PIERZCHALSKI,   Konstancya
1871 - 1912 (B)
Maryanna 1896 - 1916 (B)
Stanislaw 1909 - 1910 (B)
Wladyslaw 1878 - 1949 (B)
PIETRASZEWSKI, Pelegia 1875
- 1950 (Nee: Wegner) Mother
(B)
Frank 1873 - 1947 Father (B)
(Norbert & Leonard Golubski
same lot)
PIETRASZEWSKI, Joseph 1877 -
1946 (B)
Florentyna 1900 - 1978 (B)
(Wladyslaw & Apolonia Rewers
same lot)
PIETRASZEWSKI,   Wladyslawa
1887 - 1943 Mother (D)
PIETRASZEWSKI, Casimir no
date - 19 Mar 1935 (-)
PIETRZAK, Jan 1853 - 1926 (A)
(Antoni Lechtanski same lot)
PIETRZAK, Thomas A 1884 -
1965 (C)
Magdaline 1886 - 1960 (Nee:
Wieczorek) (C)
Sadie 1905 - 1941 (C)
Stanley no dates (C)
Edward no dates (C)
PIETRZAK, Jacob S 1887 - 1950
(E)
Mary 1888 - 1925 (E)
George W 1916 - 1965 (E)
PIETRZAK, Bronislaw S 1907 -
1973 (F)
Anna T 1913 - 19-- (Nee:

PIETRZAK (continued)
Pietraszewski) "Married 20
May 1930" (F)
PIETRZAK, Frank C 1902 - 19--
(F)
Kazimierz 1863 - 6 Jan 1933
Father (F)
Maryanna 1871 - 1934 (Nee:
Kujawski) (F)
William C 1900 - 1945 Husband
(F)
PIETRZAK, Frances L 1913 -
19-- (Nee: Glon) (F)
Joseph T 1910 - 1976 "Married
18 July 1936" (F)
PIETRZYCKI, Anton K 1872 -
1935 (C)
PILARSKI, William 1883 - 1954
(H)
Hattie 1887 - 1977 (Nee:
Sosinski) (H)
Thomas William 6 Aug 1935 -
26 Nov 1935 (H)
PILARSKI, John 1883 - 1966 (A)
Martha 1884 - 1956 (A)
Jozef 10 Mar 1861 - 3 Feb 1908
(A)
Peter 28 Apr 1894 - 1 Jan 1939
"Indiana Pvt 112 Inf 28 Div
WWI" (A)
Stanley 28 Nov 1887 - 14 Dec
1946 "Indiana Pfc Ord Dept
WWI" (A)
PILARSKI, Mary no dates (E)
(Walenty Sosnowski same lot)
PILARSKI, Napomycyna 12 Oct
1865 - 20 May 1939 (Nee:
Jaroszewski) Mother "Married
3 times" (E)
(Frank & Verna Buzalski same
lot)
PILARSKI, Casimir no date - 20
Dec 1931 (F)
PILARSKI, Valentine no date - 2
Sept 1918 "Husband of
Napomycyna Jaroszewski" (E)
PILARSKI, Joseph no date - 23
Apr 1913 (-)
PINKOWSKI, Chester 1902 - 1965
(F)
Alice 1928 - 1949 (F)
Albina 1906 - 1962 (F)

PINKOWSKI (continued)
Florence 1907 - 1946 (G)
Virginia 1911 - 1951 (G)
Catharine 1883 - 1951 Mother (G)
Arthur 9 May 1909 - 18 Oct 1950
"Indiana Pfc Hq Co 3 Bn 409
Inf BSM WWII" (G)
PINKOWSKI, Max 1881 - 1951
(B)
Mary Sept 1884 - 1971 (Nee:
Wroblewski) (B)
Leo 26 Mar 1907 - 1 Mar 1979
(B)
PINKOWSKI, Ethel M 1925 -
1926 (C)
(Jan & Stanislawa Chrobot same
lot)
PINKOWSKI, John J Sr 1890 -
1954 Father (D)
Mary C 1892 - 1974 Mother (D)
Michal J 10 May 1948 - 30 June
1948 (D)
(Nancy Kubiak Brownell same
lot)
PINKOWSKI, Jozef 1866 - 1926
(D)
Franciszka 1868 - 1918 (D)
(Marjorie Nave same lot)
PINKOWSKI, Irene Ewa 1901 -
1923 (E)
Clara 1903 - 1930 (E)
Michael 1882 - 1945 (E)
(Joseph Myslinski same lot)
PIOTRASZEWSKI, Valentine 14
Feb 1895 - 29 Oct 1911 (B)
Peter 1845 - 1920 (B)
PIOTROWSKI, Kazmiera no dates
(A)
PIOTROWSKI, Szymon May 1862
- 1936 (B)
Agnieszka July 1853 - 24 Aug
1914 (B)
(Anna Arnold same lot)
PIOTROWSKI, Wladyslaw 1874 -
1911 Father (B)
Walyntina 1883 - 1916 (Nee:
Klockowski) Mother (B)
(Bernice & Leroy Patterson same
lot)
PIOTROWSKI, Valentine 1883 -
22 July 1930 (D)
Victoria no dates (D)

PIOTROWSKI (continued)
(Frank & Bertha Wroblewski, &
John Mackowski same lot)
PIOTROWSKI, Walter no dates
(H)
PITULA, John no date - 17 Nov
1901 Reg Army (A)
PITULA, Bertha B 1911 - 19--
Mother (D)
Bert S 1909 - 1969 Father (D)
Mary 1880 - 1945 (D)
Jacob 1869 - 1932 (D)
PITULA, Michael 1862 - 1929
Father (D)
Jozef 1890 - 1923 WWI Son (D)
PITULA, Valentine no date - 18
Apr 1917 (-)
PIWOWARCZYK, George (Adal-
bert) 1858 - 7 May 1930 (D)
(Joseph & Anna Balon same lot)
PLENCNER, Lawrence 1878 -
1966 (G)
Magdalene 1883 - 1976 (G)
John P 1 Nov 1906 - 26 Feb 1969
"Sgt 1879 Svc Cmd Unit
WWII" (G)
PLENKALA, Clem J 1918 - 19--
(D)
Loretta T 1919 - 1980 (D)
PLOCKI, Michael 12 Sept 1862 -
1952 Father (B)
Marya 30 June 1872 - 1934
Mother (B)
Mary 26 Oct 1902 - 1979 Daugh-
ter (B)
(Dora Stachowski same lot)
PLONSKI, Joseph 1887 - 1960 (D)
Mary 1888 - 1951 Mother (D)
Leonard 1912 - 1957 Son (D)
PLONSKI, Pawel 7 June 1942 -
10 July 1942 (A)
(Stanislaw Kaminski same lot)
PLONSKI, Joanna 1901 - 1948 (F)
Jozef 1889 - 1962 (F)
PLONSKI, Matthew M 2 Aug 1909
- 8 Dec 1968 (H)
Helen S 5 Feb 1918 - 19-- (H)
Joseph T 22 Feb 1944 - 25 Feb
1944 (H)
PLONSKI, Wladyslaw 1889 -
1959 Father (F)
Eleanor 1893 - 1942 Mother (F)

PLONSKI (continued)
(Jozefa Makowski (Mother) same
lot)
PLUCINSKI, Martin no dates (-)
PLUTA, Wojciech 1887 - 1938
(H)
Stanislawa 1890 - 1971 (H)
Casimir A 1924 - 1976 "Pfc USA
WWII" (H)
POCZEKAJ, Josephine 1855 -
1930 (G)
(Peter & Lottie Rogalinski same
lot)
POCZESNY, Maryanna 5 July
1883 - no date "Daughter of
John & Rozalia Pocesny &
first wife of John Kwitek" (C)
(John & Frances Kwitek same
lot)
PODEMSKI, Mary 1902 - 1923
(D)
Jack 6 Nov 1909 - 19 May 1933
(D)
Frances 1879 - 1951 Mother (D)
Joseph 1882 - 21 Mar 1929
Father (D)
PODEMSKI, Mikolaj Nov 1840 -
1915 (A)
Michalina 1850 - 15 Sept 1917
(Nee: Lapczynski) (A)
(Theodore Wisler same lot)
PODEMSKI, Pauline 1877 - 1936
(Nee: Szymanowski) (C)
Stanley no dates (C)
Stanislaw no dates (C)
Anna no dates (C)
PODEMSKI, Zofia 1910 - 1937
(C)
Kazimierz 1889 - 1915 (C)
PODEMSKI, Jakob 18?4 - 2 July
1938 (PC1)
PODEMSKI, Marvin 26 Sept 1929
- 4 Sept 1957 "Indiana Pfc 655
Trans Co" (F)
Maryann 1935 - 19-- (F)
PODEMSKI, Stella Jan 1900 -
1933 (Nee: Palka) (F)
John 1898 - 1962 Father (F)
PODEMSKI, Antoni 1887 - 1941
Father (G)
Maryanna 1887 - 19-- (Nee:
Winarowicz) Mother (G)

PODLAS, Wladyslaw 1854 - 1919 (C)

Marianna 1857 - 1933 (C)

Cypryian 25 Apr 1879 - 1938 (C)

Wiktoria 26 Dec 1886 - 1930 (Nee: Wituski) (C)

PODLAS, Roman M 10 Apr 1919 - 9 Apr 1948 WWII (E) (Walter & Clara Cwiklinski same lot)

PODOLAK, Mary 19 Feb 1869 - 25 Sept 1905 (Nee: Nowicki) "Born in Greater Poland" (A)

John Apr 1869 - 28 May 1927 (A)

POLCYN, Agnes Apr 1882 - 1934 (Nee: Piotrowski) (D)

George July 1880 - 1942 (D)

POLEGA, Marcin 1858 - 23 Mar 1916 (C)

Antonette 1861 - 1957 Mother (C)

POLINSKI, Paul W 1902 - 1940 (D) (Wojciech Buszkiewicz, Hattie Dejaegher & Henry Szymczak same lot)

POPIELSKI, George 1870 - 1945 Father (A)

Cecylia 1867 - 1928 Mother (A) (A E Van Dusen same lot)

POPIELSKI, Sophie 1889 - 1977 Mother (B)

Albert 1887 - 1955 Father (B) (Peter & Petronella Rachmadzinski same lot)

POPIOLEK, Alexander 1866 - 1955 (B)

Stella 1873 - 1958 (B)

POPP, George A 2 Feb 1895 - 13 Feb 1973 "Kentucky Pvt USA WWI" (F)

Veronica 1896 - 1929 (F)

POTTS, Andrew 1900 - 1978 "Pvt USA WWI" (C) (Thomas & Frances Pacala same lot)

POTURALSKI, Jan 1859 - 21 Feb 1937 (A)

Jozefa 1864 - 1943 (A) (Frances Ginter same lot)

POTURALSKI, Mary 1890 - 1957 (H)

Chester R 1913 - 1941 (H)

POTURALSKI (continued) Roman 1891 - 1947 (H)

POWICKI, Cecylia 1885 - 1945 "Wife of Walter Powicki" (B)

Florence 1913 - 1943 (B)

PRAWAT, Stanley J 1894 - 1949 (A)

Stanislaw 1863 - 1914 1st Husband (A)

Jozefa 1869 - 1943 (Nee: Liszewski) (2nd Husband: Fred Casimir Kimmel) (A)

Mae Helen 1892 - 1967 (A)

PRAWAT, Helen 1885 - 1952 (B) (Marcin Szmanda same lot)

PREBYS, Stanley J 1912 - 1966 (E)

Harriet G no dates (E)

PRENTKOWSKI, John 1870 - 25 Jan 1934 (A)

PRENTKOWSKI, John 1891 - 14 Apr 1929 (B)

Blanche 1893 - 1976 (B)

Irene no dates (B)

John Jr no dates (B)

Bernada no dates (B)

PRENTKOWSKI, Joyce no date - 9 Feb 1964 (F) (Jacob & Zuzanna Sobczyk same lot)

PRENTKOWSKI, Mary 1903 - 19-- (F)

Jozef 1899 - 1974 (F)

Peter 1865 - 1953 Father (F)

Michalena 1865 - 1929 Mother (F)

PRENTKOWSKI, Weronika 1891 - 1927 (F) (Joseph - Walter & Joanna Kazmierczak same lot)

PROKAY, Stephen 1893 - 1927 (F) (Stanley J - Sophie Rakowski same lot)

PRUSZKOWSKI, Anthony no dates (F)

PRZEBINDOWSKI, Maryanna 1868 - 1918 Mother (B)

PRZERADZKI, Maryann 1872 - 1910 (B) (Marianna Wozniak same lot)

PRZERADZKI, Frances 21 Mar 1894 - 24 May 1921 (E) (Ludwik & Antonina Niezgodski, & Joseph Bajdek same lot)
PRZESTWOR, Jozef 1875 - 1964 (A)
Franciszka 1880 - 1912 (A)
Stanislaw 1881 - 1942 (A)
PRZESTWOR, Theresa J 1899 - no date (B)
Joseph A 1895 - 1979 "Pvt USA WWI" (B)
Jacob 1845 - 8 June 1909 (B)
PRZESTWOR, Maryanna 1861 - 1940 (Nee: Leda) Mother (C)
Steve no date - 10 Sept 1929 "Indiana Pvt 115 Inf 29 Div WWI" (C)
Antonina 1894 - 1914 (C) (Andrzej Leda same lot)
PRZESTWOR, Wladyslaw (Walter) no date - 26 Apr 1920 (D) (Joseph & Stella Lesniewski, & Joseph Michalski same lot)
PRZEZDZIENKOWSKI, Marcin 1864 - 1940 (B)
Barbara 6 Sept 1867 - 10 Apr 1929 Wife (B) (Bronislawa Wodka same lot)
PRZYBYL, Thomas 1895 - 1927 (F)
Larry 1934 - 1937 (F) (Alex & Rose Rajkowski same lot)
PRZYBYLA, Marion 1924 - 13 Feb 1925 (A)
Mary 1 Jan 1913 - 21 Aug 1913 (A)
PRZYBYLA, John 1888 - 19-- (E)
Barbara 1895 - 1966 (E)
Maryanna 1930 - 1937 (E)
Wiktoria 1932 - no date (E)
PRZYBYLA, Sylvester no date - 1929 (-)
PRZYBYLINSKI, Michael 30 July 1863 - 30 Aug 1938 (C)
Jozefa 1863 - 1948 (Nee: Jesko) "1st Husband Antoni Jasicki" (C)
Prakseda 1886 - 1974 (C) (Antoni Jasicki same lot)

PRZYBYLINSKI, Walter 1875 - 1931 (D)
PRZYBYLINSKI, Stanley M Jr 13 July 1925 - 16 Aug 1925 (G) (Franciszek & Katarzyna Jaroszewski same lot)
PRZYBYLSKI, Kaspar 1874 - 1941 Husband (A)
Apolonia 1876 - 1945 Wife (A)
PRZYBYLSKI, Andrzej 30 Nov 1893 - 11 July 1947 "Indiana Pvt USA Svc Corp WWI" (D) (Vincent Sternik same lot)
PRZYBYLSKI, Marcyanna 1866 - 1941 (Nee: Wolter) Mother (D)
Walenty 1863 - 1934 Father (D)
PRZYBYLSKI, Rosalia 4 Sept 1918 - 12 July 1953 (D)
Catharine 1883 - 1964 (Nee: Rybacki) (D)
Stanley 1881 - 1965 (D)
Anthony L no dates Indiana Tec 4 624 Ord BAS WWII (D)
PRZYBYLSKI, Walter 1875 - 1931 Father (D)
Stella 1877 - 1948 (Nee: Rafalski) Mother (D)
Frank 1909 - 1968 Son (D)
John 1905 - 1968 Son (D)
PRZYBYLSKI, Michael 1870 - 1928 Husband (E) (Stella Lemanski & Valentine Janowiak same lot)
PRZYBYLSKI, Louis 1859 - 20 Sept 1931 (E)
PRZYBYLSKI, Stanley no date - 16 Aug 1925 (-)
PRZYBYLSKI, John F 1895 - 2 Feb 1940 "Pennsylvania Pfc 338 Inf 85 Div WWI" (H)
Florence S 1899 - 1952 (Nee: Andrysiak) (H)
PRZYBYLSKI, Wladyslaw 1869 - 1961 Father (F)
Jozefa 1874 - 1936 Mother (F) (Sam S & Ronald Scanlan same lot)
PRZYBYSZ, Leo J 1882 - 9 Feb 1956 (A)
Valentine 1908 - 19-- (A)
Adeline A 1909 - 1974 (A)

PRZYBYSZ, Andrew J 29 Oct 1880 - 10 Nov 1958 "Indiana Cpl Co H 45 US Vol Inf" (B)
Rozalia B 13 Oct 1888 - 6 Sept 1956 Mother (Nee: Frankowiak) (B)
PRZYBYSZ, Kathryann 1929 - 1936 (F)
Valentine 1886 - 1949 Father (F)
Frances 1888 - 1975 (Nee: Katamoja) Mother (F)
PRZYBYSZ, Walter J Mar 1888 - 1964 Father (F)
Frances M 1891 - 1977 (Nee: Panicki) Mother (F)
PRZYBYSZ, Franciszek 1874 - 1949 (F)
Franciszka 1876 - 1946 (F)
Stanislaw 18 Apr 1904 - 2 Mar 1928 (F)
PRZYBYSZ, Malgorzata 1852 - 1939 (Nee: Frankowski) Mother (C)
Tomasz 22 Dec 1841 - 21 Mar 1926 (C)
(John Klaybor same lot)
PRZYBYSZ, Mary 1882 - 1960 (Nee: Popielski) (G)
Antoni 13 June 1915 - 6 Feb 1950 "Indiana Cpl 3883 Qm Truck Co WWII" (G)
PRZYBYSZ, Angela 13 May 1882 - 16 Aug 1954 (G)
John F 20 May 1875 - 31 Aug 1930 (G)
(Henrietta Przybysz Sherk same lot)
PRZYBYSZ, Wanda 1880 - 1959 Mother (F)
John L 3 July 1879 - 1952 Father (F)
Rozalia 17 Jan 1845 - 4 Apr 1932 Wife (F)
Stanislaw 6 May 1849 - 22 Dec 1926 Husband (F)
PRZYBYSZ, John J 1892 - 15 Aug 1936 (PC1)
PRZYGODA, Magdaline 1884 - 1952 (Nee: Nowak) Mother (F)
Ignac 1878 - 1926 Father (F)
PRZYSTAS, Ignacy 1864 - 1924 (F)

PRZYSTAS (continued)
Anna 12 Oct 1873 - 21 Aug 1959 (Nee: Salaman) (F)
PSZERADZKI, Marion 1872 - 1910 (B)
Marianna Wozniak Przeradzki 1876 - 1942 (B)
(Ed J Wozniak same lot)
PTASKIEWICZ, Stanislaw 1890 - 1918 (D)
Michalina 1893 - 1962 (D)
PUKROP, Wladyslawa 1882 - 1953 (C)
Ignacy 1880 - 1971 (C)
Joseph no date - 1909 (C)
Czeslaw no date - 1913 (C)
PUKROP, Nicholas 1898 - 1977 "Pfc USA WWI" (C)
No name no date - 20 Jan 1920 (C)
Katarzyna 1857 - 1948 Mother (C)
Michael 1853 - 20 Mar 1918 Father (C)
PUKROP, Frank 16 Nov 1895 - 27 Nov 1916 (C)
PULAWSKI, Katarzyna 1872 - 1914 (C)
Frank 1870 - 25 July 1925 (C)
Frances 1894 - 1922 (C)
PUTEK, Franciszka 1884 - 1956 Mother (G)
Ludwig 1881 - 1949 Father (G)
Franciszek 19 Jan 1913 - 8 Aug 1924 (G)
PUTRZENSKI, Alvin S 1941 - 1942 (D)
(Issac H Silva, Edward Knape, & Rose Gorney same lot)
PUTRZENSKI, Victor 1910 - 1953 (D)
(Joseph Nowastowski, Stanley Zalas, Mary Szabo Horvath, & Jan Janiak same lot)
PUTZ, Katharine 1867 - 19-- (Nee: Jasicki) Mother (D)
Florian 1860 - 27 Jan 1931 Father (D)
Stanislaw 30 Aug 1886 - 4 Nov 1931 "Placowka #125 WWI Polish Army Veterans of America" (D)

PUTZ, Mary 1886 – 1975 Mother (D)
Casimir J 1884 – 1955 Father (D) (Elizabeth Was & Marianna Kalicki same lot)
PUTZ, John J 1863 – 1928 (F)
Mary A 1876 – 1937 (Nee: Grabarz) (F)
PUZINSKI, Esther no dates (A) (Peter, Valentine, & Mary Wieczorek, & Irene Chlebek same lot)
PYCLIK, John 1890 – 1963 Father (C)
Agnes 1887 – 1 Dec 1951 (Nee: Kosik) Mother (C)
PYCLIK, Anna 1863 – 1935 Wife (C)
Jozef no dates (C)
PYCLIK, Joseph P 1899 – 1974 Father (D)
Verna M 1903 – 19-- (Nee: Nowicki) (D)
Rita 1940 – 1941 Infant (D)
PYSZKA, Stanley Aug 1878 – 25 Dec 1933 (D)
Stanley C 17 Feb 1929 – 25 Oct 1960 "Indiana Pfc Corp of Engineers Korea" (D)
Josephine P 1886 – 1970 (Nee: Brylewski) (D)
PYTLAK, Jacob 1859 – 1919 Father (E)
Mary 1865 – 1939 Mother (E)
Harvey 1895 – 1972 Son (E)
PYTLEWICZ, Marya 1890 – 1941 (Nee: Smiegielski) (F)
Andrzej 1888 – 1966 (F)
(Arthur J & Blanche V Deruyck same lot)
RACHMADZINSKI, Petronella 1870 – 1949 (Nee: Strozewski) Mother (B)
Peter 10 June 1865 – 1 June 1910 (B)
(Albert & Sophie Popielski same lot)
RACHWALSKI, Franciszek 1885 – 1925 (B)
Jozef 1884 – 3 Mar 1937 (B)
Clement 1916 – 1941 (B)
John 1 Apr 1906 – 17 Aug 1969

RACHWALSKI (continued)
"New York Pfc Co G 4 Inf" (B)
RADECKI, George A 1881 – 1961 (B)
Walentyna R 1884 – 1979 (B)
Lucy no dates (B)
Lenora no dates (B)
Irene no dates (B)
RADECKI, Anna 26 July 1858 – 1 May 1910 Mother (B)
John F 1883 – 1961 (B)
RADECKI, John 1879 – 1963 Father (B)
Catharine 1885 – 1958 (Nee: Maciejewski) Mother (B)
Frank 1904 – 3 July 1920 Son (B)
RADECKI, Anna 1 Dec 1887 – 22 Aug 1976 (Nee: Jegier) Wife (F)
David Teofil 23 Oct 1884 – 24 Aug 1971 Husband (F)
Edward J 1908 – 1981 "Tec 5 USA WWII" (F)
RADECKI, Walter no dates (-)
RADECKI, Andrew J 1907 – 19-- (H)
Carrie M 1908 – 1971 (H)
RADECKI, Jozefa 1879 – 1928 (Nee: Niespodziany) (F)
Stanislaw 1876 – 1961 Father (F)
(Joseph & Martha Yuhasz same lot)
RADZIKOWSKI, Josephine 1882 – 1939 (Nee: Poczekaj) Wife (B)
Marion 1872 – 1934 Husband (B)
RADZIKOWSKI, Mary F 1895 – 1937 (F)
(Harry F & Mary Kendziorski same lot)
RADZISZEWSKI, Cecylia 1901 – 1939 (H)
Chester R 10 Apr 1930 – 6 Feb 1953 "Killed in Action in Korea" (H)
Ben 1892 – 1969 (H)
John no date – 21 Sept 1981 (H)
RADZIUS, Paul 15 Jan 1864 – 3 June 1932 (B)
Lottie 15 Apr 1875 – 11 Mar 1963 (B)
RADZIWILL, Jakob 1871 – 1944 (A)

RADZIWILL (continued)
Helena 1871 - 1938 (A)
Andrzej 1892 - 12 Dec 1911 (A)
RADZIWILL, Ignatius 1889 -
1944 Father (C)
Mary 1895 - 1974 Mother (C)
Joseph J 25 Feb 1909 - 8 June
1952 "Indiana Pfc 435
AAA/AW BN CAC WWII" (C)
Franciszek 24 Feb 1913 - 26
July 1913 (C)
Bronislaw 1918 - 1919 (C)
RADZIWILL, Franciszka 1892 -
1919 (E)
Eleanor no date - 1964 (E)
RAFALSKI, Michael no date -
1957 Baby (D)
Cheryl 1958 - 1959 Baby (D)
(Ralph & Patricia Myszak same
lot)
RAFALSKI, Casimir 1878 - 1939
(PC1)
RAJSKI, Rozalia 26 Aug 1887 -
22 Dec 1909 (Nee: Pasket)
"Wife of Antony Rajski - born
in Greater Poland" (B)
RAJSKI, Frank no date - 10 Mar
1932 (B)
RAJSKI, Alex 22 Aug 1899 - 5
Dec 1948 Father (E)
Cecylia 4 June 1902 - 18 Aug
1976 Mother (E)
(Zygmond Sochocki same lot)
RAJSKI, Frank Mar 1863 - 1935
(H)
Rose Sept 1862 - 1942 (H)
Mary 1903 - 1951 (H)
Hattie 1888 - 1971 (H)
RAJEWSKI, Joanna 12 Aug 1932
- 17 Aug 1932 (D)
Gladys 1890 - 1967 Mother (D)
(Sabina Bartz same lot)
RAJKOWSKI, Alex 1893 - 1962
(F)
Rose 1896 - 1976 (F)
(Thomas & Larry Przybyl same
lot)
RAJTER, Stella 1900 - 1966 Wife
(G)
(John Nowakowski & Stanislaw &
Helena Manuszak same lot)

RAKOWSKI, Alexander 1872 -
1932 Father (B)
Josephine 1876 - 1965 (Nee:
Werwas) (B)
Wladziu no dates (B)
RAKOWSKI, Edward 1907 - 1930
(F)
Antonina 1865 - 26 Mar 1940
(Nee: Wlodarek) Mother (F)
Franciszek 1860 - 6 Mar 1945
(F)
John A 1894 - 1948 "Btry E FA "
(F)
RAKOWSKI, Marie 1906 - 1928
(with picture) (F)
Joseph E 1911 - 19-- (F)
Bernice H 12 Oct 1915 - 3 Feb
1981 (Nee: Zapolski) (F)
RAKOWSKI, Stanley J 1899 -
1976 "Pvt USA WWI" (F)
Sophie R 1901 - 1978 (F)
(Stephen Prokay same lot)
RAMENDA, John A 1884 - 1969
(D)
Elizabeth 1892 - 19-- (D)
RAPALSKI, Constance 1887 -
1935 Mother (H)
Casimir 1883 - 1967 Father (H)
RAPELA, Frank 1886 - 1918
(Single Grave D)
RATAJCZAK, Helen 8 Sept 1867
- 15 May 1911 Mother (B)
RATAJCZAK, Stanislawa 1878 -
1932 (D)
RATAJCZAK, Karolina 1892 -
1965 Mother (D)
Franciszek 1887 - 1930 "Reg
Army" Father (D)
RATAJCZAK, Frances 1894 -
1957 (Nee: Przybysz) (E)
Joseph 1893 - 1945 (E)
RATKIEWICZ, Alexander 30 July
1920 - 30 Sept 1920 (E)
(Victor E & Antoni Slusarek
same lot)
RAY, John H 1922 - 1948 (with
picture) (C)
REGULINSKI, Waclaw 1896 - 7
May 1918 (E)
(Matthew & Magdelena Madej
same lot)

REGULINSKI, Gladys 1914 - 1979
(-)
Joseph 1915 - 1967 (-)
Betty Ann 17 Feb 1945 - 20 Feb
1945 (-)
REITER, Theodore 1888 - 1927
(B)
Anna M 1893 - 1965 (Nee:
Starzynski) (B)
REITER, Julius J 1885 - 1939
Father (E)
Agnes 1886 - 1967 (Nee:
Kowalewski) Mother (E)
Dorothy 1918 - 1926 Daughter (E)
(Esther Krol same lot)
REITER, Stanley M 22 Oct 1903 -
9 Apr 1964 "Ohio Cpl 2002
Base Unit AAF WWII" (E)
Stanislaus B 29 Oct 1873 - 14
Dec 1954 Father (E)
Mary 25 Mar 1879 - 4 Oct 1939
(Nee: Kazmirski) (E)
Harriet 14 Oct 1914 - 12 Dec
1933 Daughter (E)
(Corrine Vargo same lot)
REJER, Lucian 1906 - 1917 (D)
Walter no dates (D)
REMBLESKI, Bartholomew 1851
- 1945 (F)
(Joseph & Victoria Olszewski, &
Stanislaw Wietrzynski same
lot)
REMS, John no date - 23 Apr
1924 (F)
RENGIELSKI, Jozef 1863 - 23
Jan 1923 Father (E)
Antonina 3 June 1859 - 1939
(Nee: Paszkiet) Mother (E)
RENES, Frederick 1867 - 5 July
1926 (F)
(Jacob Celichowski & Pauline
Brambert same lot)
RESKIEWICZ, Jozefa 1887 -
1940 Wife (E)
(John Karpinski same lot)
REWERS, Apolonia 1875 - 7 May
1909 (Nee: Szymanski) (B)
Wladyslaw 1868 - 11 Feb 1929
(B)
(Joseph & Florentyna Pietras-
zewski same lot)
REYNOLDS, Esther 1919 - 1965

(G)
(Joan & Matthew J Kasprzak
same lot)
RILEY, James F 1 Oct 1900 - 11
June 1951 "Indiana Pfc 1590
QM Sig Unit WWII" (E)
(Frank C Jenczewski same lot)
ROBAKOWSKI, no names no
dates - family (C)
(Jan Lodyga & Alex Isban same
lot)
ROBAKOWSKI, Jozef 1872 - 1941
Father (C)
Marya 1875 - 1942 Mother (C)
Leo F 20 Feb 1906 - 22 Feb
1962 "Indiana Pfc 811 Tech
School Sq AAF WWII" (C)
Franciszek 1911 - 1950 Son (C)
ROBAKOWSKI, Jozef 29 Jan 1936
- 14 June 1936 (E)
Peter June 1886 - 1969 (E)
Helen 1894 - 1942 (Nee: Ksycki)
(E)
(Antoni & Jozefa Ksycki same
lot)
ROBAKOWSKI, George 1848 - 30
June 1913 (C)
ROBAKOWSKI, Alex 1923 - 1981
Son (G)
Frank 1885 - 1971 (G)
Dorothy 1927 - 1960 (G)
Tadeusz 1920 - 1922 (G)
ROBASKI, Anna 1860 - 1944
Mother (D)
(Victor Grochowski same lot)
ROBASKI, Stanley J 1899 - 1964
Father (F)
Sophie 1903 - 1931 Wife, Mother
(F)
(Steve Wozny same lot)
ROBERTS, Clifford 1885 - 19--
(B)
Frances 1886 - 9 Aug 1936 (Nee:
Zelasko) (B)
(John Lakomski same lot)
ROBERTSON, Irene 1911 - 1933
Daughter (E)
(Leon & Lucy Kaminski same
lot)
RODRIGUEZ, Esther 23 Aug 1962
- 11 July 1963 (D)

RODRIGUEZ (continued)
(Ramiro & Maria Lopez - Mary
Filipek - Angie & Rogiella
Paloma same lot)
ROEDER, Jean J 1 Nov 1922 - 16
July 1974 (F)
ROETS, David Norbert no date - 6
Oct 1974 (H)
(Stephen A & Stella Kristofski
same lot)
ROGACKI, Katarzyna 1885 - 1918
(F)
Walenty 1882 - 1969 (F)
ROGACKI, Stanley no date - 27
July 1923 (-)
ROGACKI, Sophie 1840 - 1930
Grandmother (F)
(Joseph & Antonette Walkowski
same lot)
ROGALINSKI, Peter F 1872 -
1961 (G)
Lottie 1884 - 1942 (G)
(Josephine Poczekaj same lot)
ROGALSKI, Antoni 10 May 1855 -
23 Mar 1935 (F)
Anna 13 May 1855 - 9 July 1929
(Nee: Chojnacki) Mother (F)
William 18 July 1892 - 14 Mar
1955 (F)
ROGOWSKI, Victor 1889 - 28 Apr
1939 "Indiana Pfc 11 Bakery
Co QMC" (H)
Mary 1902 - 1974 (H)
ROMANOWSKI, Paul C 11 Oct
1894 - 1971 (E)
Stephanie M 14 Dec 1897 - 1969
(E)
Evelyn Mary 1927 - 1928 (E)
(Frank Kaluzney & Theodore
Kosch same lot)
ROSPLOCH, Martha 9 Jan 1896 -
29 Apr 1963 (G)
Walenty 1857 - 1934 (G)
Frances 1863 - 1925 (G)
ROSPLOCHOWSKI or ROZPLO-
CHOWSKI, Czeslaw 1891 - 10
Mar 1919 "New York Pvt 170
Aero Sq WWI" (B)
Boleslaw 1878 - 1948 Husband
(B)
Helena 1886 - 1951 (Nee: Woz-
niak) Wife (B)

ROSS, Virginia Ruszkowski 1921
- 1958 (A)
(Walter J & Dora Ruszkowski
same lot)
ROSZYK, Anna 1856 - 1952 (Nee:
Barczak) Mother (A)
Peter 1865 - 27 Dec 1910 Father
(A)
Ted 1901 - 1954 Son (A)
ROYTEK, Frank 1873 - 1949
Father (F)
Anna 1878 - 1946 Mother (F)
(Constance Zielinski same lot)
ROYTEK, Robert Roy 1930 - 1931
(F)
(Joseph & Mary Klosinski same
lot)
ROZANSKI, Konstanty 1881 -
1966 Father (G)
Wladyslawa 1893 - 1978 (Nee:
Kwestorowski) Mother (G)
John A 26 Mar 1923 - 31 Feb
1969 "Ohio Tec 5 18 Gen Hosp
WWII" (G)
ROZANSKI, Julius 1914 - 31 May
1937 (PC1)
ROZEK, Andrzej 1867 - 1927
Father (F)
Frank Edward 1922 - 1977 "Pfc
USMC WWII" (F)
John 1919 - 1971 Son (F)
Wiktorya 1881 - 1942 Mother (F)
ROZEWICZ, Peter no date - 5
May 1919 (-)
ROZMARNOWSKI or ROZ-
MARYNOWSKI, Wiktor 1851 -
10 June 1917 Father (A)
ROZNIAREK, Franciszek 1871 -
1935 Father (A)
Katarzyna 1872 - 1935 Mother
(A)
ROZNIAREK, Eleanora 2 Nov
1884 - 1943 Wife (F)
Franciszek 13 Aug 1895 - 1953
Husband (F)
ROZPLOCH, Valentine no dates
(-)
ROZPLOCH, John no date - 26
July 1934 (G)
ROZPLOCH, Helena 1886 - 1952
(G)
Michael 1889 - 1949 (G)

ROZPLOCH (continued)
(Ewa & Walenty Strozewski & Loretta Stypczynski same lot)
ROZPLOCHOWSKI, Jan P 24 June 1873 - 14 Aug 1941 (C)
Weronika 1883 - 1963 (Nee: Andrzejewski) (C)
ROZPLOCHOWSKI, Nick no date - 11 Aug 1916 (-)
ROZWARSKI, Michael 15 Aug 1867 - 20 June 1918 Husband (C)
Teofilia 1 July 1866 - 20 Nov 1958 Wife (C)
Leokadya 9 Dec 1903 - 4 Oct 1927 (C)
ROZWARSKI, Weronika 1867 - 1918 (Nee: Ligowski) (D)
Thomas 1870 - 1956 (D)
Georgiana no date - 17 Mar 1929 (D)
(Jozef & Carrie Nowak same lot)
ROZWARSKI, Michal A 1876 - 1953 Father (F)
Mary M 1883 - 1929 Mother (F)
ROZYCKI, ---- no dates Father (G)
---- no dates Mother (G)
(Alexander Szymanski same lot)
RUDOLFO, Martinez no date - 1 July 1951 (D)
(Mary E Gallegos same lot)
RUDYNSKI, Walter 1915 - 1978 (H)
(Andrew & Mary Stopczynski same lot)
RUDYNSKI, Stephen Oct 1892 - 6 Mar 1926 (A)
(Antony Stopczynski same lot)
RUMAK, Nicholas 1889 - 193- (not legible) (H)
RUSIECKI, Stella 1887 - 1965 (2nd Wife) Mother (E)
Joseph 1895 - 1945 Father (E)
Bronislawa 8 Dec 1892 - 10 Dec 1918 (Nee: Zamojski) First Wife (E)
RUSIEWICZ, Stanislaw 1849 - 1917 (C)
Maryanna 1855 - 1938 (C)
RUSZKOWSKI, Dora 1903 - 19-- (Nee: Wisniewski) Mother (A)

RUSZKOWSKI (continued)
Walter J 1899 - 1979 Father (A)
(Virginia Ruszkowski Ross same lot)
RUSZKOWSKI, John 22 Mar 1857 - 16 Dec 1909 (B
RUSZKOWSKI, Genofa 1920 - 1924 (E)
(Mary Niespodziany same lot)
RUTKOWSKI, Boleslaw P 21 May 1890 - 11 Dec 1963 (H)
Maryann 10 Aug 1893 - 11 Oct 1963 (Nee: Kalka)
(Steve Boniewski same lot)
RUTKOWSKI, Bernard 14 Aug 1896 - 19 Feb 1925 "New York Pvt 147 Inf 37 Div" (H)
(Peter & Lottie Grotkowski same lot)
RUTKOWSKI, Joseph 12 Mar 1891 - 1 July 1911 (A)
Nicholas no date - 1919 (A)
RUTKOWSKI, Henry no dates (C)
Stella no dates (C)
Helen 1890 - 1977 (Nee: Harmacinski) Mother (C)
Vincent 1886 - 1951 Father (C)
RYAN, Veronica D 1904 - 1979 (B)
(Stefan - Peter - Walter Kreczmer same lot)
RYBACKI, Michael 1859 - 7 Apr 1939 (A)
Maryann 1863 - 1947 (A)
Stephen 1901 - 1943 (A)
(Jakob Wierzclewski same lot)
RYBACKI, Martin no date - 21 July 1938 (A)
RYBACKI, John 1896 - 1917 (B)
Andrzej J 1858 - 20 May 1930 (B)
Katarzyna 1861 - 1917 (B)
RYBACKI, Michael 1884 - 1920 (B)
Helen 1885 - 1910 (B)
RYBACKI, Bert 1881 - no date (F)
Katarzyna 1874 - 1956 Mother (F)
Bronislaw 1897 - 1930 Son (F)
Jan 1909 - 1929 Son (F)
(Helena V Bodge same lot)

RYBACKI, Jan 1861 - 1928 (F)
RYBACKI, Casimir 18?7 - 1955
Father (H)
Josephine 1874 - 19-- Mother
(H)
(Joseph & Stella Labis same lot)
RYBAK, Tomasz M 26 Oct 1876 -
1935 Father (A)
Eleanora Z 2 Feb 1882 - 1953
(Nee: Kuczmanski) Mother (A)
Jakub 1850 - 18 Sept 1925 (A)
Michalina 1851 - 1944 (A)
RYBAK, Martin no date - 6 May
1927 (A)
Josephine no dates (Nee:
Lisiecki) (A)
(Rose Cooper same lot)
RYBAK, Wiktoria 1914 - 1941 (C)
(Franciszek & Jadwiga Lyc-
zynski same lot)
RYBAK, Franciszek 1887 - 1949
Father (F)
Antonina 1891 - 1956 (Nee:
Kujawa) Mother (F)
Mateusz 4 June 1925 - 8 June
1925 (F)
Frank J Jr 13 July 1926 - 3 Sept
1974 "Pvt USA" (F)
RYBARKIEWICZ, Agnieszka no
date - 14 June 1917 "age 67"
(D)
(Andrew & Benedict Orszulak
same lot)
RYBARKIEWICZ, Jozef no date -
1918 "Married Hattie Kam-
inski" (A)
(Jan & Pelegia Kaminski same
lot)
RYBICKI, Martin 1863 - 21 July
1938 Father (A)
Anna 1869 - 1955 Mother (A)
RYBICKI, Simon (Sam) 1873 -
1946 (B)
Bernice W 1880 - 1966 (B)
RYBICKI, Cecylia 1902 - 1922
(C)
(Michael Hudak, Stanislaw Mal-
kowski, & Theresa Miller
same lot)
RYBICKI, Lucian no dates (F)
RYBICKI, Martha 18 Jan 1909 -
18 Apr 1967 (G)

RYBICKI (continued)
(Jan & Franciszka Zastawa same
lot)
RYDZINSKI, Jakob July 1856 - 23
Sept 1934 Father (A)
Marya 31 Jan 1861 - 1937 (Nee:
Jarecki) Mother (A)
Jadwiga 1889 - 1921 (A)
RYMER, Jan 1897 - 1951 (C)
Franciszka 1871 - 1946 Mother
(C)
Marya 1895 - 1917 (C)
Hilarya 1908 - 1917 (C)
Leon 1902 - 13 May 1917 (C)
Franciszek 1869 - 18 Dec 1922
Father (C)
RYSKA, Magdalena 1834 - 1 Oct
1919 (Nee: Wozniak) "Wife of
John Ryska who died in
Poland" Grandmother (C)
(Marcin & Anna Goralczyk same
lot)
RZEPKA, Michael 1876 - 1945
(A)
Victoria 1878 - 1947 (Nee:
Bonek) (A)
Aloysius 1906 - 1967 (A)
RZEPKA, Lott F 1892 - 1968
Husband (A)
Josie A 1898 - 1971 (Nee:
Jurgonski) Wife (A)
Franciszka 1857 - 1943 Mother
(A)
Clara 13 Feb 1922 - 28 July 1929
Daughter (A)
RZEPNICKI, Wojciech 1887 -
1979 Father (C)
Stefania 1891 - 1955 (Nee:
Grochowski) Mother (C)
Wincenty no date - 1917 (C)
RZESZEWSKI, Thomas 1882 -
1910 (B)
Mary 1889 - 1951 (Nee: Wegner)
(B)
Paul 1884 - 1940 Brother (B)
Thaddeus no dates (B)
RZESZEWSKI, Stanley 1875 -
1948 Father (E)
Frances 1883 - 1958 (Nee:
Kujawski)
Evelyn no dates Baby (E)
RZESZEWSKI, T no dates (B)

SABINAS, Margaret 1885 - 1928
(F)
Joseph 1881 - 1953 (F)
Peter T 1910 - 1967 (F)
Alice 1913 - 19-- (F)
SABOSKI, Blanche L (Pelegia)
1882 - 1955 (Nee: Szulczew-
ski) Mother (E)
Edward J 1880 - 1952 Father (E)
(John Szulczewski same lot)
SADOWSKI, Andy no date - 1929
(-)
SALATA, Richard R no date (E)
Janice no date - 30 Aug 1961 (E)
SALATA, Maryann 1875 - 1944
(F)
Stanislaw 1870 - 1959 (F)
Wladyslaw 1904 - 1926 (F)
SALOMEN, Harry B 14 June 1909
- 23 Dec 1978 Son (F)
Helen 30 Mar 1888 - 27 Mar 1946
(Nee: Jegier) Wife (F)
Joseph 18 Apr 1887 - 1 Mar 1923
Husband (F)
(Katarzyna Jegier same lot)
SALWIN, Jozef 1863 - 24 Mar
1907 (B)
Antonina 1861 - 1937 (B)
SALWOWSKI, Steve 1878 - 1957
(E)
Frances 1893 - 1979 (E)
SAMP, John 1898 - 1936 (A)
(Frank J & Eleanora Golupski
same lot)
SAMULSKI, Franciszek 1902 - 13
Feb 1920 (B)
Pelagia 1904 - 1923 (B)
Leokadya no dates (B)
Heromin no dates (B)
Edmond no dates (B)
Bronislawa no dates (B)
Stanislaw no dates (B)
Bronislaw no dates (B)
Irena no dates (B)
Andrzej 10 Nov 1887 - 30 Jan
1936 (B)
SARNOWSKI, Helena 1891 - 1951
(A)
(Frank & Maryanna Barkowski
same lot)
SARNOWSKI, Frank 1896 - 1975
"Pvt USA WWI" (F)

SARNOWSKI (continued)
Lottie 1897 - 1969 Sister (F)
SAUNDERS, Maryann 5 Apr 1954
- 17 May 1954 Baby (C)
(John & Mary Piechocki, Mary
Wroblewski, Edward J Wroble,
& David Lee Carroll same lot)
SAWICKI, Thomas 1 Aug 1883 -
26 Oct 1926 (F)
(Frank & Alex W Kujawski same
lot)
SCANLON, Sam S 5 Nov 1923 -
30 Dec 1963 "Florida Pvt USA
WWII" (F)
Ronald S 9 June 1945 - 14 Mar
1970 "Indiana Sp 4 Btry C 1
MSL Bn 60 Arty" (F)
(Wladyslaw & Jozefa Przybylski
same lot)
SCHNIEDER, Lucille S 3 Apr
1906 - 11 Aug 1967 Mom (H)
(Klementyna & Stanislaw
Marszal same lot)
SCHOEN, Frank 1878 - 1961
Father (B)
Josephine 1878 - 1963 Mother
(B)
SCHULTZ, Leon 1878 - 1946
Father (B)
Maryanna 1882 - 1929 Mother (B)
SCHULTZ, Helen 1898 - 1960
(Nee: Szulczewski) (C)
(Franciszek & Victoria Szul-
czewski same lot)
SCHULTZ, John 1883 - 1975 (D)
Mary 1886 - 1978 (Nee: Piecha)
(D)
Leo 1919 - 1960 (D)
(Michael Dana McClure same
lot)
SCHWIND, Jean Ruth 17 Feb
1933 - 20 July 1934 (G)
George A 23 Nov 1891 - 21 Oct
1905 "Indiana Sgt Ord Dept
WWII" (G)
Clara 20 July 1890 - 25 Mar 1970
(G)
SCHYMANSKI, Mary 1885 - 1941
(C)
John 1877 - 1959 (C)
(Fisher, mother & father same
lot)

SCIBA, Leon 1875 - 1964 (H)
Josephine 1881 - 1968 (H)
(Albert & Frances Lukasiewicz same lot)
SCIPSKI, Frank 1866 - 1920 (Nee: Niespodziany) Father (B)
Mary 1867 - 1943 Mother (B)
SCIPSKI, Katarzyna 1819 - 1911 (B)
(Joseph & Anna Szmanski same lot)
SCZEPANSKI, ---- no dates (D)
(Anthony Witucki & Rose Witucki same lot)
SCZEPANSKI, ---- no dates (D)
(Jan & Apolonia Witucki same lot)
SCZEPANSKI, Jan 4 July 1897 - 4 Nov 1918 "Born in Poland - entered the Army the 6th of July 1917 - Died in the field of action in France for the freedom of our nation - Pfc 9 Inf 2nd Div WWI" (F)
SETLAK, Phyllis Mary 1932 - 1940 (F)
Mary C 1880 - 1945 (F)
John W 1881 - 1929 (F)
SEYMOUR, Verna no date - 2 Dec 1981 (H)
(Michael & Hattie Matela same lot)
SHADESKI, Leon 20 Dec 1899 - 19-- WWI (B)
SHERK, Henrietta 1912 - 1963 (Nee: Przybysz) (G)
(John F & Angela Przybysz same lot)
SHRINER, Patricia J 1940 - 1967 Wife (B)
(John S Sommer same lot)
SIATKOWSKI, Antonina 1871 - 1966 Mother (A)
Jan 1865 - 1928 Father (A)
SIDOR, Walter no dates (-)
SIDOROWICZ, Katarzyna 1871 - 1934 (D)
SIENKIEWICZ, Ursula 1893 - 1954 (C)
John F 1885 - 1953 (C)
Chester S 1929 - 1939 (C)
Eugene 1915 - 1915 (C)

SIERACKI, Anna 1875 - 1958 (H)
(John P Jasicki & Frank Kaminski same lot)
SIERACKI, Michael no date - 9 Apr 1911 (-)
SIERADSKI, Franciszek 1857 - 9 Feb 1929 Father (B)
Franciszka 1860 - 1916 Mother (Nee: Stroszewski) (B)
SIERADSKI, Stanislaw 9 Oct 1883 - 3 July 1918 (D)
Mary Stawska 1 Feb 1891 - 1952 (Nee: Podolak) (D)
(Wladyslaw Starczewski same lot)
SIERADSKI, Denice Dawn no date - 1 May 1958 (E)
SIEZKAREK, Jan 1884 - 12 Dec 1932 Father (D)
SIKORSKI, Antony D 21 July 1913 - 23 Oct 1980 "Pfc USA WWII" (B)
SIKORSKI, Mateusz 1856 - 25 Nov 1916 Father (A)
Stanislawa 24 Mar 1865 - 5 Sept 1939 Mother (A)
SIKORSKI, Wanda V 1914 - 19-- (Nee: Nowastowski) "Wife of Antony Sikorski" (B)
Maryanna 1872 - 1934 (Nee: Gorna) Mother (B)
SIKORSKI, Alex F 25 Jan 1894 - 25 May 1972 "Michigan Pvt Co E 339 Inf WWI" (F)
SIKORSKI, Mary 29 Oct 1888 - 19-- (Still alive in 1986) (Nee: Rybicki) (F)
Stanley 8 Sept 1886 - 1959 "Brother to Alex F Sikorski" (F)
SIKORSKI, Jan 1906 - 1936 Son (H)
Jan 16 June 1889 - 1942 Father (H)
Michalena 1878 - 1952 Mother (H)
Bronislaus J 13 Mar 1908 - 10 July 1969 "Indiana Pfc Fld Arty WWII" (H)
SIKORSKI, Boles no dates (East Fence)
SILVA, Issac H no dates (D)

SILVA (continued)
Maria no dates (D)
Esther no date - 3 May 1965
Daughter (D)
(Alvin S Putrzewski, & Edward
Knape & Rose Gorney same
lot)
SIMMONS, Mary Lee 25 Dec
1934 - 15 Jan 1938 (H)
Dorothy E 1936 - 1955 (H)
Fred N 19 Mar 1897 - 29 Feb
1960 "Indiana Wagoner Trp E
16 Cav WWI" (H)
Mary no date - 23 Oct 1981 (H)
SITARZ, Michael 1886 - 1964 (D)
Agnes 1894 - 1977 (D)
Maria 1920 - 1932 (D)
SKARUPINSKI, Michael 1847 - 9
Sept 1939 Father (A)
Apolena 1850 - 1917 (A)
(Henrietta Aranowski same lot)
SKARUPINSKI, Casimir 1888 -
1968 (C)
Rose 1893 - 1972 (C)
SKARUPINSKI, Stanley 1913 -
1933 (D)
Frances 1883 - 19-- Mother (D)
Frank J 1883 - 1960 Father (D)
SKARUPINSKI, Stella 8 May 1880
- 30 June 1966 (H)
John 5 Apr 1880 - 6 Nov 1962 (H)
SKIBA, Franciszek 1873 - 1928
(F)
Marya 1916 - 1939 (F)
Victoria 1886 - 1947 Mother (F)
SKOCZYLAS, Aleksandra 1891 -
1954 (C)
Jan 1883 - 1952 (C)
SKOROBINSKI, Stanley no dates
(D)
SKOWRONSKI, Dorothy J 1927 -
1976 (A)
Leonard 1925 - no date "Married
15 Feb 1947" (A)
SKOWRONSKI, Marya R 1867 -
1942 (Nee: Ciesiolka) Mother
(C)
Wojciech 1856 - 12 Oct 1921 (C)
Joseph C 6 Feb 1888 - 10 Aug
1964 "Indiana Pvt Co I Ord
Cas Bn WWI" (C)
Stanley C 1896 - 1976 (C)

SKOWRONSKI, John 5 May 1890
- 21 Nov 1962 "Indiana Pvt 35
Eng WWI" (G)
(John M Strojny - Allen & Wil-
bert Kozakiewicz same lot)
SKRZESZEWSKI, Nikodem 14
Sept 1861 - 7 Oct 1940 (E)
Stanislawa 10 Dec 1870 - 28 May
1951 (Nee: Palicki) (E)
SKUBISZEWSKI, Andrew 30 Oct
1883 - 1950 (D)
Maria 1 Feb 1885 - 1953 (D)
SKWIAT, Marta 1889 - 19-- (D)
Ignacy 1884 - 1932 (D)
(Adam Kapusta, brother same
lot)
SLABY, Franciszek 1868 - 1940
Uncle (E)
SLABY, John 1906 - 1969 Son (E)
Antoni 1870 - 1929 Father (E)
Maryanna 1871 - 1926 Mother (E)
SLAMPURT, Jadwiga 1884 -
1907 (Nee: Urbanski) (A)
(W Ciupinski & Joseph Fritz
same lot)
SLAZOWSKI, Jozef 1870 - 1957
Father (G)
Klara 1885 - 1937 Mother (G)
Wladyslaw S 1909 - 1930 Son (G)
John no date - 19 Feb 1925 Son
(G)
SLESINSKI, Antonina 1853 - 1918
(C)
(Jacob & Frances Gleniewicz
same lot)
SLESINSKI, Boleslaw 1918 - 1930
(D)
Ignacy J 1916 - 1944 (D)
Maximillian 1879 - 1946 (D)
Kazimiera 1888 - 1972 (D)
SLESINSKI, George 1926 - 19--
(D)
Genevieve 1916 - 19-- (D)
Ted T 1921 - 1975 "Sgt USAAF
WWII" (D)
Casimir 1929 - 19-- (D)
SLESINSKI, Gizella 1917 - 1964
(H)
Casimir J 1919 - 1978 "Pfc USA
WWII" (H)
Antony 1886 - 1969 (H)
Florence 1893 - 1951 (H)

SLESINSKI (continued)
Olga L 3 Dec 1921 - 20 June
1939 (H)
SLESSMAN, Genevieve Papczyn-
ski 1900 - 1979 (Nee: Wrob-
lewski) Mom (G)
(Alexander Papczynski Sr same
lot)
SLIPLICKI, Stanley 1878 - 1965
Father (D)
Anna C 1890 - 1948 Mother (D)
Wladyslaw 1908 - 1930 Son (D)
SLISZ, Ferdynand S 1913 - 19--
(G)
Irene S 1911 - 1975 (G)
SLISZ, Clem 4 Dec 1906 - 12 Nov
1980 (H)
Gertrude 1907 - 19-- (Nee:
Kubiak) (H)
SLISZ, Casper V 24 Dec 1881 -
25 Apr 1956 (E)
Mary 1881 - 1972 (Nee:
Andrysiak) (E)
SLOMA, Floryan 1880 - 1957 (C)
Katharine 1882 - 1970 (C)
John 12 Apr 1907 - 20 Dec 1979
"Cpl USA WWII" (C)
Leo W 1939 - 1940 (C)
SLOTT, Joseph M 1877 - 19--
(A)
Rose 1884 - 1956 (Nee: Skow-
ronski) (A)
Clem A 1920 - 1946 Son (A)
Joseph Jr 1916 - 1917 Son (A)
SLOTT, Maryanna Nov 1839 -
1914 (Nee: Leda) (A)
(Stanley & Constance Pejza
same lot)
SLOTT, Thomas W 1872 - 1943
(D)
Mary E 1877 - 1968 (Nee:
Kapalczewski) (D)
SLOTT, Hattie E 1903 - 1970 (E)
Alexis T 1900 - 1975 (E)
SLOWATYCKI, Anna 1882 - 1938
Wife (F)
Jan 1869 - 1929 Husband (F)
SLUSAREK, Victor E 1905 - 1959
(E)
Antoni 8 Jan 1878 - 26 Dec 1918
(E)
(Alexander Ratkiewicz same lot)

SMANDA, Stanislaw 1872 - 1932
(C)
Mary Dietz 1881 - 1938 (C)
(William Dietz same lot)
SMANDA, Arthur T 1915 - 1972
Husband "Husband of Alma
Beitler" (E)
(Julius & Elizabeth Beitler same
lot)
SMICHOWSKI, Stanislaw 2 May
1892 - 30 Dec 1955 "Indiana
Pfc Co G 59 Inf WWI SS PH"
(B)
SMIEGIELSKI, Albin no dates (-)
Joseph no dates (-)
Michael no date - 4 Apr 1912 (-)
Stanley no date - 1916 (-)
SMIEGIELSKI, F 8 Sept 1862 - 5
Feb 1916 (B)
(Julia Demska same lot)
SMIEGIELSKI, Leon 1854 - 1922
(B)
Gertrude 1853 - 1932 (B)
(John S & Agnes R Walewski
same lot)
SMIEGIELSKII, Wiktoria 1893 -
1927 (E)
Agnieszka 1853 - 1945 Mother
(E)
(Melchior Niemier same lot)
SMIEGIELSKI, Bernice 1917 -
1950 (E)
Mary 1898 - 1939 (E)
Max 3 Oct 1894 - 1 Apr 1954
"Indiana Cook Co C 35 Eng
WWI" (E)
Frank 10 Jan 1927 - 1 Dec 1977
"Pvt USA WWII" (E)
SMIEGIELSKI, Martha 1896 -
1981 (Nee: Lukasiewicz) (E)
Nicolas 1890 - 1944 (E)
SMIEGIELSKI, Katy 1883 - 1915
(C)
Anna 1893 - 1948 (Nee: Odynski)
(C)
John 1885 - 1971 (C)
SMITH, Joseph no dates (-)
SMITH, Julius 1869 - 1961 Uncle
(D)
(Frank & Mary Zielinski same
lot)
SMUCINSKI, John 1850 - 14 Oct

101

SMUCINSKI (continued)
1917 (C)
Agnes 1853 - 1938 Mother (C)
Maryanna 29 Aug 1882 - 4 March
1950 Daughter (C)
(Frank Czyzewski same lot)
SMUCINSKI, Leon 1888 - 1913
Son (C)
Domycela 1919 - 1920 Daughter
(C)
SMUDZINSKI, Antoni 1880 - 1968
Father (F)
Franciszka 1871 - 1970 Mother
(F)
Klemenc 1915 - 1922 Son (F)
SMOLKA, Henry J 1917 - 1963
WWII (D)
Wladyslaw 1881 - 21 July 1932
(D)
Klara 1884 - 1973 (Nee:
Cukrowicz) (D)
Clement 1911 - 1968 (D)
SNIADECKI, Stanislaw 1863 -
1910 (B)
Stanislawa 1898 - 1916 (B)
Franciszek 1893 - 1924 (B)
Leon 1899 - 1925 (B)
(Chrystina Jaremba same lot)
SNIADECKI, Jan 1865 - 1950
Father (B)
Katarzyna 1866 - 1923 Mother
(B)
Tadeusz 1915 - 1919 (B)
SNIADECKI, Wladyslaw 1890 -
1962 Father (D)
Pelegia 1891 - 1949 (Nee:
Kruszka) Mother (D)
Mary Evelyn no date - 8 Apr
1951 Infant Daughter (D)
Carl 1 Feb 1934 - 1 Feb 1935
Grandson (D)
SNIADECKI, Magdalena no dates
(B)
Franciszek no dates (B)
Maryanna no dates (B)
Bernard no dates (B)
SNYDER, Elizabeth 1911 - 19--
(Nee: Mikolajewski) (PC1)
Joseph 1910 - 19-- (PC1)
(Casimir & Catharine Mikolajew-
ski same lot)
SNYDER, Pearl Najdek 1893 -

SNYDER (continued)
1976 (C)
(Roman & Tadeusz Najdek same
lot)
SOBCZAK, Wawrzyniec 1874 -
1929 Father (A)
Wiktorya 1875 - 1948 Mother (A)
Gertruda 1912 - 1929 Daughter
(A)
SOBCZAK, Frank no date - 24
Mar 1916 Grandfather (C)
(Joseph & Cecylia Szulczyk
same lot)
SOBCZAK, Joseph Aug 1890 -
1966 (D)
Lottie 1894 - 1967 (Nee:
Pietrzak) #2 Wife (D)
Lottie 1891 - 1916 (Nee:
Switalski) Mother (D)
SOBCZYK, Zuzanna 1884 - 1970
(Nee: Gaik) (F)
Jakob 1883 - 1926 (F)
(Joyce Prentkowski same lot)
SOBECKI, Roy S no date - 11 Mar
1931 "Indiana Pfc 1 Engrs 1
Div" (F)
(Mary Boryc same lot)
SOBECKI, Franciszek 1853 - 12
Aug 1927 Father (A)
Ignace 1897 - 24 Mar 1920 (A)
SOBECKI, Eva 1854 - 1918
Mother (B)
(Jan & Maryanna & Jozefa Chrus-
towski same lot)
SOBECKI, Katharine 1889 - 1972
(Nee: Wisniewski) Daughter
(D)
(Frank & Wiktorya Konstanty -
Jozef Kruk - Casimir - Mary &
Joseph Wisniewski same lot)
SOBECKI, Benjamin Jr no date -
19 Dec 1930 (E)
Benjamin Sr 16 Oct 1898 - 7 Oct
1945 "Indiana Pvt 124 Fld Arty
33 Div WWI" (E)
SOBIECH, Janina 1903 - 1976
Wife, Mother (H)
(Andrew & Ronald Wasielowski,
& Albin Bednarek same lot)
SOBIECH, Stanislaw 1888 - 1960
(G)
Stanislawa 1893 - 1967 (G)

SOBIECKI, Joe K no date - 9 Jan 1929 "Indiana Sgt 59 Rgt Coast Arty Corp WWI" (E)
(Anna Kopczynski same lot)
SOBIERAJ, Petronella 1845 - 1938 (PC1)
(Anton & Catharine Zmudzinski same lot)
SOBIERALSKI, Chester no dates (-)
SOBIERALSKI, John 1875 - 26 Apr 1932 Father (F)
Franciszka 1874 - 1929 (Nee: Bentkowski) Mother (F)
SOBIERALSKI, Agnieszka 1893 - 1962 (B)
Lucya 1867 - 1944 Mother (B)
Andrzej 1864 - 20 Dec 1933 Father (B)
SOBIERALSKI, Frank 1861 - 1941 Father (E)
Rose 1863 - 1926 Mother (E)
Michael 1894 - 1919 Son (E)
Lottie J no date - 10 Feb 1944 "Indiana Pvt 78 Inf 14 Div" (E)
SOBIERALSKI, William J 1891 - 1956 (B)
Martin S 5 Nov 1896 - 16 Dec 1956 "Indiana M/Sgt USA WWI & WWII" (B)
Frank J 21 July 1886 - 1 Feb 1960 "Indiana Pfc 159 Depot Brigade WWI" (B)
John C 27 Dec 1904 - 5 July 1973 WWII (B)
SOBIESKI, Anna 1887 - 1939 (Nee: Winkiel) Mother (D)
John 1883 - 1932 Father (D)
SOBOLEWSKI, Franciszek X 1905 - 5 Mar 1920 (A)
Maryanna 1880 - 1943 (Nee: Przybylski) Mother (A)
Jan 1877 - 1947 Father (A)
SOCHOCKI, Tekla 1894 - 20 July 1965 (Nee: Szulczewski) (D)
Franciszek 1890 - 15 July 1958 (D)
Jerena 1915 - 30 Oct 1918 Daughter (D)
(Andrzej Szulczewski same lot)
SOCHCCKI, Zygmond 10 Jan 1922 - 1978 "Pfc USA WWII"

SOCHCKI (continued) (E)
(Alex & Cecylia Rajski same lot)
SOKOLA, Peter 1877 - 7 Dec 1910 (B)
John 1845 - 15 Mar 1916 (B)
Pauline 1835 - 1918 (B)
SOKOLOWSKI, Wojciech no date - 18 Sept 1910 (A)
Martin dates buried "WWI" (A)
Walter S no date - 13 Jan 1954 "Indiana Sgt Co H 68 Inf WWI" (A)
---- no dates Mother (A)
SOKOLOWSKI, Bert 1893 - 1931 (F)
(Stephen Grontkowski & John Zyto same lot)
SOLETA, Lawrence 1860 - 1909 Father (B)
Wladyslawa 1865 - 1959 (Nee: Ogorkiewicz) Mother (B)
Mary 1984 - 1973 (B)
SOLETA, Frank 1878 - 1941 (B)
Cecylia 1886 - 1966 (B)
Harriet no dates (B)
Tony no dates (B)
Mary no dates (Nee: Malecki) (B)
Andrew no dates (B)
SOLETA, Walter A 1892 - 1968 (C)
Martha R 1889 - 1966 (Nee: Frackowiak) (C)
SOMMER, Julius P 20 Sept 1928 - 17 Nov 1952 "Indiana Cpl Co B 23 Signal Bn Korean War" (B)
John S 1902 - 1975 (B)
Blanche H 1904 - 19-- (B)
(Patricia J Shriner same lot)
SOMOGYI, Stanley J no date - 24 Mar 1962 Baby (H)
(Jozef & Mary Bielewski same lot)
SOPCZYNSKI, John F 1890 - 1934 (C)
Theresa D 1929 - 1947 (C)
Martha 1890 - 1964 Mother (C)
SOSNOWSKI, Valentine 14 Feb 1854 - 26 Apr 1920 Father (E)
Magdelena no dates (Nee: Wesolowski) Mother (E)

SOSNOWSKI (continued)
Mary Pilarski no dates (E)
John 4 Apr 1895 - 14 Mar 1975
"Pvt Air Svc" (E)
SOTKIEWICZ, Bartholomew no
date - 4 July 1932 (-)
SOTKIEWICZ, Victoria 1847 - 3
Nov 1912 (Nee: Lemanski)
"Born in the Province of Poz-
nan, Poland" (A)
Szczepan 1884 - 1947 Father (A)
Konstancya 1891 - 1972 (Nee:
Walkowiak) Mother (A)
SOTKIEWICZ, Stanislawa 1874 -
1960 Mother (B)
Jan 1871 - 26 Dec 1939 Father
(B)
August 5 Aug 1909 - 17 Aug 1968
"Indiana Pfc Co E 137 Inf
WWII" (B)
SPARAZYNSKI, Lucyna 1889 - 17
Oct 1955 (Nee: Witucki)
Mother (C)
Wincenty 1888 - 20 Mar 1932
Father (C)
Theophil V 17 Mar 1915 - 24 Feb
1981 "Pvt USA WWII" (C)
(Wincenty Witucki same lot)
SPARAZYNSKI, Wanda 1893 -
1958 (Nee: Bojewicz) (E)
Valentine 1892 - 1959 (E)
SPILINSKI, F no dates (C)
SPILSKI, Frank 1891 - 1934 (C)
Anna 1890 - 1946 (Nee:
Pawelski) (C)
Frank Jr 1915 - 1916 (C)
Edward 1916 - no date (C)
(Hypolit & Mary Pawelski same
lot)
SPLAWSKI, Jan J 1884 - 1958
Father (E)
Teofilia 1881 - 1954 (Nee:
Jablonski) Mother (E)
Wladyslaw C 1915 - 1951 Son
(E)
SPLITT, Marcianna 1885 - 1964
(Nee: Skarupinski) Mother (A)
Adolph 1884 - 1958 Father (A)
Henry 1909 - 1910 Son (A)
---- 1878 - 1966 Daughter (A)
Andrew 1843 - 1936 Father (A)
Josephine 1856 - 1920 (Nee:

SPLIT (continued)
Kaminski) Mother (A)
(Andrzej Kaminski same lot)
SPLITT, Antony no dates (A)
SPRINGER, Ludwig 1916 - 1925
(A)
Raymond 7 Mar 1926 - 26 May
1926 (A)
(Jan Zielinski & Frank J Green
same lot)
SPRINGER, John 23 Apr 1878 -
19 Apr 1951 (A)
Jozefa 21 Feb 1885 - 23 Feb
1961 (Nee: Zielinski) (A)
Stanislaw 1915 - 23 June 1917,
age: 2 (A)
SPYCHALSKI, Leo A 1905 - 1977
(A)
Lillian G 1910 - 19-- (A)
SPYCHALSKI, Jan 1865 - 1906
(A)
Antonina 1869 - 1940 (Nee:
Krakowski) (A)
(Jozef Gabrys same lot)
SPYCHALSKI, Wincenty J 1893 -
1941 (C)
Stanislaw no dates (C)
Stanislawa no dates (C)
SPYCHALSKI, Joseph S 1907 -
19-- (G)
Clara D 1912 - 1978 (G)
(Viola G Lehman same lot)
SRODA, Walenty 17 Jan 1867 - 3
Jan 1941 Father, Husband (A)
Henrietta 1914 - 1928 Daughter
(A)
SRODA, Anton 1872 - 1951 (E)
Mary 1880 - 1919 (Nee: Rybak)
(E)
Wiktorya 1906 - 1912 (E)
Anna 1902 - 1911 (E)
SROKA, Francis 1877 - 1 Sept
1927 Father (E)
Frances 1878 - 1968 (Nee:
Thilman) Mother (E)
STABNIK, Joseph 1894 - 1946
Grandfather (G)
STACHOWIAK, Antony 27 Dec
1876 - 24 June 1940 "Married
to Valaria Krakowski" (A)
(Frank Krakowski same lot)

STACHOWIAK, Walerya 1910 -
1934 (Nee: Wroblewski) (A)
(Jozef & Maryanna Wroblewski
same lot)
STACHOWIAK, Pelegia 1882 -
1907 (B)
Eleanora 1889 - 13 Dec 1913 (B)
Jozef 1857 - 28 Oct 1922 Father
(B)
Marya Dec 1861 - 1923 Mother
(B)
STACHOWIAK, Antony 1886 -
1963 (C)
Hattie 1891 - 19-- (Nee: Brekus)
(C)
STACHOWIAK, Frank Peter 22
Sept 1882 - 24 Jan 1957 (D)
Hattie Rose 14 Oct 1892 - 4 Nov
1967 (Nee: Laskowski) (D)
(George & Mary Laskowski same
lot)
STACHOWIAK, Martin 1869 - 1
May 1933 (D)
Agnes C 21 Jan 1873 - 7 Jan
1945 (Nee: Rajter) (D)
STACHOWIAK, Peter no date -
26 Oct 1908 (-)
STACHOWIAK, John 1859 - 21
July 1927 Husband (F)
Maryanna 1863 - 1950 (Nee:
Waluszynski) Wife (F)
Phillip J 1894 - 1975 Husband
(F)
Clara 1901 - 1974 Wife "Married
21 July 1917" Wife (F)
STACHOWIAK, Stanislaw 1885 -
5 Aug 1925 WWI (F)
STACHOWIAK, Bartlomiej J
1853 - 1946 (F)
(Stanley & Victoria Makielski
same lot)
STACHOWICZ, Dorothy 10 Dec
1898 - 22 Jan 1964 (Nee:
Niespodziany) (D)
(Paul & Mary Niespodziany same
lot)
STACHOWSKI, Sylvester 7 Dec
1894 - 15 Feb 1980 "Married
to Bernice Sokolowski" (A)
STACHOWSKI, Dora (Theodosia)
25 May 1898 - 1979 (Nee:
Plocki) "Wife of John J

STACHOWSKI (continued)
Stachowski" Daughter (B)
(Michael & Mary Plocki same
lot)
STACHOWSKI, Peter P 1899 -
1965 (E)
STACHOWSKI, John 1870 - 1936
(E)
Antonette 1876 - 9 June 1961
(Nee: Graczyk) (E)
Wincenty 1837 - 1923
Grandfather (E)
(Jan Graczyk - grandfather -
same lot)
STACHOWSKI, Piotr 1872 - 1948
Father (E)
Maryanna 1870 - 1943 (Nee:
Wieczorek) Mother (E)
(Apolonia Wieczorek -
grandmother - same lot)
STACHURSKI, Gertruda 1921 -
1961 Niece (C)
(Jan & Cecylia Jankowski, &
Katharine Nowakowsk same
lot)
STACHURSKI, Thomas 29 Dec
1874 - 18 Feb 1949 (G)
STAJBACH, Jozefa 1862 - 13
Nov 1943 (Nee: Murowski) (H)
(Bert Laskowski same lot)
STANKIEWICZ, Jozefa 1871 -
1953 (Nee: Borowski) (G)
Kazimierz 1871 - 1944 Father
(G)
Michael S 1898 - 1938 (G)
STANKIEWICZ, Paulina 1861 -
1937 Mother (B)
Marcin 1851 - 1925 Father (B)
(Wladyslawa Chlebek same lot)
STARCZEWSKI, Wladyslaw 1884
- 5 June 1917 (D)
(Stanislaw Sieradski & Mary
Sieradski Stawski same lot)
STARCZEWSKI, Joseph V 1890 -
1968 (D)
Hattie 1890 - 1909 (Nee:
Sobecki) (D)
STARCZYNSKI, Antony 1860 - 28
Feb 1932 (B)
Joseph 1888 - 1909 (B)
Mary 1866 - 18 Apr 1930 (B)
Marie 1903 - 1921 (B)

105

STASINSKI, Katarzyna 25 Nov 1849 - 5 Feb 1937 (A)
Jan 20 Oct 1847 - 9 Feb 1922 (A)
(Jozef T Bolka & Mary A Bolka Huber same lot)
STASKIEWICZ, Walenty 2 Feb 1875 - 20 July 1924 (A)
STASZEWSKI, Walenty 1845 - 14 Jan 1913 (A)
(Steve & Mary Paris same lot)
STASZEWSKI, Tekla no date - 16 May 1925 (B)
(Wojciech Wolowicz & Walter Borowski same lot)
STASZEWSKI, John W 1883 - 1956 (E)
Mary R 1890 - 1900 (Nee: Jasinski) (E)
(Bernard & Theresa Lentych same lot)
STASZEWSKI, Andrew J 1895 - 1953 Father (F)
Josephine 1861 - 1921 Mother (F)
Andrew no date - 30 Mar 1930 (F)
Alojzy 1901 - 1939 Son (F)
Stanislawa 1881 - 1940 Mother (F)
Franciszek 1873 - 1958 Father (F)
STAWSKI, Mary Sieradski 1891 - 1951 (D)
(Stanislaw Sieradski & Wladyslaw Starczewski same lot)
STEDMAN, Eleanor 6 Jan 1912 - 1958 (Nee: Gorney) (A)
(Sophie & Rose Gorney same lot)
STEFANIAK, Wladyslaw 1895 - 1948 (E)
Pelagia 1896 - 1963 (Nee: Trudzinski) (E)
STEFANSKI, Julia 1873 - 1928 (Nee: Spychalski) (B)
Andrew 1866 - 1958 (B)
STEFANSKI, John 1876 - 1946 (D)
Frances 1884 - 1921 (D)
(Maryann Winkel same lot)
STEKNET, George no dates (-)
STEINBRUNNER, Matthew F 26 Apr 1971 - 26 Apr 1971 (F)

STEINBRUNNER (continued)
Julie Lynn 8 Nov 1968 - 30 Nov 1968 (F)
(Forest & Bernice Ciesiolka same lot)
STEMPINSKI, John 1866 - 4 Nov 1928 (B)
Mary 1878 - 1928 (B)
Joseph 1918 - 1977 Son (B)
STERNIK, Vincent 1878 - 1947 (D)
(Andrzej Przybylski same lot)
STESZEWSKI (Staszewski), Genowefa Leokadya 1895 - 1918 (A)
Helena Kazmiera 1892 - 1959 (Nee: Jaroszewski) (A)
Tadeusz Kazimierz 1892 - 20 Oct 1919 (A)
Stanislaw 1859 - 1940 Father (A)
Josephine 1873 - 1956 Mother (A)
STEVENS, Eleanor 1900 - 1978 (F)
John 1901 - 1970 (F)
Robert no date - 7 Aug 1981 (F)
STENGLIK, John 1892 - 1935 (H)
STOPCZYNSKI, Antony no date - 28 June 1934 Father (A)
Frank no date - 26 May 1936 Son (A)
(Steve Rudynski same lot)
STOPCZYNSKI, Ignacy 1890 - 1951 Father (E)
Jozefa 1895 - 19-- (Nee: Witkowski) Mother (E)
Edward 30 Aug 1915 - 3 May 1958 "Indiana Sgt 180 QM Baker Co WWII BSM PH OLC" (E)
Loesia 1919 - 1928 Daughter (E)
STOPCZYNSKI, Enoch no date - 1944 Father (PC1)
Lottie no date - 1944 Mother (PC1)
---- no date - 1944 Daughter "All killed in Train crash" (PC1)
STOPCZYNSKI, John 1900 - 1945 Son (H)
Mary 1873 - 1950 Mother (H)
Andrew 1896 - 1966 Father (H)

STOPCZYNSKI (continued)
(Walter Rudynski same lot)
STRANGRECIAK, Jozefa 1867 -
1942 (H)
Wojciech 1865 - 1940 (H)
Frank J 29 Nov 1897 - 31 May
1963 "Indiana Pvt USA WWII"
(H)
STRANTZ, Edmund 1897 - 3 Dec
1914 (A)
STRAUSS, Joseph 1874 - 1913 (C)
STRAUSS, Frances 1880 - 1968
(C)
(Kazimierz Muchlicki same lot)
STROJNY, John M 1882 - 1958
Father (G)
(Allen & Wilbert Kozakiewicz &
John Skowronski same lot)
STROMINSKI, Michal S 1882 -
1945 Father (D)
Jozefina 1892 - 1970 Mother (D)
(Julianna M Jurkiewicz same lot)
STROZEWSKI, John 1866 - 1927
(C)
Stella 1893 - 1919 (C)
Joseph 1898 - 9 May 1918 (C)
Angela 1881 - 1944 (C)
STROZEWSKI, Lottie 18 Oct
1900 - no date (Nee:
Celichowski) (F)
Anthony 2 Feb 1894 - 23 Jan
1973 "Indiana Pvt 36 Inf
WWI" (F)
STROZEWSKI, Ewa 1860 - 1951
(Nee: Ohocka) (G)
Walenty 1858 - 1922 (G)
(Helena - Michael Rozploch &
Loretta Stypczynski same lot)
STROZEWSKI, Frances 12 May
1913 - 22 Dec 1962 (H)
Maryanna 1873 - 1949 (Nee:
Niespodziany) (H)
Edwin 24 Nov 1913 - 19-- (H)
Peter 1865 - 1936 (H)
STROZEWSKI, Jozef 1830 - 24
Mar 1908 (B)
(Wojciech Bonek, Raymond
Luczkowski, & Susan C
Wiltrout same lot)
STRYCHALSKI, Julian 1886 -
1972 Father (A)
Theresa 1890 - 1953 Mother (A)

STRYCHALSKI, Rozalia 1852 -
1920 Mother (E)
STRZELEC, Frank no date - 1
Jan 1936 (-)
STRZELEC, Wojciech 1862 -
1938 (D)
Jadwiga 1862 - 1940 (D)
STRZELECKI, Alex 1919 - 1979
"SSgt USA WWII" (C)
Weronica Mikula 1915 - 1957 (C)
Katarzyna 1879 - 1939 (Nee:
Zalas) Mother (C)
Wincenty 1872 - 30 Nov 1930
Father (C)
STRZELECKI, Mary 1902 - 19--
(H)
John 1 July 1897 - 1936 (H)
STRZELECKI, Michael N 1902 -
1960 (H)
(Walter & Stella Jenczewski
same lot)
STRZELECKI, Mary 1896 - 1970
(Nee: Nowaczewski) (H)
Richard 1938 - 1939 (H)
Paul 1933 - 19-- (H)
Frank J 5 Oct 1895 - 3 May 1968
"Indiana Pvt Sup Co 150 Fld
Arty WWI" (H)
Joseph F 3 Mar 1923 - 1 Jan
1969 "Ohio Pfc Co H 137 Inf
WWII" (H)
STUGLIK, Magdeline 1885 - 1961
Mother (G)
Joseph 1887 - 1941 Father (G)
STUGLIK, John 1892 - 1935 (H)
Frances 1892 - 1966 (H)
(Joseph Dziedzic same lot)
STYPCZYNSKI, Jozef 1857 -
1919 Father (B)
Anna 1859 - 1934 Mother (B)
Wladyslaw 1886 - 1907 (B)
Jadwiga 1895 - 1919 (B)
Izidor 1890 - 1930 (B)
Franciszek 1898 - 1934 (B)
STYPCZYNSKI, Joseph A 1893 -
19-- (B)
Verna 1893 - 1958 (B)
STYPCZYNSKI, Stanley 2 May
1889 - 27 Dec 1912 (A)
STYPCZYNSKI, Loretta 1927 -
1928 Granddaughter (G)
(Helena & Michal Rozploch, Ewa

STYPCZYNSKI (continued)
& Walenty Strozewski same lot)
SUDOL, Josephine no dates (D)
(Catharine Tobolski same lot)
SUDOL, Joseph no dates (D)
SUPERCZYNSKI, Joseph J 26 Jan 1880 - 22 Dec 1961 "Indiana Sgt Cen Off Trng School WWI" (A)
SUPERCZYNSKI, Stanley no date - 27 Dec 1912 (-)
SUPLICKI, Stanley 1878 - 1965 Father (D)
Anna C 1890 - 1948 Mother (D)
Wladyslaw 1908 - 1930 Son (D)
(Franciszek Ratajczak same lot)
SURNICKI, Sophie 1910 - 1948 Daughter (E)
(Adam Kaczmarek same lot)
SUSKI, Jane E 1921 - 1944 (A)
Jozefa 1883 - 1974 (A)
Walenty 1885 - 1972 (A)
Waclaw 6 July 1910 - 6 July 1911 (A)
SUSZYNSKI, John no dates (A)
SWARTZ, Frank Sr 1865 - 1939 (A)
Rose 1879 - 1951 (A)
Frank Jr 1907 - 1938 (A)
SWARTZ, Clara 1905 - 1962 Mother (B)
SWARTZ, Mary 1888 - 1933 Mother (C)
---- no dates Grandmother (C)
Adam Sr no dates (C)
Adam Jr no dates (C)
SWARTZ, Alex L 10 Apr 1905 - 29 Dec 1957 "Indiana Pvt 206 Mil Police Co" (G)
Clementine 1908 - 1964 Mother (G)
SWIATOWY, Jakob 1874 - 1958 Father (A)
Rozalia 1881 - 1965 (Nee: Chojnacki) Mother (A)
Jozefa March 1913 - May 1913 Daughter (A)
Anna 1905 - 1924 Daughter (A)
(James J Lyczynski same lot)
SWIATOWY, Maryanna 1865 - 1928 Mother (F)

SWIATOWY (continued)
Antonette 1900 - 1927 Mother (F)
August 27 Aug 1895 - 13 Jan 1928 "Indiana Sgt Troop B 8 Cavalry" (F)
SWITALSKI, Rosalie 1845 - 1929 (C)
Mary 1881 - 1943 (C)
John 1865 - 1933 (C)
Michael 1873 - 1952 (C)
SWITALSKI, Sarah no dates (Nee: Szulczewski) (C)
Stanley no dates (C)
Agnes no dates (C)
SWITALSKI, Mateusz 21 Sept 1857 - 7 Aug 1913 Father (C)
Katarzyna 1858 - 1935 (Nee: Czyczewski) Mother (C)
SWITALSKI, Marya 1905 - 1942 (G)
(Stanislaw & Wiktorya Fujawa same lot)
SZAFRANSKI, Ignacy 1859 - 1937 Husband (B)
Anna 1856 - 1930 Wife (Nee: Goraczewski) (B)
(Adam & Jozefa Goraczewski, & Janina Klosinski same lot)
SZAJKO, Antonina 1892 - 19-- Mother (E)
Franciszek 1889 - 1934 Father (E)
SZALEWSKI, Rev Mieczyslaw 1 Jan 1881 - 8 Apr 1958 (A)
Wladyslawa 22 June 1879 - 30 Aug 1954 Daughter (A)
Pelegia 17 Dec 1854 - 24 Mar 1939 Mother (A)
Piotr 27 June 1845 - 11 Feb 1923 Father (A)
SZALEWSKI, Pelegia 1877 - 1950 (Nee: Niedbalski) (B)
Stanley 30 Apr 1876 - 15 Nov 1947 Father "Pvt 157 Ind Inf Spanish American War" (B)
SZARWARK, Michael 1877 - 1961 (C)
Rozalia 1877 - 1960 (C)
Apolonia 1879 - 1917 (Nee: Wroblewski) (C)
Frank S 1880 - 1976 (C)
Agnes J 1886 - 1972 (C)

SZCZECHOWSKI, Sylvester 1909
- 1978 (B)
Rose 1879 - 1962 (Nee: Kapsa)
Mother (B)
Lillian 1912 - 19-- (B)
Ignatius J 1875 - 1961 Father (B)
SZCZEPANEK, Francizek 1900 -
1931 Husband (D)
Bertha 1902 - 1976 Wife, Mother
(D)
SZCZEPANIAK, Agnieszka no
dates (A)
(Boleslaw & Jozefa Grochowski
same lot)
SZCZEPANIAK, Anna 1868 - 4
Apr 1945 (F)
Michael 1866 - 8 Feb 1938 (F)
(Stella Vander Hagen & Lisa
Marie Bochers same lot)
SZCZEPANSKI, Frank S 4 July
1897 - no date (F)
SZCZEPANSKI, John 30 Mar 1887
- 16 June 1916 Reg Army (D)
SZCZESPANKIEWICZ, Joseph
1892 - 12 Apr 1917 (A)
SZCESNY, Marcin 1867 - 1915
(B)
Piotr no date - 1908 (B)
(Wiktoria Mroczkiewicz & Prak-
seda Witkowski same lot)
SZCZODROWSKI, Joseph 2 Mar
1851 - 15 Feb 1938 (A)
Rozalia 10 Mar 1856 - 2 Oct
1918 (A)
Piotr 1893 - 1925 (A)
Geo A (Lott) 5 Jan 1884 - 15 Feb
1968 (A)
(DeLoise & Stella Ware same
lot)
SZCZODROWSKI, Michael 1843 -
25 Jan 1926 (A)
Rozalia 1847 - 1925 (Nee:
Stranc) Mother (A)
SZCZYPSKI, Frank 1866 - 1 Jan
192(Not legible) (B)
SZEFCIK, Rozalia 1881 - 1942
(H)
Jozef T 1908 - 1954 (H)
SZEPANEK, Annette Thompson
1908 - 1948 Daughter (D)
Agatha 1878 - 1953 Mother (D)
Piotr 1872 - 1938 Father (D)

SZEWCZYK, Blanche (Pelegia)
1890 - 1965 (Nee: Kaminski)
(C)
Adam 1876 - 1918 (C)
SZKIELKA, Piotr 1878 - 1938 (D)
Anastazya 1878 - 1934 Mother
(D)
SZLAFRAK, Steve 1894 - 26 July
1929 (D)
John 1867 - 1925 Father (D)
Andrzej 1901 - 1919 (D)
---- 1870 - 1918 Mother (D)
SZLAFRAK, Wladyslaw 1906 -
21 Feb 1930 (D)
Jan 1911 - 1933 (D)
Edward 1908 - 1968 (D)
SZMANDA, Frank 1897 - 1927
(B)
Marcin 1840 - 14 Feb 1922 (B)
Jozefa 1849 - 1931 (B)
Antony 1890 - 1957 (B)
Angela 1887 - 1909 (Nee: Kaczo-
rowski) (B)
Thomas 1874 - 1949 (B)
Cecylia 1881 - 1942 (Nee: Pra-
wat) (B)
(Helen Prawat same lot)
SZMANDA, Stanislaw 1872 -
1932 (C)
Mary Dictz 1881 - 1938 (C)
SZMANKOWSKI, Rozalia 1866 -
1940 Mother (Nee: Mincinski)
"Wife of Antony Szmankow-
ski" (A)
Vincent 1888 - 1917 (A)
(Mary Hasko same lot)
SZMANSKI, Jozef 1858 - 23 Feb
1928 Father (B)
Anna 1857 - 1922 (Nee:
Sczypski) Mother (B)
Franciszek 1886 - 31 Dec 1913
(B)
Stella 1899 - 1957 (B)
(Katarzyna Scipska same lot)
SZOCINSKI, Helen 1896 - 1961
(Nee: Banicki) (B)
John J 26 Aug 1897 - 5 Sept 1962
"Michigan Wagoner Utilities
Dept QMC WWI" (B)
Joseph 16 Mar 1893 - 30 Jan
1958 "Indiana Pfc Btry D 1 Fld
Arty" (B)

SZOCINSKI (continued)
(Debra Criswell same lot)
SZOCINSKI, Sylvestor 22 Dec
1901 - 21 Sept 1973 "Minne-
sota Pvt USA WWII" (B)
Marcin 1861 - 1911 Father (B)
Antonina 1867 - 1946 (Nee:
Paszkiewicz) Mother (B)
SZUBA, Jozef 1880 - 1951 Father
(E)
Maryanna 1881 - 1940 Mother (E)
Helen 1907 - 1925 Daughter (E)
Anna 1903 - 1927 Daughter (E)
Frank 2 Oct 1912 - 23 Oct 1973
"Pvt USA WWII" Son (E)
SZUBA, Edward 1917 - 1929 Son
(E)
Rose 1893 - 1977 Mother (E)
John 1892 - 1964 (E)
SZULCZEWSKI, Ludwika 1855 -
1911 Mother (B)
(Maryanna Jaskiewicz same lot)
SZULCZEWSKI, Andrzej 1880 -
18 Apr 1950 Brother (B)
(Franciszek Sochocki same lot)
SZULCZEWSKI, Franciszek 1860
- 1940 (C)
Wiktoria 1862 - 1914 (C)
Helen Schultz 1898 - 1960 (C)
SZULCZEWSKI, John 1854 -
1922 (E)
(Ed & Pelegia Sabowski same
lot)
SZULCZYK, Cecylia A 1886 -
1971 (Nee: Sobczak) Mother
(C)
Joseph M 1884 - 1946 Father (C)
(Frank Sobczak same lot)
SZULKOWSKI, Leonard 21 Oct
1891 - 7 Feb 1938 "Indiana Sgt
Motor Trans Corp" (A)
(Konstanty Wiatkowski & Frank
Kendziorski same lot)
SZULKOWSKI, Joseph no dates
(-)
SZYJA, Wladyslaw 1917 - 1917
(D)
Raymond 1919 - 1940 (D)
George 1875 - 1957 Father (D)
Angela 1887 - 1973 (Nee: Nowak)
Mother (D)

SZYMANOWSKI, Wawrzyniec J
no dates (A)
Jozefa 1876 - 1933 (Nee:
Zielinski) Mother (A)
Irena 1914 - 1914 Daughter (A)
SZYMANOWSKI, Jozef 1869 -
1949 Father (A)
Maryanna 1869 - 1940 Mother (A)
SZYMANOWSKI, Theodore 1880
- 1963 (A)
Eva 1878 - 1959 (Nee: Kasprzak)
(A)
SZYMANOWSKI, Marianna 1880
- 1942 (Nee: Merzykowski) (C)
Feliks 1875 - 1953 (C)
SZYMANOWSKI, Maryanna no
date - 9 Aug 1929 (F)
Katarzyna no date - 21 Jan 1922
Wife (F)
SZYMANOWSKI, Stanley no date
- 26 Dec 1933 (D)
SZYMANOWSKI, Marcin 1884 -
1929 Husband, Father (F)
Anna 1890 - 1961 (Nee: Biskup)
Wife-Mother (F)
(Andrzej Zyzak, 2nd Husband
same lot)
SZYMANSKI, Joseph 1858 - 23
Feb 1928 Father (B)
Anna 1857 - 1922 (Nee:
Szczypski) (B)
Franciszek 1886 - 31 Dec 1913
(B)
Stella 1899 - 1957 (B)
(Katarzyna Scipska same lot)
SZYMANSKI, Teodor 1907 - 1943
Son (B)
(Jan & Pelegia Osmanski - Ed-
ward Osmanski same lot)
SZYMANSKI, Lucya no dates (B)
Stanislaw no date - 22 Jan 1918
(B)
Wojciech no dates (B)
Marya no dates (Nee: Lodyga)
(B)
Piotr 1842 - 11 Apr 1920 (B)
SZYMANSKI, Jozef 1871 - 3 Jan
1921 Father (D)
Wiktorya 1872 - 1946 Mother (D)
SZYMANSKI, Blanche 1893 -
1963 (Nee: Brzeniak) (F)
Ladislaw L 8 Apr 1892 - 13 Feb

SZYMANSKI (continued)
1980 "Sgt USA WWI" (F)
(Rosalia Brzeniak same lot)
SZYMANSKI, Alexander 1893 -
1935 (G)
SZYMANSKI, John 1915 - 1923
(G)
Mary 1885 - 1936 Mother (G)
Antony 1884 - 1944 Father (G)
SZYMAREK, Maryanna no date -
1930 "Daughter of Frank &
Mary Paruzynski Szymarek"
(E)
(Edward & Katarzyna Paruzynski
Nowakowski same lot)
SZYMAREK, John Frank 19 Apr
1923 - 23 June 1982 "USN
WWII" "Son of Frank & Mary
Paruzynski Szymarek" (H)
Genevieve 12 May 1922 - 19--
(Nee: Stachowiak) "Daughter of
Frank & Hattie Laskowski
Stachowiak" "TSgt Womens
Army Corps 2506 SCU 17 Sig
Svc Co WWII" (H)
SZYMCZAK, Julia 1911 - 1934
Beloved Mother (A)
SZYMCZAK, Joseph 1853 - 4 Oct
1910 (A)
Apolonia 1870 - 1908 (A)
SZYMCZAK, Henry 29 June 1928
- 13 Jan 1929 (D)
(Paul W Polinski, Wojciech
Buszkiewicz, Jozef Gutek, &
Hattie Dejeigher same lot) (D)
SZYMCZAK, John no date - 1934
(A)
SZYMCZAK, Laura 1899 - 1962
Mother (F)
Bernice 1904 - 1929 Sister (F)
Casimir 2 Oct 1896 - 21 Jan
1963 "Indiana Pfc I Co 159
Depot Brigade WWI" (F)
Richard no date - 1932 Son (F)
SZYMCZAK, Lawrence no dates
Baby (H)
(Albin & Katarzyna Waluszka
same lot)
SZYMCZAK, Leon no date - 1918
(-)
SZYMKOWIAK, Sophie 1908 -
1975 (C)

SZYMKOWIAK (continued)
Tony 1906 - 1972 (C)
(John & Rose Mezykowski same
lot)
SZYMKOWIAK, Michael 1892 -
1927 (C)
Edward 1916 - 1917 (C)
Robert 1925 - 1927 (C)
(Cecylia Pacholski same lot)
SZYMKOWIAK, Stephen 1869 -
1937 (E)
Mary Nowak 1875 - 1922 (E)
SZYMONKIENIEC, Antonina no
dates (A)
Ignac no dates Son (A)
Ludwig no dates Son (A)
SZYNSKI, Edmund A 1905 - 1972
(B)
Stella S 1911 - 19-- (B)
(Marian & Alexandria Klodzinski
same lot)
SZULCZEWSKI, John 1854 -
1922 (E)
(Edward & Blanche Saboski same
lot)
SZULCZEWSKI, Franciszek 1860
- 1940 (C)
Wiktorya 1862 - 1914 (C)
Helen Schultz 1898 - 1960 (C)
TABERSKI, Franciszek 1869 -
1944 (A)
Stanislawa 1876 - 1931 (A)
Jozef A 1898 - 20 Sept 1920 (A)
Marcin 1905 - 1906 (A)
(Helen Majewski same lot)
TABERSKI, Joseph & John no
date - 21 Dec 1941 (F)
(Jan & Stanislawa Lisek same
lot)
TABERSKI, Agnieszka 1884 -
1938 (Nee: Wroblewski)
Mother (C)
Stefan 1875 - 1939 with Picture
Father (C)
Marcin 1841 - 6 Feb 1915 (C)
Katarzyna 1843 - 1922 (C)
TABERSKI, Lawrence no date -
16 Apr 1921 (-)
TAFELSKI, Maryanna 1865 -
1949 (Nee: Kajzer) Mother (B)
Wawrzyniec 1865 - 1955 Father
(B)

111

TAFELSKI (continued)
Walter 6 Mar 1896 – 23 Jan 1965
"Indiana Cpl 309 Trench Motar
Bn WWI" (B)
(Agnieszka Dereszynski & Zyg-
munt Kolczynski same lot)
TAFELSKI, Stanley E 1892 –
1970 Father (D)
Nettie H 1896 – 1972 Mother (D)
Virginia M 1921 – 1924 Baby (D)
TAKOWSKI, Ignatius no dates (C)
TALENTKOWSKI, Antony F 1868
– 1933 (D)
TALIGOWSKI, Andrew no date –
21 Mar 1925 (-)
TARWACKI, ---- no date – 1939
(PC1)
TAUCAS, Anton 1868 – 1923 (E)
Petronella 1886 – 19-- (E)
TAYLOR, Martha 1906 – 1977 (C)
(Wawrzyniec & Anna Jasinski –
Josephine Witt same lot)
TEGHON, Lee W no date – 1935
(F)
(Mary Perzak same lot)
TERLECKI, Antonina V 27 Aug
1871 – 31 Dec 1970 (E)
(Franciszek Lewiecki same lot)
THILMAN, Veronica 1879 – 1975
(E)
Leo J 1876 – 1961 (E)
Mary 1898 – 1919 (E)
THOMAS, Richard D 22 Apr 1937
– 20 July 1937 (H)
Theresa H 22 Oct 1911 – 19--
(H)
Gaston "Keystone" 7 Dec 1911 –
10 May 1979 "Married 10 Feb
1934" (H)
THOMPSON, Annette 1908 –
1948 Daughter (D)
(Piotr & Agatha Szepanek same
lot)
TOBALSKI or TOBOLSKI, Jean H
14 Dec 1939 – 11 Nov 1941 (A)
(Jozef Gawronski & Blanche J
Kuspa same lot)
TOBALSKI, Regina no date –
1919 age 7 weeks (A)
(Frank & Mary Jankowski, &
Wladyslawa Nowak same lot)
TOBOLSKI, Franciszek 1859 – 9

TOBOLSKI (continued)
Aug 1930 Father (A)
Agnieszka 1857 – 1932 (Nee:
Grabowski) Mother (A)
Zygmunt 1901 – no date (A)
(Wanda Kolesiak same lot)
TOBOLSKI, Catharine 21 Oct
1881 – 27 May 1925 (D)
(Josephine Sudol same lot)
TOBOLSKI, Joseph S 23 Nov 1893
– 20 Feb 1940 (E)
(Michael & Tillie Jerzykowski
same lot)
TOBOLSKI, Stanley H 1894 – 25
Aug 1968 (PC1)
Agnes no date – 13 June 1970
(Nee: Kuczwara) (PC1)
Eylene no date – 1956 (PC1)
John no date – 1961 (PC1)
TOBOLSKI, Edward C 1894 – 10
Feb 1928 Father (F)
(Frank J & Laura Jahnz same
lot)
TOKARSKI, Thelma C 1912 –
19-- (A)
Alex C 1907 – 1971 (A)
(John J & Eva Dietz same lot)
TOMAL, Sophie Langner no date
– 8 June 1902 (C)
(Matthew – Stella – Frank
Luczkowski same lot)
TOMASIK, Joseph 1894 – 1970
(H)
Helen E 1903 – 19-- (H)
Bernard no date – 6 Sept 1939
WWI Inf (H)
TOMASZEWSKI, Michael 1869 –
1947 Father (C)
Joanna 1876 – 1956 (Nee:
Obalski) Mother (C)
Casey 1906 – 1964 (C)
Clementine 3 Jan 1913 – 26 Oct
1914 (C)
TOMASZEWSKI, Stanley 1880 –
30 Jan 1920 (-)
TOMASZEWSKI, Martin no dates
(-)
TOMASZEWSKI, Frank 1897 –
1965 (F)
Amelia 1898 – 1926 (Nee:
Ciesiolka) (F)
Angela 1906 – 19-- (F)

TOMASZEWSKI (continued)
(Rosalie Guzicki same lot)
TOMASZEWSKI, Marion 1887 –
1928 Husband (F)
Mary 1869 – 1928 Mother (F)
TOMASZEWSKI, Franciszka
1896 – 1931 (Nee: Kuczwara)
(F)
Kathryn 1896 – 1960 (F)
Harry S 26 Dec 1895 – 14 Jan
1966 "Michigan Wagoner Co D
14 AMM TN WWI" (F)
TOMKINS, Louise 1876 – 1956
(C)
Joseph 1869 – 1950 (C)
Leonora 15 Nov 1907 – 29 Apr
1922 (C)
Bert S 9 Oct 1915 – 5 Jan 1981
"Pfc USA WWII" (C)
Sally no date – 1982 Aunt (C)
TOROWICZ, John 16 Aug 1886 –
23 June 1932 (D)
Bronislawa 7 Aug 1924 – 9 Aug
1924 Daughter (D)
(Bronislaw Kontnik, Maria Jan-
dola, & Franciszek Pawlak
same lot)
TORZEWSKI, Walter no date –
15 Sept 1927 "Indiana Pvt 78
Inf 14 Div" (B)
(Edward McCauley same lot)
TORZEWSKI, Joseph 1873 – 1939
(C)
Antonina 19 Mar 1879 – Mar 1917
(C)
(Gladys A Melton same lot)
TOTH, Clara B Wlodarski 1912 –
1964 (F)
John no date – 3 Apr 1920 (F)
(Stanley & Frances Wlodarski
same lot)
TRAFKA, Valentine no dates (–)
TRAFKA, Rose 1830 – 1925 (A)
(Frank & Agnes Graczyk, &
Josephine Zalas same lot)
TRODZINSKI, Antony no dates
(B)
TROJANOWSKI, Jozef 1866 –
1940 Father (D)
Pelegia 1877 – 1969 Mother (D)
TROK, Walter 1881 – 1956 (D)
Elizabeth M 1881 – 19-- (Nee:

TROK (continued)
Kapalczynski) (D)
John J 9 Feb 1919 – 24 Nov 1919
Baby (D)
TRYTKO, Regina 1871 – 24 Feb
1960 (D)
Piotr 1868 – 28 May 1921 (D)
(Ignacy & Mary Jankowski same
lot)
TRYTKO, Stanley 1902 – 5 May
1936 (PC1)
TRASZKOWSKI, Szczepan 1875 –
1923 (E)
Wladyslaw 1909 – 4 Apr 1930 (E)
(Franciszka Bargielski same lot)
TRASZKOWSKI, Helen 1892 –
1959 (H)
Tadeusz S 1909 – 1941 (H)
Michael 1891 – 19-- (H)
TRZCINA, Joseph 19 Mar 1896 –
15 May 1970 "Indiana Cpl Co I
67 Inf WWI" (F)
(Henrietta Grocki same lot)
TRZYBINSKI, Blazy 25 Dec 1891
– 27 Oct 1956 "Indiana Pvt 23
Co 158 Depot – WWI" (G)
(Mieczyslaw Grocki same lot)
TUCKER, Sharon J 4 June 1942 –
26 Oct 1943 "Daughter of CR &
JF Tucker" (F)
(Alex & Stella Dubicki – William
Pawlowski same lot)
TURKOWSKI, Elizabeth 1861 –
1928 Mother (C)
TURZA, Frank no dates (–)
TURZA, Anna L 13 Nov 1911 – 18
June 1934 (E)
Michael W 1906 – 1948 (E)
TURZYNSKI, Mary 1879 – 1961
(Nee: Chmielewski) Mother (C)
Joseph 1874 – 1955 Father (C)
(Michael & Maryanna
Chmielewski same lot)
TURZYNSKI, Thomas Sr 1845 –
1917 (C)
Josephine 1851 – 1923 (Nee:
Smorowski) (C)
Thomas Jr 1878 – 1958 (C)
Mary 1883 – 1969 (Nee: Stach-
owiak) (C)
TURZYNSKI, Martha 1880 – 1967
(Nee: Nowak) (C)

TURZYNSKI (continued)
Jacob 1876 - 1947 (C)
Albert J 1910 - 1974 Husband (C)
Erwin 1908 - 1914 (C)
TURZYNSKI, Maryann 22 May
1932 - 6 Aug 1935 (H)
John D 1894 - 1972 (H)
Blanche H 1899 - 1974 (H)
TWARDOWSKI, Margaret 1856 -
1924 Mother (Nee: Wasicki)
(E)
(John & Agnes Kush same lot)
TYLKI, Jakub 1851 - 18 Nov 1916
Father (A)
Franciszka 1851 - 1923 Mother
(A)
Wladyslaw 1890 - 1 Sept 1911
(A)
(Franciszka Niezgodski same
lot)
UMINSKI, Edward 11 Sept 1917 -
12 Jan 1960 "Indiana Cpl 11
FTR Contl Sq USAAF WWII"
(G)
UMINSKI, James Edward 1949 -
1952 Son (G)
(Henrietta Jendrzejewski same
lot)
UNIEWSKI, Bill J 1893 - 1975
"Pfc USA" (D)
Catharine 1883 - 1966 (D)
UNIEWSKI, Helena 1899 - 1935
(E)
(Vincent & Stephaniw Degus
same lot)
URBAN, Peter 1887 - 28 Mar
1930 (E)
URBAN, Helen 1927 - 1934 (F)
(Romnald & Eulalia Parafinowicz
same lot)
URBAN, John 1894 - 1958 (F)
Regina 1892 - 1968 (F)
(Peter J Holtz same lot)
URBANSKI, Mikolaj no date -
1912 (A)
(Teodor & Katarzyna Ewald &
Carrie Mejer same lot)
URBANSKI, Peter 1885 - 1960 (A)
Casimir 1897 - 1970 (A)
Mary 1865 - 1948 Mother (A)
Jacob 1863 - 1945 Father (A)

URBANSKI, Klemens 1900 - 20
Oct 1918 (A)
Stanislaw 1866 - 7 Nov 1913 (A)
Rozalia 1870 - 1946 (A)
URBANSKI, Nicholas 2 Dec 1836
- 1912 (A)
URBANSKI, Theodore 1887 - 19--
Father (E)
Stella 1887 - 1953 (Nee:
Tobolski) Mother (E)
URBANSKI, Joseph 1861 - 1943
(H)
Maryanna 1865 - 1947 (E)
URBANSKI, Josephine 1897 -
1973 (Nee: Stachowiak) (D)
Gracie 1932 - 1932 (D)
Steve 24 Dec 1893 - 7 May 1960
"Indiana Sgt Hdq Co 46 Inf
WWI" (D)
URBANSKI, Stephen 1894 - 1966
Father (E)
Jane 1895 - 1951 Mother (E)
Mary 1903 - 1976 (E)
VALLEJO, Guadelupe L "Nacio
31 Falecio 27" - Enero 1935
(D)
Agosta no date - 1953 (D)
(Theresa Gramza same lot)
VANDUSEN, A E 1901 - 1952 (A)
(George Popielski same lot)
VANEK, John 1860 - 1939 (F)
Teofilia 1870 - 1927 Mother (F)
Michael & Stanley no dates
Brothers (F)
VANDERHAGEN, Stella 1898 -
1940 Wife (F)
(Michael & Anna Szczepaniak
and Lisa Marie Bocher same
lot)
VAN HOKE, Isadore 18 May 1890
- 31 Dec 1967 (A)
Helen 10 July 1887 - 4 May 1965
(Nee: Markiewicz) (A)
(Franciszek & Katarzyna Markie-
wicz, & Genevieve Leonard
same lot)
VARGO, Carrie 29 Sept 1891 -
1958 (Nee: Jablonski) (D)
Alex 1889 - 1931 (D)
VARGO, Corrine no date - 8 Nov
1946 (E)
(Stanislaw & Mary Reiter same

VARGO (continued)
lot)
VARGO, Eugene J 1931 - 1957 (F)
(Casimir Dombrowski same lot)
VARGYAS, Frank P 1917 - 1969 (F)
(George & Martha Gadowski same lot)
VERBEKE, Irene M 1906 - 1978 (D)
(Joseph & Agnes Niezgodski same lot)
VERMILYER, Robert E 16 Jan 1921 - 6 Sept 1970 "Pvt Hq Det 1 Med Sec WWII" (E)
Violet 14 May 1918 - 17 June 1919 (E)
WACHOWIAK, Anna 1873 - 1913 (B)
John 1873 - 1946 (B)
Mary 1891 - 1973 (B)
WACUNAS, Paul 1885 - 1958 (E)
Aniela 1891 - 1972 (E)
WADZINSKI, Leon 1918 - 1940 (F)
Henry 1871 - 1949 (F)
Jozefa 1882 - 1962 (F)
Joseph 1911 - 1977 WWII USA (F)
WALCZAK, Stanislaw 1883 - 1935 (E)
(Samuel Zukowski & Jan Haluda same lot)
WALCZAK, Stanley 1863 - 1935 (G)
WALCZAK, Bert no date - 14 Aug 1932 (D)
WALCZAK, Jozefa 1887 - 28 Nov 1959 (Nee: Kielszek) (H)
John 1882 - 18 Mar 1938 (H)
Leon Francis 11 Feb 1921 - 28 Apr 1921 (H)
WALEWSKI, Agnes R 17 Jan 1895 - 6 Mar 1980 (Nee: Smigielski) (B)
John 25 Dec 1891 - 2 Jan 1962 "Illinois Sgt USA WWI" (B)
(Leon & Gertrude Smiegielski same lot)
WALIGORSKI, Walenty 1856 - 1939 (B)

WALIGORSKI (continued)
Jozefa 1858 - 1942 (B)
WALINSKI, August 1875 - 1953 (B)
Apolonia 1875 - 1958 (Nee: Wroblewski) (B)
WALKER (Named changed was Chodzinski), John 1879 - 1967 Father (C)
Catharine 1879 - 20 July 1962 (Nee: Kolacz) Mother (C)
Harry 1912 - 1920 Son (C)
Casimir 1913 - 6 Sept 1914 Son (C)
Clem no date - 3 Mar 1911 (C)
Joseph 24 Feb 1925 - 19 July 1971 (C)
WALKOWIAK, Piotr 1860 - 1933 Father (B)
Michalena 1876 - 1930 (B)
WALKOWIAK, Veronica 1896 - 1916 (B)
Michael 1859 - 1 Nov 1938 Father (B)
Katarzyna 1869 - 1951 (Nee: Przybysz) Mother (B)
WALKOWIAK, Vera 1902 - 1945 (D)
(Victor Barber, A Gaik, A Wrotnowski, B Wrotnowski, & Louis M Hanyzeski same lot)
WALKOWIAK, Jozef 27 Sept 1865 - 27 Aug 1913 Father (C)
Joseph 2 Dec 1895 - 10 Dec 1919 (C)
Cathrine 1875 - 1962 (Nee: Kazmierczak) Mother (C)
(Cecylia Hes same lot)
WALKOWIAK, Michael 1849 - 1933 Father (D)
Rose 1855 - 1945 Mother (D)
WALKOWSKI, Antonette 1874 - 1969 Mother (F)
Joseph 1869 - 1943 Father (F)
(Sophie Rogacki same lot)
WALKOWSKI, Bronislaw 25 Sept 1897 - 8 Apr 1913 (A)
WALKOWSKI, Peter 19 Feb 1900 - 1959 Father (D)
Jennie 1902 - 19-- Mother (D)
Ralph P 28 Oct 1942 - 24 Feb 1970 "Indiana Pvt USA" (D)

WALKOWSKI, Michael 1851 -
1933 (-)
WALORSKI, Katarzyna no dates
Grandmother (B)
(Szczepan & Agnes Laskowski
same lot)
WALORSKI, Henrietta 8 Apr 1921
- 25 May 1922 (C)
Franciszek 1882 - 6 Feb 1929
(C)
Mary 1889 - 1971 (Nee: Lodyga)
(C)
Jozef 1885 - 1957 Brother (C)
Rose 1892 - 1970 (Nee: Lodyga)
Wife-Sister (C)
(Wojciech Leda & Michael, &
Apolonia Lodyga same lot)
WALOWSKI, Joseph A 27 Feb
1915 - 29 May 1972 "Indiana
1Sgt Co C 152 Inf WWII PH"
(C)
(Frank and Victoria Markiewicz
same lot)
WALOWSKI, Julia 1873 - 1915
(C)
WALSH, Erin Marie 17 Aug 1972
- 21 Aug 1972 Baby (G)
(Edward & Irene Witucki same
lot)
WALUSZKA, Katarzyna 1898 -
1943 Mother (H)
Albin 1889 - 19-- Father (H)
Sophie 1906 - 1970 (H)
(Lawrence Szymczak same lot)
WALTERS, William no date - 13
May 1919 (-)
WANTUCH, Anna 1879 - 1953
Mother (F)
Antoni 1877 - 1962 Father (F)
WARANOWYCZ Family, ---- no
dates (G)
(Zubras Family same lot)
WARE, Deloise no date - 20 May
1940 Husband (A)
Stella no dates Wife (A)
WARUSZAK, Jacob no date - 22
Apr 1918 (-)
WAS, Elizabeth 1877 - 1930 (D)
(Maryanna Kalicki & Casimir J -
Mary Putz same lot)
WAS, Aloysius 1906 - 1955 (F)
Mary M 1909 - 19-- (F)

WASIELEWSKI, Andrew 1890 -
1944 (H)
Ronald 1937 - 1938 (H)
(Janina Sobiech & Albin Bed-
narek same lot)
WASIKOWSKI, Richard J 12 Mar
1917 - 6 Dec 1974 "SSgt
USAAF" (C)
John J 1887 - 1972 (C)
Helen I 1888 - 1977 (Nee:
Cholewczynski) (C)
WASIKOWSKI, John 1862 - 1944
(C)
Agnes 1860 - 1952 (C)
WASLICKI, Stanley 1893 - 1954
(F)
(Casimir & Magdelena
Hanyzewski, & Felix & Mary
Drajus same lot)
WAWRZYNIAK, Anna 1889 -
1940 (Nee: Sosnowski) (B)
Ignacy 1887 - 1964 (B)
WAWRZYNIAK, John 6 May 1890
- 1 Nov 1948 "Indiana Pvt 333
Inf 84 Div WWI" (D)
Michael no dates (D)
John 16 May 1861 - 8 Feb 1928
(D)
Val 19 Feb 1902 - 8 Apr 1924 (D)
WAWRZYNIAK, Vincent 1890 -
1977 (H)
Stella 1889 - 1970 (H)
WAWRZYNIAK, Lucian J 14 May
1916 - 15 Jan 1944 "Indiana
TSgt 69 Armd FA WWII" (F)
Vincent F 1889 - 1965 (F)
Alfreda 1917 - 1917 (F)
Michaline 1890 - 1970 (Nee:
Kaczmarek) (F)
Stanley 1928 - 1929 (F)
WCISEL, Franciszek 1867 - 1953
Father (D)
Madgelena 1875 - 1928 Mother
(D)
Weronika 1900 - 1973 Daughter
(D)
John 1893 - 1907 Son (D)
WCISEL, Andrew 1906 - 12 Aug
1936 (PC1)
M no dates (PC1)
WECHNEROWSKI, Jan 1871 -
1939 (H)

116

WECHNEROWSKI (continued)
Franciszka 1873 - 1958 (Nee:
Kozlowski) (H)
WEGENKA, Franciszek 1856 -
1933 (C)
Maryanna 1861 - 1943 (C)
WEGENKA, Sylvester W 25 Aug
1890 - no date "Indiana Cpl
USA WWI" (F)
Tadeusz 1924 - 1929 Son (F)
WEGENKA, Steve 6 Sept 1894 -
15 Sept 1974 Father "Pfc USA"
(F)
Clara L 20 June 1900 - 19--
(Nee: Spychalski) Mother (F)
(Christine Deanna - Michael Al-
len - Wm Michael Krill same
lot)
WEGNER, Pawel 1869 - 1955
Father (A)
Franciszka 1877 - 1929 Mother
(A)
(Aloysius & Lillian Lewinski
same lot)
WEGNER, Gloria no date - Sept
1929 (F)
WEGNER, Michael 1872 - 12
July 1920 (C)
Katarzyna no dates Wife (C)
(Klementyna Horka same lot)
WEGNEROWSKI, Maryanna 1850
- 1911 Grandmother (B)
Ignacy 1853 - 19 Mar 1929
Grandfather (B)
Stanislawa 1881 - 1947 Mother
(Nee: Wyremblewski) (B)
Wincenty 1880 - 1957 Father (B)
WEGNEROWSKI, Stanley no date
- 17 Mar 1931 (D)
WENDOWSKI, Stefan 1872 - 1920
Father (C)
(Franciszek Kmitta same lot)
WENDLAND, Frank 10 Sept 1892
- 6 Nov 1960 "Indiana Pvt Trp
C 12 Cavalry" (B)
(Charles Bock & Jan Witucki
same lot)
WENTLAND, Anna July 1844 -
12 July 1912 (Nee: Gnoth)
Mother (A)
Florentyna no dates (A)

WENTLAND, Felix 1865 - 14
Dec 1931 (B)
Mary 1870 - 1936 (B)
Constance 1915 - 1975 (B)
Casimir 1902 - 6 Oct 1982 (B)
WENTLAND, Agnes 1872 - 15
Feb 1932 Mother (D)
Frank 1863 - 30 Nov 1936 (D)
Blase S 10 Jan 1894 - 16 Jan
1961 "Indiana Pvt USA WWI"
(D)
Aloysius 6 Nov 1902 - 26 Sept
1977 (D)
WENTLAND, Stella 1881 - 1952
Mother (D)
Steve 1880 - 1959 Father (D)
Henry T 1915 - 1916 (D)
WENTLAND, Sylvester 25 Dec
1896 - 12 Aug 1950 "Indiana
Seaman USN" (F)
(Antony F Kolesiak same lot)
WERWINSKI, Joseph A 14 Jan
1882 - 1943 (B)
Ignatius 2 July 1886 - 15 Nov
1958 "Indiana 1Lt USA WWI &
WWII" (B)
(Antoni & Emilia Beczkiewicz
same lot)
WESOLOWSKI, Frank 1885 - 13
Nov 1925 (A)
Mary 1864 - 1943 (Nee: Rybak)
(A)
Stanley 1893 - 22 Mar 1914 (A)
Jan 18 Nov 1861 - 11 June 1911
(A)
WESOLOWSKI, Nicholas 1897 -
1973 (A)
Nettie 1898 - 19-- (Nee: Cwidak)
(A)
WESOLOWSKI, Frank R 1888 -
1914 (A)
(Julia & Jan Elantkowski - Albin
S Nowinski same lot)
WESOLOWSKI, Catharine 1906 -
1962 (D)
Joseph F 1895 - 1976 (D)
WESOLOWSKI, Bronislawa 1877
- 1943 (H)
Wladyslaw 1880 - 1944 Father
(H)
John P 26 June 1914 - 24 Aug
1955 "Indiana Cpl Co A 33

WESOLOWSKI (continued)
Tank Bn WWII" (H)
WHITE, Martin 1878 - 1953
Father (E)
Stella 1884 - 1944 (E)
WIATROLIK, Kathryn M 1903 -
1971 (F)
Bert J 1903 - 1956 (F)
(Walter & Anna Bednarek same
lot)
WIATROLIK, Edward 1896 - 1961
(D)
Alex 1900 - 1947 (D)
Josephine 1866 - 1938 (Nee:
Maternowski) (D)
Cyryl 1866 - 11 Dec 1930 (D)
WIATROWSKI, Konstanty 1873 -
19 Sept 1912 (A)
Roman 1906 - 1955 (A)
(Frank Kendziorski & Leonard
Szulkowski same lot)
WIDOWSKI, Hipolit 1881 - 1956
(D)
Lillian 1883 - 1965 (D)
WIECZORKOWSKI, Szcepan no
date - 1923 (C)
Angela 26 Jan 1878 - 10 May
1951 (Nee: Mackowski) (C)
Maryanna 1872 - 1915 (Nee:
Raider) Wife (C)
Stanislaw 1912 - 1913 Son (C)
(Rozalia Jaworski same lot)
WIECZOREK, Peter 1907 - 1936
Son (A)
Valentine 1873 - 21 July 1952
Father (A)
Mary 1881 - 1948 (Nee: Andrze-
jewski) Mother (A)
(Esther Puzinski & Irene Chlebek
same lot)
WIECZOREK, Apolonia 1845 -
1925 Grandmother (E)
(Piotr Stachowski same lot)
WIECZOREK, Franciszek 1916 -
1919 (E)
Gabryela 1876 - 1950 Mother (E)
Franciszek 1876 - 1925 Father
(E)
WIELGASZ, Stanley no date - 22
Sept 1922 (-)
WIELGOSZ, W no dates (D)
WIELGOS, Paul 1896 - 19-- (H)

WIELGOS (continued)
Stella 1902 - 19-- (H)
WIERZBICKI, Julianna 16 Feb
1863 - 12 July 1907 (A)
WIERZBINSKI, Heronim S 1907 -
8 Nov 1933 (D)
Walter H 1900 - 1956 (D)
WIERZBINSKI, William 23 Mar
1898 - 9 Dec 1975 (C)
Michaline 1865 - 1950 (C)
Michael 1861 - 1935 (C)
Hilary 1912 - 1913 (C)
(Elzbieta Wojciechowski same
lot)
WIERZBINSKI, Vincent no date -
15 Dec 1917 (-)
WIERCLEWSKI, Jakub 1825 - 11
Mar 1913 (A)
(Michael Rybacki same lot)
WIETRZYNSKI, Stanislaw 1868 -
1922 (F)
(Joseph & Victoria Olszewski, &
Bartholomew Rembleski same
lot)
WIKTOROWSKI, Lott 24 June
1893 - 21 July 1949 (A)
John no dates (A)
WILCZEWSKI, Frances 1882 -
1962 Mother (D)
Frank 1913 - 1932 (D)
(Balbina Gierszewski same lot)
WILCZEWSKI, Wladyslaw no
date - 2 Nov 1943 "Placowka
No 125 Polish Soldier" (D)
WILCZYNSKI, Leo J 1912 - 19--
(H)
Lottie A 1906 - 1969 (H)
Elvin 1935 - 1936 (with Picture)
Baby (H)
WILCZYNSKI, Felix no date -
1927 (E)
WILTROUT, Susan C no date -
1949 (B)
(Wojciech Bonek, Jozef Strozew-
ski, & Raymond Luczkowski
same lot)
WINDYKOWSKI, Frank no date -
4 Aug 1922 (-)
WINKEL, Karol 1879 - 1935
Father (A)
Katarzyna 1882 - 1956 Mother
(A)

118

WINKEL (continued)
Gordy 1918 - 5 Aug 1931 Son (A)
WINKEL, Mary Ann 1933 - 1933
(D)
(John & Frances Stefanski same
lot)
WINKEL, Albert 1884 - 1945 (H)
Frances 1883 - 1938 (H)
Edwin 1910 - 1961 (H)
WINKIEWICZ, Clem 1913 - 1979
(G)
Gertrude 1916 - 19-- "Married 18
May 1935" (G)
(Antony & Mary Kanczuzewski
same lot)
WINKOWSKI, Zygmunt 27 Mar
1911 - no date (B)
Aniela 1872 - 1949 (Nee:
Nowaczewski) Mother (B)
Eligiusz 9 June 1901 - 22 June
1934 Son (B)
Maksymilian 1869 - 1921 Father
(B)
WINKOWSKI, Edwin 8 Mar 1914
- 19-- Husband (E)
Mary Helen 12 July 1911 - 25
June 1977 (Nee: Dzikowski)
Wife (E)
Valaria 9 Feb 1909 - 19--
Daughter (E)
Mildred B 1894 - 1973 Daughter
(E)
Mary 12 July 1893 - 19 Jan 1979
(E)
(Casimir & Sophie Kukla, &
Wladyslaw J & Seweryna Las-
kowski same lot)
WINNICKI, Salomea 1882 - 1972
(Nee: Dalkowski) (B)
John T 1882 - 1959 (B)
WINTER, Leo 1896 - 1964 (D)
Mary 1896 - 1933 (D)
WIRANT, Jozef Z 15 Sept 1912 -
8 Feb 1924 (D)
WISKATONI, Ignatius 1893 -
1945 Father (C)
WISLER, Theodora 1905 - 1934
(A)
(Mikolaj & Michalena Podemski
same lot)
WISLEWSKI, Joseph no date -
1910 (-)

WISNIEWSKI, Antoni 1872 - 1956
Husband (A)
Maryanna Wlodarek 1865 - 1943
(Nee: Modracki) Wife (A)
(Michael Wlodarek same lot)
WISNIEWSKI, Blanche 1885 -
1952 (Nee: Zalas) (A)
John B 27 July 1889 - 18 Feb
1969 "Indiana Cook USA
WWI" (A)
(Blanche & John Zalas same lot)
WISNIEWSKI, Frances 1850 -
1908 Mother (B)
(William & Katharine Hosinski -
Florence Wroblewski same
lot)
WISNIEWSKI, Frank 1894 - 22
Dec 1913 (C)
Jozef 1846 - 28 Mar 1928 Father
(C)
Teofilia 1856 - 1929 Mother (C)
Leon A 1899 - 1952 Son (C)
WISNIEWSKI, Mary 1868 - 1945
Mother (D)
Kazimierz 1865 - 17 Apr 1919
Father (D)
Jozef F 5 July 1894 - 21 Nov
1918 "Veteran"
(Frank & Victoria Konstanty,
Jozef Kruk, & Katharine
Sobecki same lot)
WISNIEWSKI, John no dates (D)
Joseph 20 Jan 1889 - 24 Apr
1970 "Indiana Cook USA
WWI" (D)
WISNIEWSKI, Andrew S no date -
15 Feb 1932 "Indiana Sgt 18
Fld Arty 3 Div" (F)
WISNIEWSKI, Josephine 13 Sept
1900 - 22 May 1963 Mother (F)
Stanley 19 May 1894 - 11 Aug
1953 "Indiana Pvt Co I 337 Inf
WWI PN" (F)
WISNIEWSKI, Maryanna 1874 -
1949 Mother (F)
Franciszek 1869 - 1936 Father
(F)
Martin no date - 7 Aug 1925
"Indiana Pfc 15 Fld Arty" (F)
Zygmunt 1901 - 1922 (F)
WISNIEWSKI, Michael no date -
27 Feb 1929 (D)

WISNIEWSKI, Alex F 31 Oct 1890 - 11 Oct 1936 (PC1)
Victoria J 16 Jan 1899 - 30 Jan 1982 (PC1)
WISNIEWSKI, Kasper 1889 - 1960 Father (F)
Boleslawa 1889 - 1960 (F)
Marya no date - 31 July 1928 (F)
(Henryk Moczdlowski same lot) (F)
WISNIEWSKI, Frank W 1902 - 1937 Brother (H)
Michael 1854 - 1934 (H)
WITKOWSKI, ---- 1861 - 1933 Mother (A)
Stanislaw 1859 - 2 Mar 1912 (A)
John 13 Jan 1876 - 24 July 1925 "Indiana Cpl Trench Mortar Btry 1 Div" (A)
(Carrie Campbell same lot)
WITKOWSKI, Franciszka 1870 - 1961 (Nee: Wituski) Mother (A)
Jan 1874 - 1943 Husband (A)
(Leon & Jan Wituski same lot)
WITKOWSKI, Stanley no date - 3 July 1918 (A)
WITKOWSKI, Prakseda 1881 - 1930 (Nee: Mroczkiewicz) Mother (A)
(Marcin Szczesny & Wiktoria Mrockiewicz same lot)
WITKOWSKI, Antony 1889 - 10 Jan 1973 "Indiana Pvt 14 Cav" (B)
(Jan Lentych & Mary Kieloch same lot)
WITKOWSKI, Agnes no dates (Nee: Malicki) "Wife of George Witkowski interred at Cedar Grove Cemetery" (C)
(Casimir & Rose Malicki same lot)
WITKOWSKI, Walter no date - 27 May 1925 (-)
WITT, Josephine 26 Jan 1885 - 9 Feb 1966 (C)
(Wawrzyniec & Anna Jasinski & Martha A Taylor same lot)
WITUCKI, Rosemary 1919 - 1964 (A)
Leonard S 1918 - 1978 (A)

WITUCKI (continued)
Theresa 19 Oct 1903 - 4 Nov 1906 (A)
WITUCKI, Leon 2 Jan 1859 - 2 Jan 1913 (A)
WITUCKI, Jan 1879 - 1925 Husband (B)
Mary 18 Dec 1878 - 2 Feb 1954 (B)
Cecylia 21 Oct 1886 - 25 June 1966 (Nee: Wentland) (B)
Walter F 28 Apr 1886 - 14 Nov 1974 (B)
(Charles Bock & Frank Wendland same lot)
WITUCKI, Louis no date - 5 Mar 1925 (-)
Nick no dates (-)
Sylvester no dates (-)
WITUCKI, Sophie 1898 - 1940 (B)
(Casimir & Catharine Balka, & Helena Niedbalski same lot)
WITUCKI, Franciszek W 25 Aug 1876 - 23 Aug 1912 (B)
Eleanor 25 Sept 1910 - 5 Nov 1910 Granddaughter (B)
Eleanora 18 Mar 1890 - 10 Oct 1910 Daughter (B)
Alexander W 25 Jan 1882 - 6 Apr 1908 Son (B)
Magdelina W 20 May 1858 - 6 Nov 1915 Mother (B)
Teofil V 26 Feb 1853 - 26 May 1923 Father (B)
Anna W 1 July 1885 - 26 Jan 1939 Wife (B)
Steve 9 Sept 1894 - 7 June 1958 "Indiana Pvt 17 Co Coast Arty WWI" (B)
Loretta 1886 - 1971 (B)
Frank 1921 - 19-- (B)
WITUCKI, Wincenty no date - 22 Jan 1916 (C)
(Wincenty & Lucy Sparazynski same lot)
WITUCKI, Stanislaw 1879 - 1914 Husband "Veteran of Spanish American War" (C)
WITUCKI, Rose 1883 - 1962 (D)
Jan 1887 - 1916 (D)
Antony 1880 - 1963 (D)

WITUCKI, Thomas no date - 1
Sept 1915 (-)
WITUCKI, Casimir J 1905 - 19--
(F)
Martha M 1914 - 19-- (F)
Leona 1904 - 1928 (F)
WITUCKI, Edward F 26 Aug 1904
- 29 Dec 1977 Father (G)
Irene F 22 Oct 1904 - 2 Feb 1975
Mother (G)
Patricia J 5 Aug 1932 - 19 Aug
1949 (G)
(Erin Marie Walsh same lot)
WITUSKI, Konstanty 1880 - 1964
Father (A)
Urszula 1889 - 1945 (Nee:
Lisniewicz) (A)
Stanislaw 1912 - 1914 Son (A)
Stanislaw 1879 - 1912 Brother
(A)
WITUSKI, Leon 2 Jan 1859 - 2
Jan 1913 Father (A)
Jan 1905 - 1921 Son (A)
(Jan & Franciszka Witkowski
same lot)
WITUSKI or WITUCKI, Frank J
1892 - 1967 (F)
Sophie M 1895 - 19-- (Nee:
Borlik) (F)
(Casimir & Hattie Budzinski
same lot)
WLODAREK, Maciej 1836 - 15
Feb 1923 Father (A)
Agnieszka 1842 - 1925 Mother
(A)
Stanislaw 14 Aug 1879 - 7 Jan
1933 (A)
WLODAREK, Michal 1862 - 17
June 1906 (A)
Maryanna Wisniewski 1865 -
1943 (Nee: Modracki) Wife (A)
(Anton Wisniewski - 2nd Hus-
band - same lot)
WLODAREK, Lillian M no dates
Infant (C)
(John & Bernice Karczewski
same lot)
WLODAREK, Lillian 1921 - 19--
(Nee: Karczewski) (C)
Matthew F 2 Feb 1917 - 14 June
1980 "Cpl USA WWII" (C)
WLODAREK, Antony J 6 June

WLODAREK (continued)
1912 - 6 June 1944 "Indiana
Pfc 116 Inf" (H)
Stanislaw 1875 - 1950 Father (H)
Maryanna 27 July 1880 - 26 June
1939 (Nee: Grzegorek) (H)
WLODARSKI, ---- no dates (B)
(Martin Giest same lot)
WLODARSKI, Eleanora 13 June
1892 - 1958 (Nee: Borowski)
(C)
Antoni 1884 - 1944 (C)
Wladyslaw 1917 - 1918 (C)
(Antoni Borowski same lot)
WLODARSKI, Frances 1887 -
1976 (Nee: Rydzinski) Wife
(F)
Stanley 13 May 1886 - 4 Mar
1925 Husband (F)
(Clara B Wlodarski Toth same
lot)
WODKA or WOODKA, Bronislawa
1891 - 1923 (Nee: Przezdzien-
kowski) (B)
(Marcin & Barbara Przezdzien-
kowski same lot)
WOELFEL, Rose 1899 - 1922 (E)
(Joseph S Jeziorski same lot)
WOJCIECHOWSKI, Konstanty
1888 - 1963 (A)
Stefan 1913 - 1971 (A)
Katarzyna 1885 - 1957 (A)
Edward 1910 - 1911 (A)
Edwin 1916 - 1918 (A)
Alojzy 1918 - 1918 (A)
WOJCIECHOWSKI, Maryanna
1868 - 1918 (C)
(Bertha Kozach same lot)
WOJCIECHOWSKI, Marya 1861 -
1937 Mother (B)
Szczepan 1861 - 1928 Father (B)
Franciszek 1891 - 1949 (B)
Wojciech 1892 - 1918 "Cpl WWI
died in France" (B)
WOJCIECHOWSKI, Jozef 1860 -
1929 Father (B)
Marcyanna 1868 - 1935 Mother
(B)
---- 1898 - 1925 Son (B)
(Clara Swartz same lot)
WOJCIECHOWSKI, Mical (Mi-
chael) no date - 1956 Dad (C)

Victoria 1869 - 27 Sept 1916
(Nee: Jenczak) (C)
(Agnes Jenczak same lot)
WOJCIECHOWSKI, Elziebieta
1840 - 1927 Mother (C)
(Michael & Michaline Wierzbin-
ski same lot)
WOJCIECHOWSKI, Rozalia 1888
- 1979 (E)
Stanislaw 1887 - 1948 (E)
Feliksa 1896 - 1920 (E)
WOJCIECHOWSKI, Jozefa 1828
- 1943 (age 115 yrs) (A)
(Ignacy Liszewski same lot)
WOJCIECHOWSKI, Jozefa 1889
- 1937 Mother (H)
WOJCIECHOWSKI, Casimir no
dates WWI (B)
Simon no dates (B)
WOJCIK, Ludwika 1893 - 1979
(Nee: Mytyk) (D)
Wojciech 1885 - 1942 (D)
(Walenty Mytyk same lot)
WOJCZAK, John no dates (-)
WOJTYSIAK, Leo 1887 - 1938
(A)
Mary 1889 - 18 Feb 1916 (Nee:
Karczewski) #1 Wife (A)
Katharine 1889 - 27 Aug 1927
(Nee: Przybylski) #2 Wife (A)
WOJTYSIAK, Josephine 1855 -
1930 (E)
(Vincent Kuspa same lot)
WOLAK, Helen Belakovich 1911
- 19-- (H)
(John & James T Belakovich
same lot)
WOLKIEWICZ, Adam 1887 -
1971 Father (G)
Anna 1891 - 1960 (Nee: Kapsa)
Mother (G)
(John Kapsa same lot)
WOLOWICZ, Wojciech 1867 - 6
Aug 1927 Father (B)
Jan 20 Feb 1901 - 22 Nov 1938
Reg Army (B)
Franciszek no dates (B)
Joanna no dates (B)
(Tekla Staszewski & Walter M
Borowski same lot)
WOLOSZYN, Mary 1866 - 1932
(With Picture) Wife, Mother

WOLOSZYN (continued)
(D)
Adam 1869 - 1949 Husband,
Father (D)
WOLTER, Tomasz 1875 - 1954
(A)
Helena 1882 - 1958 (Nee:
Michalski) (A)
WOLTER, Jozef 1837 - 22 Aug
1909 (A)
(Jan & Jozefa Cwidak same lot)
WOLTMAN, Joseph 1904 - 1955
Son (B)
Helen 1875 - 1955 (Nee:
Lesiecki) Mother (B)
Martin 1869 - 1954 Father (B)
Sr M Immaculate 1899 - 1922
Daughter (B)
WOLTMAN, Jozef 1828 - 25 Feb
1914 (B)
Lucya 1827 - 1920 (B)
Tomasz 1881 - 1935 (B)
WOLTMAN, Casimir 1867 - 1944
Father (B)
Mary 1873 - 1945 Mother (B)
WOLTMAN, Maciej 1846 - 1919
(C)
Antonina 1851 - 1933 (C)
WOLTMAN, Helen H 1 Aug 1895
- 26 Apr 1950 (D)
(Jan & Mary Komasinski same
lot)
WOLTMAN, Severyna 1874 -
1948 Mother (F)
Ludwik 1870 - 1929 Father (F)
WOLTMAN, Henry 1872 - 1971
(G)
Kate 1891 - 1977 (G)
Alice 1913 - 1930 "Murdered"
Daughter (G)
WOODKA, Kazimierz 1902 - 1918
(D)
Mateusz 1903 - 1928 (D)
Jozef 1905 - 1923 (D)
---- 1867 - 1936 Mother (D)
WOODKA, Marion 1895 - 1976
(E)
Veral 1900 - 1972 (Nee:
Wroblewski) (E)
Jerome no date - 1923
(A Wroblewski same lot)
WOODS, Eric R no date - 25 Jan

WOODS (continued)
1945 (A)
(Ralph J Jasinski same lot)
WOZNIAK, Stanislaw 1877 - 1930
Father (A)
Salomea 1879 - 1938 Mother (A)
Eligiusza 1902 - 1912 (A)
Benedict L 31 Mar 1923 - 15
May 1974 "Tec USA WWII"
(A)
WOZNIAK, Stanislaw 1858 - 2
Jan 1935 Father (A)
Anna 1862 - 1936 (Nee: Gnoth)
Mother (A)
John P 1892 - 1972 Son (A)
WOZNIAK, Edward J 1907 - 1977
(B)
(Maryan & Marianna Pszradski
same lot)
WOZNIAK, Jan 1874 - 16 May
1926 Father (B)
Teofilia 1879 - 1912 (Nee:
Niezgodski) Mother (B)
Kazimierz 1905 - 1942 Son (B)
Bert 1914 - 19-- (B)
WOZNIAK, Adalbert 1879 - 1967
(C)
Mary A 1888 - 1976 (C)
Jerome no date - 1 May 1980 (C)
Amilya 15 July 1906 - 20 June
1913 (C)
WOZNIAK, John P 1887 - 1974
(D)
Teofilia 1885 - 1966 (Nee:
Grieger) (D)
WOZNIAK, Mary J 1906 - 1939
(D)
(Antoni P Mroczkiewicz same
lot)
WOZNIAK, Henry T 1901 -
197(Not legible) "Seaman 2c
USN WWI" (F)
Anna M 1905 - 19-- (F)
WOZNIAK, Franciszek 1889 - 8
Jan 1928 (With Picture) Father
(F)
Arthur S Jr 1937 - 1956 (with
picture) (F)
WOZNIAK, Richard J 28 July
1930 - 30 Jan 1953 "Indiana
Sgt 5 Inf Korea" (H)
Joseph 1893 - 1936 Father (H)

WOZNIAK (continued)
Nora 1893 - 1971 Mother (H)
WOZNIAK, Andrew no date -
1938 (PC1)
WOZNIAK, Stanley 8 May 1889 -
6 Mar 1925 (East Fence)
WOZNICKI, Theodore 1899 - 26
Oct 1935 (H)
Clara 1900 - 1962 (H)
WOZNICKI, Russell R 2 Sept
1960 - 4 Nov 1960 Twin -
James J (H)
James J 2 Sept 1960 - 4 Nov
1960 Twin - Russell R (H)
WOZNICKI, Frank no dates (-)
WOZNY, Michal 1860 - 27 Dec
1930 Father (B)
Teofilia 1866 - 1950 Mother (B)
WOZNY, Steve 13 Sept 1892 - 5
Mar 1929 "Indiana Stable Sgt
USA" (F)
Junior 23 June 1926 - 5 Jan 1929
(F)
(Stanley J Robaski same lot)
WROBEL, Karol 1878 - 1957 (A)
Jozefa 1888 - 1958 (Nee:
Wilusz) (A)
Petronella 1909 - 1916 (A)
Wiktorya 1911 - 1912 (A)
WROBLEWSKI, Mikolaj 1831 -
15 Oct 1921 Father (B)
Jozefa 1842 - 1928 (Nee:
Pijanowski) Mother (B)
David 1876 - 1970 (B)
WROBLEWSKI, Jozef 8 Mar 1842
- 25 Jan 1941 (A)
Antonina Dec 1842 - 1914 (A)
WROBLEWSKI, Edward 1913 -
1913 (A)
Casimir 1908 - 14 Jan 1937 (A)
Andrew J Sr 1880 - 1954 (A)
Rose 1878 - 1959 (Nee:
Zytowski) (A)
WROBLEWSKI, Stanley 6 May
1913 - 6 June 1931 (A)
Wladyslaw 1903 - 1906 Son (A)
Edward 1916 - 1917 Son (A)
Leon 1868 - 1958 Father (A)
Bronislawa 1876 - 1961 (Nee:
Chmielewski) Mother (A)
WROBLEWSKI, Ed no dates (A)
Alex E 1911 - 1972 (A)

WROBLEWSKI (continued)
Michael 1882 - 1955 (A)
Magdalene 1887 - 1958 (A)
WROBLEWSKI, Jozef 1866 - 1933 Father (A)
Maryanna 1869 - 1949 (Nee: Schoinski) Mother (A)
(Valaria Stachowiak same lot)
WROBLEWSKI, Franciszek 1836 - 21 Dec 1917 Father (A)
(John Mackowski same lot)
WROBLEWSKI, Florence M 29 Jan 1907 - 18 Nov 1977 (Nee: Hosinski) (B)
(William & Katarzyna Hosinski, & Frances Wisniewski same lot) WROBLEWSKI, Kazmierz 1 Feb 1935 - 11 Mar 1941 (B)
James 1874 - 1951 (B)
Carrie 1882 - 1970 (B)
WROBLEWSKI, Michael no date - 5 Feb 1908 (B)
Frank G 1882 - 1958 (B)
Joanna 1880 - 1964 (Nee: Rembenda) (B)
Thomas 21 Feb 1921 - 21 Mar 1921 Baby (B)
WROBLEWSKI, Rev John J "Pastor for 25 years at St. Stanislaw Kostka Church Terre Coupe, Ind" b 8 May 1883 ordained 21 June 1912 d 30 Sept 1956 (C)
Wojciech 23 Apr 1839 - 29 June 1929 Father (C)
Franciszka 13 Aug 1854 - 21 Jan 1921 (Nee: Prawat) (C)
WROBLEWSKI, Frank 13 Mar 1890 - 21 Feb 1956 "Indiana Seaman USN WWI" (C)
(Antony & Stanislawa Leda same lot)
WROBLEWSKI, Mary 1843 - 1926 Mother (C)
(John & Mary Piechocki, Edward Wruble, Maryann Saunders, & David Lee Carroll same lot)
WROBLEWSKI, Joseph 1886 - no date (H)
WROBLEWSKI, Raymond 1921 - 23 June 1936 (PC1)

WROBLEWSKI, Frank no dates (D)
Bertha no dates (Nee: Piotrowski) (D)
(Valentine & Victoria Piotrowski same lot)
WROBLEWSKI, Antonette 14 May 1860 - 25 Jan 1934 (Nee: Holewinski) Mother (D)
Peter 24 June 1860 - 26 Mar 1930 Father (D)
Michael 1889 - 1930 Son (D)
WROBLEWSKI, Antonia Zaworski 1864 - 1946 (Nee: Nowasczewski) (E)
Andrew 1860 - 1920 #1 Husband (E)
(Marion Woodka same lot)
WROBLEWSKI, Hedwige 25 Aug 1900 - 28 Apr 1936 Mother (E)
(Stanislaw Zalas same lot)
WROBLEWSKI, Sylvia 1908 - 1927 (F)
Jozef A 1871 - 1930 Father (F)
Marya 1873 - 1930 (Nee: Kapsa) Mother (F)
(Leonard F Falda same lot)
WROBLEWSKI, Stanley 5 May 1855 - 6 Aug 1941 (F)
WROBLEWSKI, Joseph no dates Baby (F)
(Margaret Kominowski same lot)
WROBLEWSKI, Walter P 22 Jan 1895 - 22 Feb 1973 "Ohio Pfc Btry F 69 Arty CAC WWI" (G)
Bernice 1 Apr 1895 - 19-- "Born at Rhode Island" (Nee: Przystas) (G)
WROBLEWSKI, Edward 1 Aug 1911 - 22 Mar 1968 "Indiana EM 3 USNR WWII" (G)
WROBLEWSKI, Michael H 12 Jan 1954 - 10 Apr 1954 (H)
Henry M 29 Feb 1924 - 21 Dec 1944 "Indiana Pfc 511 Inf WWII" (H)
Frances S 1896 - 1970 (Nee: Leda) (H)
John J 1892 - 1941 (H)
WRUBEL or WROBEL, Edward J 1925 - 1927 (C)
(John & Mary Piechocki, Mary

WRUBEL (continued)
Wroblewski, Mary Ann Saunders, & David Lee Carroll same lot)
WRUBLE - WROBEL, Frank 1884 - 1957 Father (G)
Frances 1894 - 1972 Mother (G)
(Emilia Pawlak, & Wojciech & Stanislawa Pendzinski same lot)
WROTNOWSKI, A no dates (D)
B no dates (D)
(Vera Walkowiak, Victor Barber, A Gaik, & Louis M Hanyzewski same lot)
WRZESIEN, Richard J Jr 1951 - 1953 "Son of John & Mary Wrzesien" (G)
(Louis T & Chester Nowakowski same lot)
WYREMBLEWSKI, Josephine 1873 - 1951 Mother (D)
Peter 1871 - 21 Nov 1932 Father (D)
WYREMBLEWSKI, Sylvester 1900 - 1951 (F)
Louise 1897 - 1936 Mother (F)
WYRUSLAK, Edward no dates (D)
Helena no dates (D)
---- no dates Infant Son (D)
WYSOCKI, Antoni 5 May 1879 - 7 Apr 1914 (D)
YOUTS, Edward L 1916 - 1942 (G)
YUHASZ, Martha 5 Sept 1902 - 1979 (Nee: Radecki) (F)
Joseph 1909 - 19-- (F)
(Jozefa & Stanislaw Radecki same lot)
ZABLOCKI, Adam no date - 18 May 1915 (H)
Thomas 12 Aug 1858 - 4 July 1935 (H)
Agnes 1863 - 28 Nov 1926 (Nee: Karaczewski) (H)
ZACK (name was Zakrzewski), Richard Edward 1 Dec 1943 - 27 Dec 1965 "Indiana SP4 USA" (PC1)
(Frank & Mary Zakrzewski same lot)

ZAKOWSKI, Wojciech 1874 - 1955 (PC1)
Sabina 1881 - 1951 (PC1)
Aurelia 1910 - 1931 (PC1)
ZAKROCKI, Jozef 1862 - 1941 (C)
Ludwika 1861 - 1943 (Nee: Rzczeska) Mother (C)
Dorota 1917 - 1947 Daughter (C)
ZAKROCKI, Theodore 1887 - 1976 (C)
Eleanor 1890 - 1961 (C)
Regina 1911 - 16 Dec 1939 (C)
Dennis no date - 1915 (C)
ZAKROWSKI, Maria 1918 - 1919 (E)
Walenty 1880 - 1929 Father (E)
ZAKRZEWSKI, Jake no date - 5 Mar 1933 (C)
ZAKZEWSKI, William 1887 - 1933 (C)
Frank no dates Infant (C)
Carrie 1891 - 1924 (Nee: Marshal) (C)
ZAKRZEWSKI, Valentine 1856 - 1916 Father (D)
Mary 1880 - 1930 Mother (D)
Margaret Ann 1908 - 1929 Daughter (D)
Andrew B 1898 - 1969 Son (D)
ZAKRZEWSKI, Antony H 1884 - 1940 Father (E)
Mary A 1885 - 1965 Mother (E)
Esther Barbara 1912 - 1969 Daughter (E)
ZAKRZEWSKI, Bronislaw no dates Father (F)
Helena Davis 1901 - 1928 Daughter (F)
ZAKRZEWSKI, Stanislaw 1874 - 19 Aug1927 Father (F)
ZAKRZEWSKI, Mary 1888 - 1951 (PC1)
Frank 1885 - 1946 (PC1)
Roman 1927 - 1931 Son (PC1)
(Richard Edward Zack same lot)
ZALAS, Blanche no dates (Nee: Sieradzki) (A)
John no dates (A)
(John - Blanche Wisniewski same lot)
ZALAS, Josephine 1885 - 1964

125

ZALAS (continued)
"Wife of Stanley F Zalas" (A)
(Frank & Agnes Graczyk & Rose Trafka same lot)
ZALAS, Stanley F 1888 - 1953 WWI (D)
(Joseph Nowastowski, Jan Janiak, Mary Szabo Horvath, & Victor Putrzewski same lot)
ZALAS, Joseph 1890 - 1953 Father (C)
Helen 15 Apr 1891 - 1974 (Nee: Bolka) Mother (C)
ZALAS, Ludwik no dates "Placowka #125 - Polish Soldier" (E)
(Ludwik Buda same lot)
ZALAS, Joseph 1 Mar 1867 - 3 Jan 1927 (E)
Victor 13 Sept 1900 - 26 Oct 1929 (E)
ZALAS, Kuneguda 1874 - 1953 Mother (E)
Stanislaw 1866 - 1950 Father (E)
ZALAS, Stanley no date - 19 Jan 1917 (E)
(Hedwidge Wroblewski same lot)
ZALAS, Tomasz 1872 - 1947 Father (H)
ZALEWSKI, Chester no date - 1933 (A)
ZALEWSKI, Jan 1870 - 30 Apr 1920 Father "Born in Poland" (A)
ZAMIATOWSKI, Helena 8 Jan 1883 - 1936 (B)
Wawrzyniec 10 July 1872 - 1947 (B)
(Teresa Olejniczak same lot)
ZAMIATOWSKI, Stephen 10 July 1898 - 29 Nov 1921 (B)
ZAPALSKI, Anny 2 Aug 1906 - 9 Aug 1906 "First Burial on this Cemetery" (A)
Teresa 1876 - 1937 Mother (A)
Jan 1872 - 1955 Father (A)
Jadwiga 1909 - 1952 Daughter (A)
ZAPARTY, Margaret 1896 - 1967 (F)
(Piotr & Maryanna Maciulski same lot)

ZAREMBKA, Teofil 1889 - 12 June 1936 (A)
ZAREMBKA, Kazimierz 4 Mar 1883 - 22 May 1941 Father (B)
Rozalia 16 July 1883 - 23 Mar 1974 Mother (B)
George 1910 - 1973 (B)
ZAREMBKA, J no date - 30 Jan 1932 "Sokol ZB No 1" (C)
(F Cholewczynski & F Mrockiewicz same lot)
ZAROBINSKI, Stanley 1878 - 1966 (G)
Stella 1877 - 1961 (G)
Pelagia 4 July 1905 - 4 May 1923 (G)
ZASTAWA, Jan no date - 1933 (G)
Franciszka no dates (G)
(Martha Rybicki same lot)
ZAWACKI, Teofil 1855 - 21 Feb 1932 Father (F)
Maryanna 1867 - 1955 Mother (F)
ZAWACKI, Antony 1888 - 1948 (G)
Alexandria 1883 - 1956 (G)
ZAWACKI, Dorothy L 1914 - 1955 Mother (G)
Stanley A 9 Aug 1916 - 1971 Father (G)
---- no date - 23 June 1967 Infant (G)
ZAWIERUCHA, Jan 1869 - 1918 (C)
Jozefa 1881 - 1960 (Nee: Wlodarski) (C)
Stanislaw no date - 1916 (C)
ZAWODNY, Stanislaw 1869 - 26 Sept 1915 Father (A)
Theophilia 1874 - 1947 Mother (Nee: Grocka) (A)
Frank 1906 - 19-- Son (A)
ZAWORSKI, Michael no date - 9 Jan 1924 (-)
Francis no date - 2 Jan 1913 (-)
ZBIERALSKI, Casimir 1916 - 20 May 1932 (D)
ZBIERANSKI, Jozef 4 Mar 1862 - 9 Feb 1938 (F)
Maryanna 9 Aug 1858 - 1 June 1922 (F)

ZBIERANSKI, Edward 1910 - 1924 (F)
Frances 1888 - 1935 (Nee: Wisniewski) (F)
Frank 1886 - 1964 (F)
ZBRZEZNY, Stanislaw 1884 - 1952 (D)
(Antony Bargielski same lot)
ZBRZEZNY, Borek 1894 - 1947 Father (E)
Maryanna 1895 - 1919 (E)
ZDONIAK, Stanley 1909 - 19-- (F)
Lillian 10 Apr 1914 - 21 Apr 1980 (F)
(Jozef & Rozalia Olsowski same lot)
ZEBROWSKI, Jozefa 1863 - 1938 Mother (E)
Felix 1859 - 1922 Father (E)
ZELASKO, Constance 1859 - 1934 (Nee: Ciapnik) Mother (B)
Andrew 1849 - 30 Nov 1917 Father (B)
Carl 1917 - 1917 (B)
ZELAZKO, Peter no date - 23 Jan 1910 (-)
ZEMANEK, Amanda Marie no date - 1961 (F)
Mary no date - 1955 (F)
(Veronica & John Kloska same lot)
ZIARNIAK, Konstanty 1887 - 1949 (D)
Franciszka 1894 - 1918 (D)
ZIELINSKI, Adalbert no date - 5 Apr 1916 (A)
Antony no date - 21 Oct 1927 (A)
Stanley no date - 18 Dec 1935 (A)
ZIELINSKI, Jan 1855 - 26 May 1931 Father (A)
Rozalia 1860 - 1935 Mother (A)
Stanislaw 1914 - 1917 (A)
(Ludwig Springer & Frank J Green same lot)
ZIELINSKI, Pelegia 3 Mar 1885 - 13 Sept 1906 (A)
ZIELINSKI, Klemens 1914 - 1919 (C)
Louise 1895 - 9 Nov 1924 (C)

ZIELINSKI (continued)
John 1865 - 1947 (C)
Antonette 1869 - 1934 (C)
ZIELINSKI, Stanley 1873 - 1960 (C)
Hattie 1884 - 1968 (C)
Joseph 1907 - 1915 Son (C)
Cecylia 18 Nov 1917 - 18 Nov 1977 Sister (C)
ZIELINSKI, Stanislaw 1886 - 19-- Father (C)
Maryanna 4 Mar 1888 - 1936 (Nee: Golubski) Mother (C)
Heromin 1909 - 1917 Son (C)
Stefan 15 Mar 1885 - 31 Mar 1953 "Indiana Bugler Co D 16 Bn US Guards WWI" (C)
ZIELINSKI, John III 1953 - 1955 (D)
John S 10 Dec 1892 - 10 Apr 1973 "Indiana Pfc USA WWI" (D)
Vincent 1882 - 1974 (D)
Bert C no date - 16 Feb 1933 "Indiana Pvt 39 Inf" (D)
ZIELINSKI, Frank 1863 - 1953 Father (D)
Mary 1874 - 1944 (Nee: Bikowski) Mother (D)
Edward 1901 - 1946 Son (D)
(Julius Smith same lot)
ZIELINSKI, Antonina 5 Apr 1863 - 21 Oct 1921 (Nee: Inoralski) (E)
Rev Jozef A 28 Jan 1881 - 20 July 1953 "Ordained 21 June 1912" (E)
Sophie 1887 - 1966 (E)
ZIELINSKI, Maryanna 1885 - 1925 (E)
Tekla 1882 - 1948 (E)
Marion 1885 - 1968 (E)
ZIELINSKI, Constance 1854 - 1926 (F)
(Frank & Anna Roytek same lot)
ZIELINSKI, John E 1883 - 1951 (F)
Mary S 1889 - 1962 (Nee: Gruza) (F)
ZIELINSKI, Catharine 1884 - 1957 (F)
Albert 1876 - 7 Aug 1938 (F)

ZIELINSKI (continued)
Chester 1924 - 1978 (F)
Sylvester 1911 - 1928 (F)
ZIELINSKI, Stanley 1898 - 1935
(H)
Tony 1909 - 1939 (H)
George 1902 - 1979 (H)
ZIOLKOWSKI, Jacob 1850 - 24
Jan 1917 (C)
Michalena 1859 - 18 Mar 1923
Mother (C)
Antony 1892 - 1958 (C)
Stella 1899 - 1978 (C)
ZIOLKOWSKI, Frank J 1880 -
1965 Father (C)
Blanche V 1883 - 1969 (Nee:
Jankowski) Mother (C)
Gabriella 1904 - 1905 Daughter
(C) ·
ZIOLKOWSKI, Mae L 1907 -
1977 (Nee: Niezgodski) (C)
Eugene J 1905 - 14 Feb 1982 (C)
ZIOLKOWSKI, Maryanna 1885 -
1932 (Nee: Drews) Mother (F)
Jan 1882 - 11 June 1926 Father
(F)
ZMUDZINSKI, John no date - 7
July 1919 (A)
ZMUDZINSKI, Marta 1887 - 1971
Mother (A)
Stanislaw 1886 - 1928 Father (A)
ZMUDZINSKI, Wincenty 6 July
1879 - 23 Dec 1947 (C)
Salomeja 11 Dec 1882 - 10 Sept
1961 (Nee: Kazmierczak) (C)
ZMUDZINSKI, Edward J 1906 -
1977 (E)
Minnie A 1907 - 19-- (E)
ZMUDZINSKI, Anton 1881 - 1974
(PC1)
Catharine 1880 - 1965 (Nee:
Sobieraj) (PC1)
(Petronela Sobieraj same lot)
ZMUDZINSKI, George J 1883 -
1965 (PC1)
Mary 1885 - 1962 (Nee: Gorka)
(PC1)
Alice 1918 - 1978 (PC1)
ZMYSLO, Peter no dates (-)
ZUBRAS FAMILY, ---- no dates
(G)
(Waranowycz Family same lot)

ZUK, Jadwiga Apolonia 1913 -
1931 (G)
Marya 1912 - 1933 (G)
Pauline 1889 - 1971 Mother (G)
Michael K 1881 - 1940 Father
(G)
Henryk M 1917 - 1945 Son (G)
ZUKOWSKI, Samuel 1882 - 1973
(E)
Jozefa 1891 - 1977 (E)
(Stanislaw Walczak & Jan
Haluda same lot)
ZULTANSKI, Stanley 1879 - 1932
(with picture) Father (C)
Sophie 1889 - 1938 (with picture)
Mother (C)
Irene Molly 1924 - 1950 (with
picture) Daughter (C)
Lottie 1910 - 1917 (C)
Alice 1923 - 1923 (C)
ZURAT, Katharine 1872 - 1939
(F)
Lillian 1899 - 1930 (F)
Joseph 1865 - 5 May 1930 (F)
John 1900 - 1944 (F)
Aloysius no date - 1927 9m old
(F)
ZURAWSKI, John no date - 20
Sept 1934 (PC1)
ZUROMSKI, K 1848 - 1917 (A)
ZWIERZYNSKI, Frank no date -
28 Mar 1918 (B)
ZWIERZYNSKI, Laura 1893 -
1963 Mother (G)
Peter 1882 - 1951 Father (G)
ZYGULSKI, Stanislaw 1885 - 30
Aug 1938 (B)
Jadwiga 1890 - 1945 Mother (B)
Raymond R Jr no date - 1948
Grandson (B)
Ceasor S 22 July 1912 - 30 Apr
1959 "Indiana Pvt Co B 777
MP BN WWII" (B)
ZYGULSKI, Ludwik 1878 - 1954
Father (D)
Maryanna 1887 - 1952 Mother (D)
Walenty 1911 - 23 July 1938 Son
(D)
ZYGULSKI, Michael 1906 - 14
Feb 1938 (PC1)
ZYSKI, John 1881 - 1 May 1933
(D)

ZYIO, Antonina 1868 - 1935 Mother (C)
Franciszek 1871 - 1950 Father (C)
ZYTO, John 1896 - 19-- (F)
Bertha 1896 - 1973 (Nee: Grontkowski) (F)
(Bert Sokolowski & Stephen Grontkowski same lot)

ZYTOWSKI, Wojciech 1831 - 4 Feb 1928 Father (F)
Maryanna Herman 1850 - 13 July 1939 (Nee: Wisniewski) (F)
Tomasz 1877 - 1941 Son (F)
(Andrzej Herman same lot)
ZYTOWSKI, Jozef S 1882 - 1923 Son (B)
ZYZAK, Andrzej 1887 - 1944 Husband, Father (F)

INDEX

This index lists women with maiden names and individuals found in the "same lot".

BLASCZYK, Salomea 41 Teofil
41
BLOMBERG, Thaddeus 71
BOBOWSKI, Amelia 52 Antoni 33
52 Emilia 33
BOBROWSKI, Michael 82
Petronella 82
BOCHER, Lisa Marie 114
BOCHERS, Lisa Marie 109
BOCK, Charles 117 120
BODGE, Helena V 96
BOJARSKI, Maryann 17
BOJEWICZ, Helen 71 Wanda 104
BOKOWSKI, Reginia 36
BOLKA, Alfred 22 Helen 126
Jozef 22 Jozef T 34 106 Mary
A 106 Stanislaw 51
BONCZYNSKI, Cecylia 38 Fran-
ciszek 38 Stella 38 Walenty 38
BONEK, Hattie 6 Victoria 97
Wojciech 64 107 118
BONIEWSKI, Steve 96
BORKOWSKI, Agnes 79 Andrew
79 Wojciech 22
BORLIK, Helen T 30 Klara
Grzesk 30 Martha 35 Sophie
121 Stanislawa 13
BOROWSKI, Antoni 121 Eleanora
121 Jozefa 105 Walter 106
Walter M 122
BORYC, Agnes 12 Mary 102
BORZESKOWSKI, Anna 34
BOTKA, Helen 3 Mary 80
BRABAREK, Elizabeth 70
BRAMBERT, Alice 38 Ignace 38
Laura 11 Pauline 11 94
BRANSON, Cecylia 9 Clara 9
BREKUS, Eleanor 36 43 Hattie
105
BRIAN, Fritz 84
BROCZINSKI, Anna 56
BRODOWSKI, Theresa 77
BRODZINSKI, Rose 25
BROWNELL, Nancy Kubiak 87
BRUSICK, Joseph 29 65
BRYLEWSKI, Agnes 9 Josephine
92 Szymon 9
BRYSKI, F 77
BRZENIAK, Rosalia 110 111
BRZEZINSKI, Bernice 26 Frank
26 Ignatius 44 Rose 44

BRZUSZKIEWICZ, Hattie 12
Stanislaw 12 Victoria 12
BUCHOLTZ, Agnieszka 30 An-
tonina 49 Frances 12 Valentine
12
BUCZKIEWICZ, Jozefa 67
BUDA, Ludwik 126
BUDZIANOWSKI, Jadwiga 84
BUDZINSKI, Casimir 121 Hattie
121 James J 24
BURLINGTON, Rosalie Elizabeth
32
BURZYNSKI, Mary K 41 Salomea
3
BUSZKIEWICZ, Wojciech 89 111
BUYSSE, Leonard 17
BUZALSKI, Frank 87 Verna 87
CADUFF, Rita Muszynski 41
CAMPBELL, Carrie 120
CARROLL, David Lee 85 98 124
125
CASNER, John William 79
CASSLER, Wladzia 83
CELICHOWSKI, Jacob 8 94
Lottie 107
CENCELEWSKI, Mary 71
CHAVIS, Edward 10 Henrietta 10
CHLEBEK, Irene 92 118 Wladys-
lawa 105
CHMIEL, Amelia 29 Apolonia 29
Stella 48 Victoria 68 Vincent
48 Wanda 48
CHMIELEWSKI, Bronislawa 123
Emilia 85 86 Frances 39 Mary
113 Maryanna 113 Michael 113
CHMILEWSKI, Wladyslawa 46
CHODZINSKI, Hattie 9 Stanislaw
9
CHOJNACKI, Anna 95 Rozalia
108
CHOLAJ, Alexander 73 Helen 73
CHOLAZ, Magdelena 2
CHOLEWCZYNSKI, F 126 Helen
116 Mary 33
CHRAPEK, Aloysius 74 Harriet
74
CHROBOT, Jan 87 Stanislawa 87
CHRUSTOWSKI, Jan 102 Jozefa
102 Maryanna 102
CHRZAN, Edward 75 Jennie 66
Mary 57 Pelegia 42 Stella 73

CHUDZICKI, Katarzyna 83 Kenneth 64
CIAPNIK, Constance 127
CICHOS, Mary 40 Thomas 40
CIERNIAK, Konstanaty 73 Zofia 73
CIESIOLKA, Amelia 112 Anthony A 1 Bernice 5 106 Forest 5 106 Mary 24 Marya R 100
CIUPINSKI, W 23 100
CLINE, Max A 20
COOK, Frederich 63
COOPER, Rose 97
CRISWELL, Debra 109 110
CUKROWICZ, Anna 24 Franciszek 24 Klara 102 Tadeusz 24 Zygmond 24
CWIDAK, Jan 122 Joseph 31 Mary B 20 Nettie 117
CWIKLINSKI, Clara 89 Konstanty 20 Walter 89
CYGART, Adam 84 Frances 84 Peter 84 Stella 84
CYMAN, Francis 35 Jadwiga 35
CYNDROWSKI, John 30 Rose 30
CYRANOWSKI, Agnieszka 1 Constance 73
CZERNIAK, Antonina 54 Katarzyna 54 Sally 52
CZEWINSKI, Sophie 42
CZYCZEWSKI, Katarzyna 108
CZYZEWSKI, Frank 102
DALDOWSKI, Pelegia 76
DALKA, Mary 31
DALKOWSKI, Emelia 17 Salomea 119 Konstancia 86 Konstancya 84 Mary 69 Piotr 84 86
DASZYNSKI, Albert 25 William 25
DAVIS, Milton 56
DEGUS, Stephaniw 114 Vincent 114
DEJAEGHER, Hattie 11 89
DEJEIGHER, Hattie 111
DEKA, Bernard 11 Clara 8 Esther 11 Margaret 11 Richard W 53 Stella 23
DELINSKI, Sophia 4
DEMBICKI, Frank 45 85
DEMBINSKI, Andrew 28 Rozalia 9
DEMKIEWICZ, Marya 16
DEMSKA, Julia 101

DERANEK, Katarzyna 34
DERDA, Mary 48
DERESZYNSKI, Agnes 49 Agnieszka 41 111 112
DERUYCK, Arthur J 92 Blanche V 92
DeSHONG, Virginia 76
DIETZ, Anna 82 Eva 112 John 112 John J 112 William 101
DLUGOSZ, Caroline 6 Wojciech 6
DOMBROWSKI, Alexander 74 Bernice 74 Casimir 115 Mateusz 27
DOMSKI, Sylvester 4
DOPIERALSKI, William Stanislaw 51
DRAJUS, Felix 116 Julia 18 Katarzana 15 Mary 116
DREJER, Frank 20
DREW, 31
DREWS, Helena 12 Maryanna 128
DUBICKI, Alex 85 113 Stella 85 113
DUDEK, Jacob 5 Stella 43
DUDKA, John 30
DUDZINSKI, Antony 15 Joseph 15 Mary 15
DURSKI, Mary M 69
DUSZYNSKI, Marya 68 Maryanna 75 Michael 32
DYNARSKI, Victoria 42
DYSKIEWICZ, Josephine 58 Peter 58
DYSZKIEWICZ, Maryanna 64
DZIEDZIC, Joseph 107
DZIEWA, Katarzyna 3
DZIKOWSKI, Mary Helen 119
DZIUBINSKI, Joseph 57
EBEL, Constance P 46
EITLER, Bernice 81 Paul 81
ELANTKOWSKI, Jan 117 Julia 117
ELANTOWSKI, Jan 79 Julia 79
ERNSDORF, Antonina 25
EWALD, Agnes 56 Agnieszka 40 Arthur 56 Augustyna 43 Herbert 56 Jozef 56 Katarzyna 114 Katharine 69 Maryanna 40 Michael 40 Paulina 37 Teodor 114 Teodore 69
FALDA, Leonard F 124
FELDMIER, Dallas 82

FENWICK, Helen 7
FIGORSKI, Katarzyna 38
FILIPEK, Mary 95
FILIPIAK, Magdelena 80 Mary 83
FISCHER, Clementine 72 Roman
  27 Stanley 27
FISHER, Boleslaw 34 Father 98
  Mother 98 Stanley 3
FLEUGAL, Clara M 7
FLORKOWSKI, Bridget 7
FLOWERS, Peter 58
FOLEY, Domocela 45
FORECKI, Maryanna 47
FOX, Christopher 63
FRACKOWIAK, Martha R 103
  Rozalia 91
FRANKOWSKI, Malgorzata 91
FRITZ, Brian C 15 Joseph 15 100
FUJAWA, Anna 61 Maryanna 41
  Rudolph 61 Stanislaw 108 Stan-
  ley B 34 Wiktorya 108
FUTA, Harriet 78 Mary 78
  Walenty 78
GABRYS, Jozef 104
GADACZ, Agnes 74 John 45 Mary
  45 Maryanna 25 26 Pelagia 13
  Wiktorya 23 Wladyslaw K 17
GADOWSKI, George 115 Martha
  115
GAEBLER, Frank E 26
GAIK, A 4 115 125 Zuzanna 102
GALLEGOS, Mary E 96
GALUS, Mary 10 Michael 10
GALWAS, Wladyslaw 15
GASIOROWSKI, Balbina 46 Hilary
  9 Joe 9 Rose 9
GAWRONSKI, Adeline 30 Jozef
  58 112 Theresa 30
GEABLER, Agnieszka 17 Andy 17
  Frank E 23
GERYK, Julianna 20
GIERSE, John 5 Josephine 5
GIERSZ, Veronica 38
GIERSZEWSKI, Balbina 118
GIERYK, Martha 30
GIERZYNSKI, Julia 79
GIEST, Martin 121
GILAS, Stanislaw 77
GINTER, Bronislawa 49 Frances
  89
GISZEWSKI, Helena 34

GLENIEWICZ, Bernice 19
  Frances 100 Jacob 100
GLON, Frances L 87 Joanna C 58
  Michalena 37 Paul 25 Paul R
  23
GNIOT, Mary 16 Marya 36
GNOTH, Anna 123
GOLUBIC, Clementine 9
GOLUBSKI, Barbara 4 Irene 53
  Leonard 86 Maryanna 127 Nor-
  bert 86
GOLUPSKI, Eleanora 98 Frank J
  98
GONIA, Catharine 51
GONSIOROWSKI, Antony 83
  Hilary 9 Joe 9 Lottie G 62
  Mary 83
GORACZEWSKI, Adam 48 108
  Anna 108 Josephine 48 Jozefa
  108 Klemens 50
GORAJEWSKI, Stanley 19
GORALCZYK, Anna 97 Anna
  Ryska 24 Marcin 97
GORECKA, Marcyanna 53
GORKA, Helen 59 Mary 128 Syl-
  vester 59
GORNA, Maryanna 99
GORNEY, Eleanor 106 Mary Rose
  48 49 Rose 91 100 106 Sophie
  106
GORNIA, Francis 37
GORNIAK, Prakseda 2 3
GORNIEWICZ, Ignacy 48 Mar-
  cyanna 48
GORNY, Helena 84
GORSKI, Bertha 84 Casimir 18
GOTH, Anna 123
GRABAREK, Anna 52 Elizabeth
  70 Maryanna 22 Vincent 70
GRABARZ, Mary A 92
GRABOWSKI, Agnieszka 112
GRACKOWSKI, Stella K 83
GRACZYK, Agnes 113 125 126
  Antonette 105 Frank 113 125
  126 Jan 105 Stanislaw 45 Stan-
  ley 37
GRAMZA, Stella 27 Theresa 114
GRATZIELLA, Julianna 6
GREEN, Frank J 104 127
GREENWALD, Mary 38
GREMBOWICZ, Maryanna 81
  Wawrzyniec 81

GROCHOLSKI, Marya 70
GROCHOWSKI, Boleslaw 109
Jozefa 109 Stefania 97 Victor
94
GROCHULSKI, Jozefa 70
GROCKA, Theophilia 126
GROCKI, Henrietta 113 Julianna
63 Mieczyslaw 113
GRODZICKI, Vincent 9
GRONTKOWSKI, Bertha 129 Har-
riet 61 Jozef 12 Stephen 103
129
GROTKOWSKI, Lottie 96 Peter
96
GRUDZICKI, Joseph 65 Vincent
65
GRUSZYNSKI, Maryanna 70
GRUZA, Mary S 127
GRYCKA, Rose 9
GRZECHOWIAK, Mary 34
GRZEGOREK, Angela 6 Anna 48
Mary 43 Maryanna 121 Tomasz
31 Walenty 43 Wiktoria 43
GRZEGOZEWSKI, Mary 35
GRZELEWSKI, Jozef 39 Wladys-
lawa 39
GRZESK, Eleanora 46 Klara 8
Leokadya 13 Martha 8 Wladys-
law 8
GRZESKOWIAK, Agnes 69
Andrzej 79 Katarzyna 55 Mar-
cin 69 Maryanna 79
GRZEZINSKI, Catharine 40
GUENTHER, Clara 37
GURCZAK ,Joseph 20
GUSICKI, Rosalie 112 113
GUTEK, Jozef 25 111
GUZICKI, Adalbert 51 65 An-
tonina 51 Antony 16 Hedwige
16 Joseph 42 Michael 35 51
Rose 16 Veronica Janczak 51
GUZOWSKI, Alice 30
HAGEN, Stella Vander 109
HAHN, Henry 56 Henry X 17
HAINES, Emma 1 2
HAJDUK, Wiktorya 34
HALAS, Frances 61
HALUDA, Jan 115 128
HANYZESKI, Louis M 115
HANYZEWSKI, Aniela 12 Anna
46 Carrie 86 Casimer 20
Casimir 116 Ignatius 86 John

HANYZEWSKI (continued)
31 Jozef 46 Leokadya 55 Louis
4 Louis M 24 125 Magdelena
116 Mary Herman 15 Michael
48
HARMACINSKI, Helen 96 Martha
76
HASKO, Mary 109
HAZINSKI, Joan F 52
HECHLINSKI, Antonina 85 Jan 85
HEGEDUS, Helen L 47
HELMINIAK, Mary 33
HENCELEWSKI, Bernice 45 84
Frances 84 Francis 45
HENNET, Magdaline 3
HERMA, Elizabeth 10 Joseph 10
HERMAN, Andrzej 129 Elizabeth
20 Eugene 76 John 20 Mary A
31 Maryanna 20 Michalena 51
Pelegia 56
HES, Agnieszka 56 Cecylia 115
Wladyslaw 82
HESS, Mike 44 Victoria 75
HOFFMAN, Alex P 78 Andrzej 31
Frank 31 Helena 59 John 31
Mary 31 Rozalia 31
HOJNACKI, Boleslaw 83 Bronis-
law 3 Clara 83 Jozefa 6 Tekla
54 70
HOLEWCZYNSKI, Jozef 13
Maciej 13
HOLEWINSKI, Antonette 124
Carrie 5 Mary 23 Victoria T 10
HOLTZ, Peter J 114
HORKA, Klementyna 117
HORNUNG, Matthew 25
HORVATH, Mary Szabo 91 126
Mary Szako 79
HOSINSKI, Cecylia 51 Edmund 23
Florence 124 Jan 18 Joan 45
Katarzyna 18 124 Katharine
119 Victoria 18 William 119
124
HOUSER, Wiktorya 22
HUBER, Mary A Bolka 106
HUDAK, Anna 68 72 Michael 68
72 97
IIYEKIEL, Wladyslaw 29
INORALSKI, Antonina 127
ISBAN, Alex 94 Alex A 64
IZDEPSKI, Praxida 73
JABLOCKI, Stephania 17

JABLONSKI, Antonette 60 Carrie
114 Teofilia 104
JACHIMIAK, Antonette 75
JACKMOVICH, Joseph 60 Joseph
S 52
JACKOWIAK, Cecylia 67
JAGLA, Catharine 29 Lottie 69
Stella 16
JAGODITS, Dorothy 75
JAGODZINSKI, Hedwige 6
Julianna 59 Marcelli 51 Stanis-
lawa 51
JAHNZ, Frank 112 Laura 112
JAKUBIAK, Micheline 55
JAMROZY, Catharine 69 Jozef 69
JANCZAK, Stanislaw 30 51
JANDALA, Marya 84
JANDOLA, Maria 113 Marya 50
JANIAK, Jan 79 91 126
JANICKI, Bernice 31 Pauline 8
JANISZAK, Jozefa 19
JANISZEWSKI, Bronislawa 9 43
Nicesor 9
JANKOWIAK, Bernard 70 Frances
A 45 Josephine 71
JANKOWSKI, Anna 2 Antony 80
Cecylia 78 105 Frank 77 112
Helen 80 Ignacy 113 Jan 78
105 Jozef 75 76 Konstancia 78
Louis 71 Martin 62 76 Mary 61
77 112 113 Maryann 84
Michalena 15 Sophia 62 Sophie
76 Stanislawa 51 Tillie 76
Tomasz 15 Wladyslawa 77
JANOWCZYK, Leokadya 6
JANOWIAK, Franciszka 24 Helen
M 39 Konstancia 85 Valentine
90
JANOWSKI, Joseph J 86
Konstancia 86
JAREMBA, Chrystina 102
JARONIK, Walter A 30
JAROSZEWSKI, Christine 13
Clara W 48 Franciszek 90
Frank 28 45 Helena Kazmiera
106 Jozefa 28 45 Katarzyna 90
Martha 48 Napomycyna 87
Veronica 28 William J 28
JASICKI, Antoni 90 John P 43 99
Katharine 91 Mary 8
JASINSKI, Agnieszka 51 Anna 112
120 Ewa 10 Mary R 106

JASINSKI (continued)
Maryanna 65 Ralph J 122 123
Wawrzyniec 112 120
JASKIEWICZ, Helena 7 Maryanna
110
JAWORSKI, Katarzyna 56
Marianna 45 Rozalia 118
JEDRACZKIEWICZ, Michalia 53
JEDRZEJCZAK, Maryann 18
JEDRZEJEWSKI, Catharine 71
JEGIER, Anna 92 Helen 98 Katar-
zyna 98
JENCZAK, Agnes 121 122 Vic-
toria 121 122
JENCZEWSKI, Frank C 94 Stella
107 Walter 107
JENDRZEJEWSKI, Catharine 70
Henrietta 114 Magdolina 79
JERECKI, Marya 97
JERZEKOWSKI, Marya 83
JERZYKOWSKI, Jan 29 Michael
112 Tillie 112
JESKO, Jozefa 90
JEZIORSKI, Bernice M 9 Elzbieta
2 Joseph S 121 Martha E 73
JOACHMIAK, Martin 59
JONAS, Stanley J 58
JORDANEK, Isadore 82
JOZWIAK, Ernest 64 Florence 64
Frank 30 Maryanna 14 Stanley
C 52
JULKOWSKI, Wladyslawa 69
JURCZYK, Agnieszka 21
JUREK, Antonina 35
JURGONSKI, Jan 6 Josie A 97
Maryanna 6 Salomea 6
JURKIEWICZ, Julianna 82
Julianna M 107
KACZMAREK, Adam 108 Jakub
11 70 74 Michaline 116 Tekla
62
KACZOROWSKI, Angela 109
KAISER, Emilia 5 Katarzyna 42
KAJZER, Helena 24 Jozef 18 49
Jozefa 49 Maryanna 111
KALAMAJA, Hattie 63 Jozef 56
Katarzyna 56 Stella 69
Theodora 51
KALAMAJSKI, Julia I 64 Leonard
J 64
KALAWAGA, Cora 49
KALICKI, Marianna 92 Maryanna

KALICKI (continued)
116
KALINSKI, Emilia 6
KALKA, Frances 31 Maryann 96
KALUZNEY, Frank 95
KALUZNY, Frank 51
KAMINISKI, Andrzej 104 Blanche
(Pelegia) 109 Josephine 104
KAMINSKI, Clara 51 Frank 38 99
Jan 97 Jan F 47 Leon 94 Lucy
94 Maryanna 18 Pelegia 97
Stanislaw 88 Stanislawa 47
Walter 51
KANCZCZEWSKI, Alicya 74
Walenty 74
KANCZUCZEWSKI, Alicya 50
Walenty 50
KANCZUZEWSKI, Antony 119
Mary 119 Walter P 57
KANIEWSKI, Bronislawa 36
Eleanora 9 Mary 29 Rose 27
Valentine 29 Vincent K 9 36
KAPALCZEWSKI, Mary E 101
KAPALCZYNSKI, Antonina 82
Elizabeth M 113 Jozef 76
Magdalena 76
KAPSA, Andrzej 59 Anna 122
John 122 Jozefa 59 Mary 124
Marya 124 Rose 109 Stanis-
lawa 56
KAPUSTA, Adam 100 ·
KARASCEWSKI, Agnes 125
KARBOSKI, Bert 32
KARBOWSKI, Lorraine Rose 32
Rose 32
KARCEWSKI, John 2
KARCZEWSKI, Bernice 121 John
121 Lillian 121 Martin J 45
Mary 122
KARPINSKI, Genewefa 58 John 94
KASPRZAK, Eva 110 Felex 84
Felix 32 Joan 94 Joseph J 22
Leonard 44 Matthew J 94
Teofil 50
KASUIRSKA, Martha 9
KATAMOJA, Frances 91
KAY, Antonette 18 Antonette H 85
KAZMIERCZAK, Blanche G 54
Cathrine 115 Joanna 89 John
81 Joseph 89 Mary 81 Patricia
Ann 28 37 Phyllis 4 Salomeja
128 Ted 24 Theodore 4 Walter

KAZMIERCZAK (continued)
89
KAZMIERSKI, Blanche 47
KAZMIRSKI, Mary 94
KENCKA, Mary 54
KENDZIORA, Frank 84 Mary 84
KENDZIORSKI, Frank 110 118
Harry F 92 Helen 7 Mary 92
KIELOCH, Mary 120
KIELOCK, Marie 61
KIELSZEK, Jozefa 115
KIELTON, Evelyn 31 Helen 31
Joseph 31 Melvyn 31
KILMER, Walter 47
KIMMEL, Fred Casimir 89 Jozefa
89
KIMNICZ, Josephine 67
KISKA, Dorothy 42
KITKOWSKI, Maryanna 68 Stanis-
lawa 12
KLAYBOR, Jan F 47 John 91
KLEIN, J Roman 32
KLEMCZEWSKI, 47
KLIMCZUK, Felix 1
KLOCKOWSKI, Maryanna 47
Mikolaj 47 Walyntina 87
KLODZINSKI, Alexandria 111
Blazy 31 Marian 111 Marion 47
Stefen 14 Zofia 31
KLOS, Pelegia 27 Weronika 8
KLOSINSKI, Hattie 41 Janina 27
108 Joseph 95 Mary 3 95 Wal-
ter 4
KLOSKA, John 127 Veronica 127
KLOSOWSKI, Blanche 11
KLOTA, Blanche 6 Walter 12
Wanda 12
KLUGA, JAN 18
KLUSZYNSKI, Cecylia 70
KLYSZ, Bert 52 61 80 Clara 38
KMITTA, Franciszek 117
KNAPE, Edward 27 91 100
KNOTH, Anna 117
KOLACZ, Agnieszka 1 Balbina 77
Catharine 115
KOLCZNSKI, Casimir 85 Hattie
85
KOLCZYNSKI, Zygmont 41 Zyg-
mund 18 Zygmunt 111 112
KOLECKI, Cora 11 Franciszka 67
Frank 11 Joseph 11 William
11

KOLESIAK, Antony F 117 Katar-
zyna 19 Wanda 112
KOLO, Madelena Marya Mul-
tanski 43
KOLOCZYK, Balbina 53 Joseph
53
KOLUPA, Harry 67 Mary 67
KOMASINSKI, Jan 122 Jessie 53
Mary 122 Stanley 53
KOMINOWSKI, Kasimir 70 Mar-
garet 124
KONIECKA, Antonina 73 74
KONSTANCIA, Joseph J 86
KONSTANTY, Frank 54 102 119
Jozefa 52 Victoria 54 119 Wik-
torya 102
KONTNIK, Bronislaw 113
KOPCZYNSKI, Anna 103
Teodozia 45
KOPINSKI, Agnieszka 37
KORN, Veronica 35 Veronica
Janczak 30
KORPAL, Helen C 54
KOSCH, Josephine 42 Theodore
42 95
KOSIAK, Franciszek 19 Karolina
19
KOSIK, Agnes 92
KOSTRUV, Steve 7
KOSZEWSKI, Paul 43
KOVACH, Karen M 30 65
KOVACS, Karl 35
KOWALEWSKI, Agnes 94 Joseph
J 40 Mary 40 Myrtle E 66
KOWALSKI, Casiemiera 10 Joan
J 31 Petronella 9
KOZACH, Bertha 121
KOZAKIEWICZ, Allen 100 107
Wilbert 100 107
KOZLOWSKI, Alexandria
Lasowicki 60 Franciszka 116
117 Julian 6 33 Szymon 60
KOZUCH, Patricia May 48 61 80
KRAKOWSKI, Adalbert 4 An-
tonina 104 Frank 104 Joseph 4
Sally 4
KRAMASZEWSKI, Konstanty 66
Pelegia 66
KRANTZ, Bronislawa 17 Jan 17
KRASINSKI, John 33
KRECIOCKI, Ann Koloczyk 50
KRECMER, Helen 6

KRECZMER, Bronislawa 17
Helen 76 Peter 96 Stefan 96
Walter 96
KREMPETZ, Thaddeusz 50
KRILL, Christine Deanna 117
Michael Allen 117 Wm
Michael 117
KRISTOFSKI, Stella 95 Stephen A
95
KROL, Esther 94 Marcyanna 26
Michael 26
KROMKOWSKI, Franceszek 16
Jan 16 Katarzyna 16 Maryanna
18
KROTNIK, Bronislaw 35 84
KRUK, Anna 73 Anna R 72 Jozef
50 102 119
KRUSZEWSKI, Jan 46 Katarzyna
46 Marta 20 Mary 35
KRUSZKA, Pelegia 102 Teresa 41
42 Weronika 33 70
KRUSZYNSKI, Josephine Jan 45
KRYCH, Piotr 35
KSYCKI, Antoni 94 Helen 46 94
Jozefa 94
KUBACKI, Rev John F 10
KUBIAK, Gertrude 101 Katarzyna
38 Martin 42 Michael 38 Syl-
vester F 67
KUBISIAK, Leo 17 31
KUCHARSKI, Frances 50
KUCZMANSKI, Eleanora 97
KUCZWARA, Agnes 112 Fran-
ciszka 113 Mary 12
KUJ, Jan 44 Victoria 44
KUJAWA, Antonina 97 Cecylia J
64 Mary 21 Pelegia 50
KUJAWSKI, Alex W 98 Antony 18
Celia 28 Frances 97 Frank 98
John 61 Jozefa 61 Maryanna 87
Walentyna 68
KUKLA, Casimir 60 119 Sophie
60 119
KULEBERDA, Franciszek 64
Franciszka 64
KULIBERDA, Franciszek 68
Franciszka 68
KULIBERSKI, Pearl 74
KURAKIEWICZ, Stella 5
KURASZ, Magdalena 60
KUREK, Victoria 76
KUROWSKI, Joseph 21

KUS, Agnes 72
KUSH, Agnes 114 John 114 Mary
    45 Maryanna 78
KUSMIEZ, Wojciech 40
KUSPA, Blanche J 25 112
    Petronella 8 Vincent 122
KUZUCH, Jozef 50
KWASNECKI, Bert 21 Stella 21
KWASNIEWSKI, Joseph 79
KWESTOROWSKI, Maryanna 49
KWIATKOWSKI, John 22 Mary 22
    Vincent 22
KWITEK, Frances 88 John 72 88
    Rozalia 72
LABIS, Henrietta 40 Joseph 97
    June Marie 40 Stella 97
    Thomas 40 Walter 40
LABODA, Agnieszka 17
LACHOWSKI, Verna 39
LAKOMSKI, John 94
LAPCZYNSKI, Frances 25
    Michalina 88
LASECKI, Apolonia 71
LASKOWSKI, Agnes 116 Apolonia
    58 Bert 105 Franciszek 43
    Frank 60 George 105 Hattie 60
    Hattie Rose 105 Joanna 41
    Jozef 86 Jozefa 43 60 Kate 63
    Marcyanna 86 Marta 5 Mary
    105 Maryanna 34 Seweryna 119
    Stella K 47 Szczepan 116
    Veronica 86 Wladyslaw 119
    Wladyslaw J 57
LASOWICKI, Alexandria 35
    Konstanty 35 52 Szymon 35
LATKOWSKI, Marcelli 68
    Veronika 68
LE VAN, Blanche 62 Charles 62
LECHTANSKI, Antoni 86 Elfreda
    Butts 76
LEDA, Al J 57 Andrzej 90 Antony
    124 Apolonia 64 Elizabeth 29
    Frances S 124 Henry 23 Joseph
    29 Maryanna 90 101 Stanislawa
    71 124 Wladyslawa 11 Woj-
    ciech 64
LEHMAN, Viola G 104
LEMANSKI, Stella 52 90 Victoria
    104
LENCKI, Ludwig 48 80 Ludwik 52
LENTYCH, Bernard 106 Jan 120
    John 46 Theresa 106

LEONARD, Genevieve 68 114
LESIECKI, Helen 122
LESNIEWICZ, Jozef 71
LESNIEWSKI, Joseph 90 Stella
    90
LESZCZ, Stella T 37
LEWANDOWSKI, Anastazya 62
    Helena 21 26 Katharine 36 76
    Michael 62
LEWIECKI, Franciszek 112
LEWINSKI, Aloysius 117 Lillian
    117 Praxeda (Sadie) 1
LIGOWSKI, Weronika 96
LIS, Anna 53
LISEK, Jan 111 John 72
    Josephine 45 76 Rose 70
    Stanislawa 72 111
LISIECKA, Maryanna 1
LISIECKI, Josephine 97 Ray 23
LISNIEWICZ, Urszula 121
LISZEWSKI, Ignacy 122 John 85
    Jozefa 89 Mary 85 Maryanna 4
    Sophie 15
LIWOSZ, Florence 40 Katarzyna
    40 Stanislaw 40
LODYGA, Apolonia 61 116 Jan 34
    94 Jozef 14 Jozefa 34 Leda
    116 Mary 116 Marya 110
    Michael 61 116 Pelegia 81
    Rose 14 116 Wojciech 116
LONG, Stella 57
LOOMIS, Cecylia 9 Helen 9
LOPEZ, Maria 83 95 Ramiro 22
    83 95
LOUCK, Josephine 42
LUCZKOWSKI, Anna 70 Frank
    112 Matthew 59 112 Raymond
    7 107 118 Stanley J 70 Stella
    59 112 Teresa 73 Vern S 73
LUKASIAK, Leonard 51
LUKASIEWICZ, Albert 99
    Frances 99 Martha 101
LUKASIK, Leonard 30
LUKASZEWSKI, Nancy 48
LUKOWSKI, Clara Paris 33
LUPA, Alice 9 29 Stanley 9 29
LUPINSKI, Anna 29
LUSA, Maryanna 66
LUZNY, Joseph 55 Pelegia 55
LYCZYNSKI, Franciszek 97 Jad-
    wiga 97 James J 108
LYKOSKA, Constance 23

139

MROCZKIEWSKI, Franciszka 79
MUCHA, Anna 73 Ludwik 73
MUCHLICKI, Kazimierz 107
MUROWSKI, Jozefa 105
MUSZYNSKI, Michael 68 Pearl 68
  Rita 70
MYSLINSKI, Joseph 87
MYSZAK, Patricia 24 93 Ralph 24
  93
MYTYK, Ludwika 122 Walenty
  122
NAJDEK, Roman 102 Tadeusz
  102
NAPIERALSKI, Maryanna 20
NASH, Stephen 74
NASZTKA, John 74 Josephine 74
NAVE, Marjorie 87
NAWROCKI, Franciszek 84 Mal-
  gorzata 84
NDIEDBALSKI, Helena 120
NEMETH, Zigmond 13
NICESOR, 43
NIEDBALSKI, Helen 3 Helena 120
  Martha 53 54 Pelegia 108 Wit
  35
NIEMIER, Agnieszka Magdelena
  71 George 68 Lucy 32 Mary 45
  68 Melchior 101 Victoria 68
NIESPODZIANY, Antony 36
  Dorothy 105 Franciszka 72
  Frank 46 99 George 11 60
  Joanna 18 Jozefa 36 92 Mary
  96 99 105 Maryanna 107
  Michael 18 Paul 105 Pearl 11
  60
NIESPODZINANY, Robert D 63
NIEZGODSKI, Agnes 115 An-
  tonina 3 90 Barbara M 60
  Franciszka 114 Frank 36
  Joseph 115 Lillian M 57 Lud-
  wik 3 90 Mae L 128 Nettie 67
  Patricia 43 Teofilia 123
  Thomas 36 Tillie 36 62
NIJAK, Anna 32 Clement 32
  Katharine 63
NITKA, Helen 40
NOWACZEWSKI, Aniela 119
  Helen M 43 Mary 107
NOWACZYK, Wladyslawa 86
NOWADOWSKI, Stella 68
NOWAK, Alexander 78 Angela
  110 Antonette 81 Carrie 96

NOWAK (continued)
  Edward 68 Frances 1 56 83
  Helen 36 Jan 9 Joseph 75 81
  Jozef 25 33 96 Jozefa 25 68
  Magdaline 91 Marianna 3 Mar-
  tha 113 Mary H 59 Marya A 50
  Maryanna 74 Raymond 68
  Wladyslawa 36 112
NOWAKOWSKI, Chester 125 Ed-
  ward 111 Franciszka 57 Harriet
  R 23 Jack 79 Joan 22 John 68
  93 John J 23 Katarzyna 111
  Katharine 105 Konstancia 36
  77 Louis T 125 Steve 77
NOWASCZEWSKI, Antonia
  Zaworski 124
NOWASTOWSKI, Joseph 91 126
  Pearl 3 Wanda 99
NOWICKI, Alvina 19 Bernard 78
  Bernice 78 Frances 7 Helena
  11 Jan 11 Julianna 30
  Katharine 20 Mary 89 Michael
  45 Mike 58 Verna 92
NOWINSKI, Albin 21 Albin S 117
NOWROCKI, Franciszek 53 Mal-
  gorzata 53
O'CHAP, Evelyn 48 52 61
OBALSKI, Joanna 112
OBARSKI, Anna 66 Carrie 22 Mar-
  tin 66
ODUSCH, Minnie A 45
ODYNSKI, Anna 101 Jadwiga 26
OGORKIEWICZ, Josephine 19
  Michalina 40 Wladyslawa 103
OHOCKA, Ewa 107
OLEJNICZAK, Bernadette 36
  Krystina 66 Mary 43 Maryanna
  3 Stanley 36 Teresa 126
  Waclaw 3
OLSOWSKI, Jozef 127 Rozalia
  127
OLSZEWSKI, Joseph 94 118 Vic-
  toria 94 118
OPACZEWSKI, Edmund 77 Violet
  77
ORSZULAK, Andrew 97 Benedict
  97
ORZECHOWSKI, Marion 45
OSINSKI, Stella 44
OSMANSKI, Edward 110 Jan 110
  Pelegia 110 Theodosia 29
OSOWSKI, Boleslaw 21

141

OTOLSKI, Joseph F 33 Sophia 54
OZDYCH, Helena 39
PABIS, Jan 40
PACALA, Frances 89 Thomas 89
  Wanda 37
PACAYTES, Stanislaw 6
PACHOLSKI, Cecylia 111
PACZESNY, Maryanna 59
PACZKOWSKI, Lucya 84
PAEGE, Helen 2 Martha 2 50
  Natalie 57 Rudolph 22
PALICKI, Stanislawa 100
PALKA, Leo 24 Mary 24
  Maryanna 21 Stella 88
PALOMA, Angie 22 95 Rogiella
  95
PALUSZEWSKI, Michael 11 Vic-
  toria 11
PANICKI, Agnes 84 Frances 91
  Franciszek 84
PAPCZYNSKI, Alexander Sr 101
PARAFINOWICZ, Eulalia 114
  Romnald 114
PARIS, Mary 106 Steve 106
PARUZYNSKI, Edward 111 Katar-
  zyna 111 Katharzyna 78 Mary
  111
PASKET, Rozalia 93
PASKIEWICZ, Konstancya 17
PASZKIET, Agnieszka 83 An-
  tonina 94 Frances 72 Fran-
  ciszka 83 Harriet 24 Mar-
  cyanna 59 Stella Cygert 23
PASZKIEWICZ, Antonina 110
  Konstancia 86 Konstancya 17
PATTERSON, Bernice 87 Leroy
  87
PATURALSKI, Jan 25 Jozefa 25
PAWELSKI, Anna 104 Hypolit
  104 Mary 104
PAWLAK, Emilia 85 125 Fran-
  ciszek 50 54 113 Lucya 82
  Martha C 34 Michalina 46
  Wojciech 27
PAWLEK, Frank 35
PAWLICKI, Joseph 49 Rose 49
PAWLOWSKI, Helen 18 45
  Michael 18 45 William 20 113
PECZKOWSKI, Marya 36
PEJZA, Constance 101 Eleanor
  10 Stanley 101
PENDZINDSKI, Stanislawa 84

PENDZINSKI, Stanislalwa 125
  Wladyslaw 84 Wojciech 84
  125
PENNFIELD, Mary E 63
PEROSKA, Pauline 77
PERZAK, Mary 112
PIASECKI, Jan 86 Joseph J 50
  Konstancia Janowski
  Piechorowski 50 Malgorzata 62
  Stella 17
PIECHA, Mary 98
PIECHOCKI, John 11 98 124 125
  Marcin 32 Mary 11 98 124 125
  Stella 38
PIECHOROWSKI, 86 Harriet T
  Kolupa 85 Helena 68 Leon 50
  85 Stanislaw 85 Wladyslawa
  85
PIECHOSKI, Antonina 32
  Veronica Laskowski 59
PIECHOWIAK, Regina 17 84
PIECHOWICZ, Barbara Ann 31
PIEKARSKI, Helen 65
PIERZOROWSKI, Marya 67
PIETRASZEWSKI, Anna T 86 87
  Florentyna 94 Frank 26 Joseph
  94 Pelegia 26
PIETROSZEWSKI, Walenty 52
PIETRZAK, Jan 60 Lottie 102
PIETRZYK, Stella May 75
PIJANOWSKI, Jozefa 123
PILARSKI, Napomocyna 11
PINKOWSKI, Ethel 13 John J 9
  56 Jozef 75 Michael 74
PIOTR, Adam Frances 23
PIOTROWSKI, Agnes 89 Ag-
  nieszka 2 Anna 2 26 Bernice R
  84 Bertha 124 Katharine 69
  Ksaweryna 15 Szymon 2 Valen-
  tine 84 124 Victoria 124
  Wladyslaw 84
PIWOWARCZYK, George 3
PLENCNER, Katharine 75
PLOCKI, Dora (Theodosia) 105
  Mary 105 Michael 105
PLONSKI, Eleanor 67 Pawel 42
  Wladyslaw 67
PLUCINSKI, Rozalia 60
POCZEKAJ, Josephine 92 95
PODEMSKI, Michalena 119
  Mikolaj 119 Wiktorya 41
PODLAS, Aniela 35 Roman W 15

PODOLAK, Mary 54 Mary
Stawska 99
POLAK, Maryann 40
POLEGA, Agnes 69
POLINSKI, Paul W 11 17 111
POMTASKA, Catharine 8
POPIELSKI, Albert 92 Georg 114
Mary 91 Sophie 92
POSTULA, Agatha 7
POTTS, Andrew C 82
POTURALSKI, Mary A 52
PRAWAT, Alexandria 25 Cecylia
109 Franciszka 124 Helen 109
PRENTKOWSKI, Joanna 45 Joyce
102 Weronika 45
PROKAY, Stephen 93
PRZBYLSKI, Hattie 81
PRZERADZKA, Franciszka 3 76
PRZESTWOR, Antonina 61
Catharine 60 Steve 61 Walter
62 71
PRZEZDZIENKOWSKI, Barbara
121 Bronislawa 121 Marcin 121
PRZYBLYSKI, Anna 73
PRZYBYL, Larry 93 Thomas 93
PRZYBYLINSKI, Jozefa 38
Michael 38 Stanley 38
PRZYBYLSKI, Andrzej 106
Jozefa 98 Katharine 122
Maryanna 103 Michael 37 Vic-
toria 61 Wladyslaw 98
PRZYBYSZ, Angela 99 Frances
93 Henrietta 99 John F 99
Jozefa 57 Katarzyna 115 Mal-
gorzata 47 Tomasz 47
PSSZRADSKI, Marianna 123
PSZRADSKI, Maryan 123
PULASKI, Frances 3
PUTREWSKI, Alvin 48 49
PUTRZEWSKI, Alvin 27 Alvin S
100 Victor 79 126
PUTZ, Casimir J 42-116 Mary 42
116
PUZINSKI, Esther 12 118
RACHMADZINSKI, Peter 89
Petronella 89
RADECKI, Jozefa 125 Kate 47
Martha 125 Stanislaw 125
RADOMSKI, Katarzyna 39
RADZIKOWSKI, Frances 46
RAFALSKI, Cheryl 74 Michael 74
Michal 24 Stella 90

RAIDER, Maryanna 118
RAJEWSKI, Gladys 4
RAJKOWSKI, Alex 90 Rose 90
RAJSKI, Alex 103 Cecylia 103
RAJTER, Agnes C 105 Stella 68
78
RAKOWSKI, Marian 82 Sophie 89
Stanley J 89 Valaria 62
RATAJCZAK, Franciszek 108
RATKIEWICZ, Alexander 101
REGULINSKI, Walter 67
REITER, Agnes 54 Esther 54
Julius 54 Mary 114 115 Stanis-
law 114 115
REMBENDA, Joanna 124
REMBLESKI, Bartholomew 81
118
RENES, Frederick 8 11
RENGIELSKI, Frances 59 Rose
58
RESKIEWICZ, Jozefa 44
REWERS, Apolonia 86 Wladys-
law 86
REYNOLDS, Esther A 45
ROBAKOWSKI, 34 64 Helen 55
Josephine 82 Peter 55
ROBASKA, Anna 29
ROBASKI, Stanley J 123
ROBERTS, Clifford 59
ROBERTSON, Irene 42
ROBOKOWSKI, Antoni 46 Jozefa
46
RODRIGUEZ, Esther 22 83
ROETS, David Norbert 53
ROGACKI, Sophie 115
ROGALINSKI, Lottie 88 Peter 88
ROGALSKI, Maryanna 47
ROMANOWSKI, Paul C 51 Paul J
42
ROSE, Lorraine 44
ROSS, Virginia Ruszkowski 96
ROYTEK, Anna 127 Frank 127
Robert Roy 48
ROZEK, Prakseda 8
ROZNIAKOWSKI, Petronella 3
ROZPLOCH, Helena 107 Michael
107 Michal 107
ROZPLOCHOWSKI, Franciszka
53 Jan 50 Maryanna 27 Tekla 5
ROZPLOCY, Helena 107 108
ROZWARSKI, Sophie 66 Thomas
77 Veronica 77

RUDYNSKI, Steve 106 Walter 107
RUSIEWICZ, Pelagia 36
RUSZKOWSKI, Dora 95 Genofa 76
  Walter J 95
RUTKOWSKI, Bernard 29 Boles-
  law 7 Maryanna 7
RYAN, Veronica D 53
RYBACKI, Bronislaw 6 Casimir
  59 Catharine 90 Jan 6
  Josephine 59 Katarzyna 6
  Maryanna 23 Michael 118
RYBAK, Anna 23 Josephine 15
  Jozefa 5 Martin 15 Mary 1 104
  117 Pelegia 49 Wiktoria 66
RYBARKIEWICZ, Agnieszka 81
  Jozef 42 Mary 63
RYBICKI, Cecylia 34 68 72 Mar-
  tha 126 Mary 99 Victoria 49
RYDZINSKI, Frances 121
RYSKA, Anna 27 Magdaline 27
  Michalina 35
RZCZESKA, Ludwika 125
RZEPKA, Mary 49 Stella 58
RZYCKA, Hattie 4
SABOSKI, Blanche 111 Edward
  111
SABOWSKI, Ed 110 Pelegia 110
SALAMAN, Anna 91
SALOMEN, Harry 39 Helen 39
SAMP, John 26
SARNOWSKI, Helena 4
SAS, Frances 8
SASS, Jozefa 76
SAUNDERS, Mary Ann 124 125
  Maryann 124 Maryanna 11 85
SAWICKI, Helen 85 Tomasz 57
SAWINSKI, Elizabeth 61
SCANLAN, Sam S 90 Ronald 90
SCHOINSKI, Maryanna 124
SCHULTZ, John 69 Josephine 44
SCHYMANSKI, John 22 Mary 22
SCIBA, Josephine 65 Leon 65
SCIPSKA, Katarzyna 109 110
SCZYPSKI, Anna 109
SEKENDI, John (Mooney) 26
SEYMOUR, Verna 69
SHERK, Henrietta Przybysz 91
SHRINER, Patricia J 103
SIERACKI, Anna 38 43
SIERADSKI, Stanislaw 105 106
SIERADZKI, Blanche 125
SILVA, Issac 27 Issac H 91

SKARUPINSKI, Apolonia 2 Mar-
  cianna 104 Michal 2
SKIBINSKI, Maryanna 37
SKOWRONSKI, John 52 107 Rose
  101
SKWARCAN, Blanche 66
SKWIAT, Ignacy 44 Marta 44
SLABY, Josephine 39
SLAMPURT, Jadwiga 15 23
SLESINSKI, Antonette 25
SLESSMAN, Papczynski 83
SLOT, Maryanna 85
SLOTT, Pelegia 58
SLUSAREK, Antoni 93 Victor E
  93
SMANDA, Arthur T 5
SMIECINSKI, Maria 4
SMIEGIELSKI, Bertha 34 Gertrude
  115 Julia 18 Leon 115 Marya
  92 Maryann 3 Wanda 36
SMIGIELSKI, Agnes 115 Ag-
  nieszka 75 Wiktorya 75
SMITH, Julius 127
SMOROWSKI, Josephine 113
SMUCINSKI, Agnieszka 17 Jan 17
  Maryanna 16
SNIADECKI, Maryann 19 Stanis-
  law 37 Stanislawa 37
SNYDER, Elizabeth 71 Joseph 71
SOBCZAK, Cecylia A 110 Frank
  110 Jacob 89 Zuzanna 89
SOBECKI, Anna 59 Eva 13 Hattie
  105 Katharine 54 119 Maryanna
  13 Ray S 8
SOBIECH, Janina 5 116
SOBIECKI, Joe K 50
SOBIERAJ, Catharine 128
  Petronela 128
SOCHOCKI, Franciszek 110 Zyg-
  mond 93
SOJKA, Jozefa 83
SOKOLOWSKI, Bert 29 129
SOMMER, John S 99
SOMOGYI, Stanley J 5
SORDEL, Bronislawa 23
SOSINSKI, Bronislawa 39 Hattie
  87
SOSNOWSKI, Anna 116 Walenty
  87
SPARAZYNSKI, Lucy 120 Win-
  centy 120
SPILSKI, Anna 84 Frank 84

SPLAWSKI, Victoria 66
SPLITT, Adolph 42
SPRINGER, Ludwig 28 127
SPYCHALSKI, Clara D 61 Clara L
  117 Jan 23 Joseph S 61 Julia
  106 Stella 10
STACHOWIAK, Antony 52 Bar-
  tholomew J 67 Doris Victoria
  Rose 26 Franciszka 66 Frank
  Laskowski 60 Genevieve 111
  Hattie Laskowski 60 Josephine
  114 Laskowski Hattie 60 Mary
  113 Pearl 79 Sophie 64 Valaria
  124 Victoria 67
STACHOWICZ, Dorothy 76
STACHOWSKI, Dora 88 Jan 28
  Piotr 118
STACHURSKI, Gertruda 78
  Gertrude 36
STAJBACH, Jozefa 60
STANKIEWICZ, Marcin 12
  Paulina 12
STARCZEWSKI, Wladyslaw 99
  106
STARZYNSKI, Anna M 94
STASINSKI, Jan 7 34 Jozefa 15
  Mary A 34 Marya 7
STASKINSKI, Anna 62
STASZEWSKI, John W 61 Katar-
  zyna 19 Marya 83 Tekla 8 122
  Walenty 83
STAWSKI, Mary Sieradski 105
STEDMAN, Eleanor 27
STEFANSKI, Chesterine 83
  Frances 119 Helena 59 John
  119
STEINBRUNNER, Matthew F 5
STERNIK, Vincent 90
STOPCZYNSKI, Andrew 96 An-
  tony 96 Mary 96
STOPKA, Anna 74
STRACHONOWSKI, Anna May 85
STRANC, Rozalia 109
STRANTZ, Monica 72
STRAUSS, Frances 74 Joseph 74
STROJNY, John 52 John M 100
STROMINSKI, Josephine 41
  Michael 41
STROSZEWSKI, Franciszka 99
STROZEWSKI, Ewa 96 107 108
  Jozef 7 64 118 Maryanna 7
  Petronella 92 Walenty 96 107

STROZEWSKI (continued)
  108
STRYCHALSKI, Apolonia 54
STRZELECKI, Hattie 14 Michael
  39
STRZELICKI, Alex 71 Katarzyna
  71 Wincenty 71
STUGLIK, Frances 21 John 21
STULL, Hazel 74
STYPCZYNSKI, Antonette 10
  Eleanora 1 Loretta 96 107
SUDEL, Josephine 112
SUDOL, Josephine 112
SUMMERS, Weronika
  (Latosinski) 32
SURNECKI, Sophie 41
SWARTZ, Clara 121
SWIATOWY, Jakob 65
SWIDAK, Jozefa 122
SWITALSKI, Lottie 102 Marya 23
  Maryanna 59
SZAFRANSKI, Anna 27 Ignacy 27
SZAJKO, Antonina 20 30 Francis-
  zek 30
SZARLETTA, Magdalina 3
SZCESNY, Marcin 73
SZCZEPANEK, Agnieszka 29
SZCZEPANIAK, Anna 114
  Michael 6 114
SZCZESNY, Marcin 120
SZCZYPSKA, Catharine 49
SZCZYPSKI, Anna 110
SZEMEK, Victoria 7
SZEPANEK, Agatha 112 Jozefa S
  16 Piotr 112
SZEPERSKI, Agnieszka 43
SZEWCZYK, Mary 28
SZMANDA, Catharine 20 Marcin
  89 Stanislaw 18
SZMANKOWSKI, Rozalia 31 Vin-
  cent 31
SZMANSKI, Anna 99 Joseph 99
SZMKOWIAK, Pearl 76
SZOCINSKI, Anna 31 Helen 15
  Joseph 15
SZOTKOWSKI, Maryanna 42
SZULCZEWSKI, Andrzej 103
  Blanche L (Pelegia) 98 Fran-
  ciszek 98 Helen 98 John 98
  Ludwika 38 Sarah 108 Stella 59
  Tekla 103 Victoria 98
SZULCZYK, Cecylia 102 Joseph

WOZNIAK (continued)
73
WOZNY, Steve 94
WROBEL, Anna 53
WROBLE, Edward 85 Edward J
98
WROBLEWSKI, A 122 Agnieszka
111 Anastazia 69 Apolonia 108
115 Bertha 66 88 Cecylia 38
Florence 34 119 Franciszek 66
Frank 61 88 Genevieve 83 101
Hedwidge 126 Hilarya 62
Joseph 50 Josephine M 54
Jozef 22 105 Jozefa 64 Mar-
garet 27 Mary 11 70 85 87 98
124 125 Maryanna 105 Teofilia
63 Veral 122 Walerya 105
WROTNOWSKI, A 4 24 115 B 4
WRUBLE, Edward 124 Edward J
11 Frances 85 Frank 85
WRZESIEN, Richard J 78
WYREMBLEWSKI, Stanislawa
117
WYRUSLAK, Edward 21 Helena
21
YUHASZ, Joseph 92 Martha 92
ZACK, Richard Edward 125
ZAKOWSKI, Mary 62
ZAKRZEWSKI, Anna 63 Frank
125 Mary 125

ZALAS, Blanche 119 John 119
Josephine 28 113 Katarzyna
107 Ludwik 10 Maryanna 36
Stanislaw 124 Stanley 91 Stan-
ley F 79
ZALISKA, Constance 1
ZAMIATOWSKI, Helena 80
Teresa 80 Wawrzyniec 80
ZAMOJSKI, Bronislawa 96
ZAPOLSKI, Bernice H 93
ZASTAWA, Franciszka 97 Jan 97
ZAWACKA, Victoria 4
ZAWISZA, Michalena 71
ZBRZEZNY, Stanislaw 4
ZDONIAK, Lillian 80 Stanley 80
ZELASKO, Frances 94
ZELL, Maryanna 60
ZEMANEK, Amanda Marie 48
ZIELINSKI, Antonina 16 Con-
stance 95 Frank 101 Jan 28
104 Jozefa 104 110 Mary 101
ZIEROMSKI, K 4
ZIOLKOWSKI, Frances 72
ZMUDZINSKI, Anton 103
Catharine 103 Valaria 16
ZUBRAS, 116
ZUKOWSKI, Samuel 31 115
ZULKOWSKI, Victoria 32
ZYTO, John 29 103
ZYTOWSKI, Jozef S 32 Rose 123
ZYZAK Andrzej 110